THE GIVENNESS OF DESIRE

Concrete Subjectivity and the
Natural Desire to See God

In *The Givenness of Desire* Randall S. Rosenberg constructs a multifaceted exploration of the human desire for God through the lens of Bernard Lonergan's notion of "concrete subjectivity." Mindful of renewed attention to the groundbreaking work of Henri de Lubac, Rosenberg, in his development of concrete subjectivity, offers a reconciling voice to a variety of neo-Thomist and *ressourcement* responses to de Lubac's legacy.

The book integrates in a new way the power of other-mediated, mimetic desire in our lives, illuminating the role of the religious experience of concrete models of holiness, such as Saint Thérèse of Lisieux and Holocaust victim Etty Hillesum, in eliciting the human desire for God. The theme of concrete subjectivity helps to resist the tendency of equating too easily the natural desire for being with the natural desire for God, without at the same time acknowledging the widespread distortion of desire found in the consumer culture that permeates contemporary life. With Lonergan as an integrating thread, Rosenberg engages a variety of thinkers, including Hans Urs von Balthasar, Jean-Luc Marion, René Girard, Lawrence Feingold, John Milbank, John Paul II, and Benedict XVI. Boldly challenging yet deeply rooted in longstanding theological debates, *The Givenness of Desire* suggests that the desire for God is paradoxically both natural and supernatural, "a given" and "a gift."

(Lonergan Studies)

RANDALL S. ROSENBERG is an associate professor in the Department of Theological Studies at Saint Louis University.

RANDALL S. ROSENBERG

The Givenness of Desire

Concrete Subjectivity and
the Natural Desire to See God

UNIVERSITY OF TORONTO PRESS
Toronto Buffalo London

© University of Toronto Press 2017
Toronto Buffalo London
utorontopress.com

Reprinted in paperback 2018

ISBN 978-1-4875-0031-3 (cloth) ISBN 978-1-4875-2367-1 (paper)

(Lonergan Studies)

___

Library and Archives Canada Cataloguing in Publication

Rosenberg, Randall S., author
The givenness of desire : concrete subjectivity and the
natural desire to see God / Randall S. Rosenberg.

(Lonergan studies)
Includes bibliographical references and index.
ISBN 978-1-4875-0031-3 (bound). ISBN 978-1-4875-2367-1 (pbk).

1. Lonergan, Bernard J.F. (Bernard Joseph Francis),
1904–1984–Criticism and interpretation. 2. Subjectivity. 3. Desire.
4. God. 5. Natural theology. I. Title. II. Series: Lonergan studies

BX4705.L75R67 2017   230'.2092   C2017-900486-7

___

University of Toronto Press acknowledges the financial assistance to its publishing program of the Canada Council for the Arts and the Ontario Arts Council, an agency of the Government of Ontario.

For Susanne, Luke, and Anna

Contents

Acknowledgments xi

Introduction 3

Part 1: De Lubac, *Ressourcement*, and Neo-Thomism

1   **De Lubac's Lament: Loss of the Supernatural**   13
    The French Social and Political Context   14
    Three Centuries of Neo-scholasticism: Separation of
       Nature and Grace   18
       The Thomistic Consensus: The Silver Age of Scholasticism   18
       Baius, Jansenius, and the State of Human Misery   20
    De Lubac's "Natural Desire for the Supernatural"   21
    Impoverished Rationalism and a Return to Mystery   26
    Surnaturel amid Theological Tensions: Daniélou and
       Garrigou-Lagrange   29
    A Note on De Lubac's Theological Style   35
    A Different Kind of Lament: De Lubac after the Council   36
    Conclusion   38

2   ***Ressourcement* and Neo-Thomism: A Narrative under
    Scrutiny, a Dialogue Renewed**   39
    Neo-scholastic Counter-narrative: Feingold's Challenge   40
    Natural and Supernatural Ends   46
    Pure Nature and Concrete Historical Nature   51
    Obediential Potency and the Aesthetic Compromise   57
    The Intelligibility of Nature and the Human Good   59
    Conclusion   61

viii Contents

Part 2: A Lonergan Retrieval: Pure Nature to Concrete Subject

3   **The Erotic Roots of Intellectual Desire**   65
   Analogy and Dialectic: Two Theological Trajectories   66
   The Diminishment of Intellectual Desire   68
   Beyond the "Erotic Cemetery": Critical Realism and the
      Challenge of Intellectual Conversion   70
   Eros of the Mind I: Natural Theology   77
   Eros of the Mind II: The Emergence of the Question of God   79
   Eros of the Mind III: The Challenge of Bias and the
      Human Good   84
   Conclusion   86

4   **Concretely Operating Nature: Lonergan on the Natural Desire to See God**   88
   Nature I: Lonergan's Scholastic Context   89
   The Natural Desire to See God   92
   Twofold End of the Human Person: Beyond Static
      Essentialism   98
   Nature II: Lonergan on Emergent Probability   100
   The Intelligibility of Nature and the Human Good Revisited   103
   Obediential Potency and Vertical Finality in the Concrete
      World Order   107
   The Aesthetic Compromise Revisited   112
   Conclusion   114

5   **Being-in-Love and the Desire for the Supernatural: Erotic-Agapic Subjectivity**   116
   The Extrinsicism of Supernatural Desire   118
   Sanctifying Grace and the Habit of Charity   120
   The Four-Point Hypothesis: Trinitarian Structure of the
      Supernatural   122
   The Shift to Interpersonal Relations: New Relation to the
      Same End   123
   Metaphysical and Phenomenological Accounts of Love   124
      Metaphysics of Love: Vertical Finality and a Critique of
         Extrinsicism   125
      Phenomenology of Love: Lonergan and Marion   127
   Erotic Subjectivity and Divine Grace   130

Desire to Be Loved　131
　　　Loving in the Flesh: Sexual Pattern of Experience　132
　　　You Have Loved Me First: Human Oath and Divine Love　134
　　Conclusion　135

**Part 3: Mimetic Desire, Models of Holiness, and the
　　Love of Deviated Transcendence**

6　**Incarnate Meaning and Mimetic Desire: Saints and the
　　Desire for God**　139
　　Intellectual Desire and Mimetic Desire　140
　　Lonergan on Incarnate Meaning　144
　　An Expansion of Incarnate Meaning: Girard's
　　　Mimetic Desire　148
　　Girardian Sanctity: Pacific Mimesis and the Graced
　　　Resistance to Violence　152
　　Sacrificial Violence, Self-Transcendence, and Self-Sacrifice　154
　　Conclusion　155

7　**The Metaphysics of Holiness and the Longing for God in
　　History: Thérèse of Lisieux and Etty Hillesum**　157
　　The Four-Point Hypothesis and the Metaphysics of Holiness　159
　　Thérèse of Lisieux: Love in the Heart of the Church　162
　　　Contemplative Life and Openness to the World　162
　　　Little Way as Sanctity *Simpliciter*　163
　　　Contemplation and Action: Sanctity *Simpliciter* as
　　　　Apostolic Sanctity　166
　　　Habit of Charity: Feasting at the Table of Unbelief　167
　　Etty Hillesum: The Thinking Heart of the Barracks　170
　　　Universal Activity of the Spirit　171
　　　The Little Way of Etty: Quest for Simplicity and
　　　　Contemplative Rest in God　174
　　　Habit of Charity: "A Balm for All Wounds"　178
　　Conclusion　182

8　**Distorted Desire and the Love of Deviated Transcendence**　184
　　A Civilization of Consumption: The Challenge of Catholic
　　　Social Teaching　185

Idolatry and Deviated Transcendence: Consumerist Practice
   in the Realm of the "Sacred"   187
Consumerism as a "Sacralization to Be Dropped"   190
Girard on Consumerism and Mimetic Desire   194
Consumerist Idolatry and the Distortion of the
   Scale of Values   197
Conclusion   200

Conclusion   201

Notes   207

Bibliography   253

Index   267

Acknowledgments

Theology is a conversational venture. I am grateful for the opportunity to engage colleagues over the last few years at the following venues: Leuven Encounters in Systematic Theology, Lonergan Workshop at Boston College, Catholic Theological Society of America, the systematic theology colloquium at Marquette University, the West Coast Methods Institute, the Colloquium on Violence & Religion, and the Agora Institute for Civic Virtue and the Common Good.

I owe a particular debt of gratitude to the work of Robert Doran, SJ, Neil Ormerod, and John Dadosky. Engagement with their respective scholarly contributions helped me to chart out my own voice in this conversation. Their generosity over the years has been immeasurable.

I am thankful for the support of my department chair, Peter Martens, and acknowledge especially the thoughtful feedback received from members of the "Monography Club": Mary Dunn, William O'Brien, SJ, and Grant Kaplan. During the gestation of this book, Mary was writing *The Cruelest of All Mothers: Marie de l'Incarnation, Motherhood, and the Christian Tradition* and Grant was completing *René Girard, Unlikely Apologist: Mimetic Theory and Fundamental Theology*. Their insight and creativity were both inspirational and contagious.

Writing can often be a lonely exercise. I want to thank those colleagues and friends who offered support in special ways, including Christopher Collins, SJ, Gregory Beabout, Thomas Lally, Jason Sengheiser, Kurt Schreyer, Daniel Smith, Monsignor Michael Turek, Kevin Vander Schel, Leonard McKinnis, Joe Mudd, and Jay Hammond. I also express my gratitude to many other colleagues at SLU and beyond: Donald Patten, Tobias Winright, Wayne Hellmann, Matt Theissen, Geoff Miller, Julie Rubio, Jeff Wickes, David Meconi, SJ, Ken Parker, Darren Dias, David

Oughton, Jeremy Wilkins, Mark Miller, Christian Krokus, Pauline Lee, Jeremy Blackwood, Elizabeth Block, Rubén Rosario Rodriguez, Pat Byrne, Kerry Cronin, R.J. Snell, Alden Bass, Jen Popiel, Tom Finan, Mark Morelli, Erik Moser, Fred and Sue Lawrence, Heather Venable, Mike McClymond, Jack Renard, Fr Nicholas Smith, Brian Sholl, Ken Steinhauser, Ben Asen, Brian Robinette, and Dan Finucane. I have profited from memorable conversations on the subject of this book with David Bentley Hart and Lawrence Feingold. I have also benefitted immensely from the assistance of and scholarly conversations with many graduate students, current and former, at Saint Louis University, especially James Lee, Stephen Lawson, Jonathan King, Joshua Schendel, Michael Pilato, and Caleb Little.

A generous Mellon Faculty Development Award at Saint Louis University enabled me to work on this project during the summer of 2014.

I thank my copyeditor, Terry Teskey, and the staff at University of Toronto Press, especially Anne Laughlin. I am obliged as well to the blind peer reviewers for their critical and constructive feedback. I am particularly indebted to acquisitions editor Richard Ratzlaff for his insight and suggestions as well as his encouragement and support.

I am grateful for the love and support of my parents, Bob and Mary, and my in-laws, Larry and Ann.

Finally, the book is dedicated to my wife, Susanne, and my children, Luke and Anna. Their daily support, good humour, and enduring love through the moments of clarity and the long "dark nights" of writing offered sustenance that was surely undeserved but profoundly appreciated. I am reminded of these consoling lines from Marilynne Robinson's novel *Gilead*: "Love is holy because it is like grace – the worthiness of its object is never what really matters."

THE GIVENNESS OF DESIRE

Concrete Subjectivity and the
Natural Desire to See God

Introduction

Human desire in the concrete world is intensely dialectical. Its complexity is captured with unparalleled insight in Augustine's *Confessions:* his account of the "restless heart" has animated the theological imagination and nourished a wellspring of reflection on the human longing for rest in God.[1] Although he profoundly recognized the ultimate desire of the human heart, Augustine was not blind to the persistent temptation to idolatry, to our all-too-often distorted love of deviated transcendence: "There is no rest where you seek for it ... You seek the happy life in the region of death; it is not there. How can there be a happy life where there is not even life?"[2] Thus is the human desire for God in all its concreteness.

Renewed attention to Henri de Lubac's treatment of the natural desire to see God and his widely accepted dismantling of "pure nature" from its neo-scholastic edifice has awakened the theological community from its historical-contextualist slumber. On the one hand, many thinkers have attempted to rescue, secure, and develop de Lubac's *ressourcement* revolution in twentieth-century Catholic thought. Against the rationalistic foundations of modern neo-scholasticism, such critics have hailed de Lubac's Catholic organic integration of natural desire and supernatural destiny as an antidote to extrinsicist and dualist understandings of nature and grace, enabling the religious to penetrate the whole of human reality.[3] On the other hand, some have attempted to call this entire thesis into question, and others have attempted to provide certain correctives.[4] This line of thought has exhibited a renewed interest in securing more intentionally the "intelligibility of nature" in its own right – whether articulated as "pure nature" or "integral nature." Only a retrieval of the authentic wisdom of Aquinas, along with his faithful, but unfairly maligned, sixteenth- and seventeenth-century commentators, will enable us to discern a pastoral and spiritual solution to the contemporary loss of the authentically sacred. The solution to this crisis "cannot lie in weakening the distinction between nature and grace," one scholar argues, "or diminishing the coherence of the natural order, but only in rightly understanding how the Christian promise opens the horizon to what we already naturally desire in a dim and inefficacious way."[5] My own engagement with de Lubac echoes the suggestion of Toulouse Dominican Gilbert Narcisse: on the one hand, de Lubac's considerable theological contribution "must be read, reread, and meditated upon"; on the other hand, his arguments were rooted in theories that are "much more debatable – and not debated enough."[6]

The central question of this book can be stated as follows: How might we understand, in a systematic-theological manner, the human desire for God when it is explored with particular attention, not only to human nature, but also to concrete subjectivity?

In answering this question, the book is guided heuristically by the often neglected yet highly relevant framework set forth by the Jesuit philosopher and theologian Bernard Lonergan (1904–84), as well as by contemporary developments of his work.[7] This book identifies Lonergan's shift of emphasis from human nature to historically conscious subjectivity and traces its influence on his developing position on the "natural desire for God," attentive to both his earlier presentation of this natural desire within a scholastic context and his later, more phenomenologically informed emphasis on the emergence of the question of God within the conscious horizon of the concrete subject. Lonergan's contribution is often ignored in the scholarship.[8] My aim is to illuminate the vitality of his work, but also to complement his contribution with insights from other thinkers. Having Lonergan as an integrating thread enables the analysis to selectively turn to other thinkers for this complementary and corrective work, especially Hans Urs von Balthasar, Jean-Luc Marion, and René Girard.

The theme of concrete subjectivity is especially pertinent to the debates over the natural desire to see God. As will become clear in the first two chapters, Henri de Lubac privileged concrete, historic nature over an abstract, hypothetical claim about what we would be in a purely natural universe – the maligned theory of "pure nature." Humanity as it is, de Lubac insists, cannot be equated with a hypothetical nature *not* called to the vision of God. Even so, neo-Thomists have criticized de Lubac's position for its lack of metaphysical precision. In Aristotelian-Thomist terms, a *nature* is the same in all who participate in that nature. It is the *individual*, the *person*, that is historical and concrete, not the nature itself.

Lonergan's work has special bearing on this question, due to its explanatory attempt to do justice to both human nature and concrete subjectivity.[9] Despite the tendency to explain human reality solely in terms of human convention, the discovery of human nature affirmed the existence of a certain permanence and universality inherent in the person that endures beneath the multiplicity of human lifestyles and customs. Aristotle defined such a nature as an "immanent principle of movement and rest."[10] Human nature, in light of this Aristotelian development, is marked, for Lonergan, by the intellectual movement and rest of the asking and answering of questions – the very spirit of inquiry that transcends human cultural differences. To consider the subject as a knower is to be cognizant of the rich unity of the unfolding of cognitional process. The spontaneously operating spirit of inquiry – the desire to know, the eros of the mind – carries the subject from experience of the data of sense and of consciousness to understanding, and from understanding to judgment. In short, this constitutive intellectual dimension of human nature reveals that human beings have a natural desire for God – a claim that we consider at more length in the first half of the book.

But this claim about the permanence of human nature admits of two interpretations. It may be framed in terms of universal propositions, self-evident truths, and naturally known certitudes; or it may be considered as a part of human nature itself, but nature "not abstractly conceived, but as concretely operating."[11] Lonergan opts for the latter. His account of the concrete subject ensures the permanence of human nature, but at the same time it accentuates the way intellectual movement and rest operate concretely in human historical life.

This move to concreteness requires a shift from understanding the human being as an individual substance of a rational nature to understanding him or her as a concretely operating subject. When conceived as substance, human nature is understood as always the same "whether [the individual] is awake or asleep, young or old, sane or crazy, sober or drunk, a genius or a moron, a saint or a sinner."[12] From the perspective of metaphysical substance, these differences are accidental. For Lonergan, however, the subject is not an abstraction but a "concrete reality" – a "being in the luminousness of being."[13]

Concrete subjectivity attends to the complexity of human living: biological, psychic, and intersubjective; intellectual, moral, and loving; interpersonal, historical, and hermeneutical.[14] This fuller view considers the "intimately related moments in the organic unfolding of a consistent and ever more comprehensive understanding of the elusive and polymorphic reality to which each of us is ever present" in the conscious reality of our lives.[15] As concrete human subjects, we are called to self-transcendence, to an ongoing intellectual, moral, and religious conversion. Concrete human existence is a "dramatic enterprise that embraces all aspects of human living – personal, communal, ethical, religious – and it unfolds in time."[16] The subject as subject is an embodied, engaged entity, embedded in time and subject to death.[17] As Lonergan put it, "we live and die, love and hate, rejoice and suffer, desire and fear, wonder and dread, inquire and doubt."[18] How might we reimagine and articulate the human desire for God, this book asks, in light of the polymorphic reality of human consciousness?

Lonergan's emphasis on concreteness is due, in part, to his critical integration of phenomenological insights. Phenomenology prioritizes the truth of disclosure – the intelligible object or state of affairs as it is presented to us and unfolds before us.[19] It acknowledges the quest for truth, but also the limitations of this search in the concrete life world – "the inescapable 'other sides' that keep things from ever being fully disclosed, the errors and vagueness that accompany evidence, and the sedimentation that makes it necessary for us always to remember again the things we already know."[20] In addition, phenomenology gives more explicit attention to human embodiment, intersubjectivity, and the gift-character of human interpersonal life.

Lonergan's turn to more sustained emphasis on intersubjectivity and interpersonal relations is especially important to the argument of this book.[21] While some work has been done to reframe the natural desire for God debates in light of phenomenology, the relevance of Lonergan's contribution in this regard has been undertreated.[22] As Lonergan notes, intersubjective disclosure is "not an object to be apprehended," but a presence that "works immediately upon my subjectivity, to make me share the other's seriousness or vivacity, ease or embarrassment, joy or sorrow; and similarly my response affects his intersubjectivity."[23] Thus, phenomenology, for Lonergan, explores "the whole drama of our interpersonal relations" and makes thematic "the preconceptual activities of our intellects, the vertical liberty by which we may emerge out of prevoluntary and prepersonal process to become freely and responsibly, resolutely yet precariously, the persons we choose to be."[24]

If the primary aim of this book is to show the relevance of Lonergan's concrete subjectivity for the natural desire for God debate as it is cast within the neo-scholastic/Lubacian frame, the secondary aim is to investigate, in light of the emphasis on the interpersonal above, how attention to concrete subjectivity prompts us to take seriously the other-mediated, mimetic character of human desire and its impact on conversations about the human desire for God. Little attention has been given to René Girard's intriguing assertion that "mimetic desire is also the desire for God."[25] Accordingly, this book – especially part 3 – engages, as an underlying thread, the ongoing Lonergan-Girard conversation.[26] It responds to Kevin Lenehan's suggestion that Girard's emphasis on "social relations" instead of "individual subjectivity" offers much raw material for theological transposition. Girard's anthropological emphasis on intersubjectivity, relationality, and the phenomenon of "knowing and willing according to a model" as a ground for "human openness to divine revelation" might complement, Lenehan suggests, "the more cognitive approaches of scholasticism and transcendentalism."[27]

Robert Doran has offered a framework – to be revisited in chapter 6 – for integrating natural desire and mimetic desire.[28] According to Doran, Girard's mimetic desire penetrates – for better or worse – our spiritual orientation to meaning, truth, and goodness. In other words, distorted mimetic desire can infect the unfolding of the eros of the human spirit, while positive mimesis may strengthen, enhance, and deepen our commitment to the exigencies of the mind.[29] Positive models have the power to elicit the desire to be faithful to the natural desire for meaning, truth, and goodness. The intersubjective and interpersonal presence of the other may evoke our innate drive for self-transcendence, for being more authentically oneself.[30] This theme will be treated in the last part of this book, which considers the relationship between the saints and the human desire for God, on the one hand, and the love of deviated transcendence, on the other hand.

Outline of the Book

This book constructs a multifaceted language for the human desire for God in the context of concrete subjectivity. Part 1 considers the animating force behind the work of Henri de Lubac and the critical scrutiny of his work that has re-emerged in contemporary theology. Chapter 1 captures de Lubac's critique of the scholastic theory of "pure nature" and his account of the "natural desire for the supernatural" with attention to his social, political, and ecclesiastical milieu. It considers his lament over the loss of the sacred in the modern world and situates his work within the theological and ecclesial tensions that emerged between *ressourcement* thinkers and neo-Thomists. This is particularly evident in the Daniélou/Garrigou-Lagrange exchange in 1947, an exchange that illuminates some of the key themes in this book: an openness to the categories of subjectivity, historicity, and culture (Daniélou), on the one hand, and the wisdom of a metaphysical account of the natural-supernatural relationship (Garrigou-Lagrange), on the other hand. Chapter 2 captures the contemporary neo-Thomist/Lubacian debate. It first examines Lawrence Feingold's critique of de Lubac and brings to light several key tensions in light of the work of many contemporary scholars on this topic: the relationship between natural and supernatural ends; pure nature and concrete nature; obediential potency and the "aesthetic compromise"; and the intelligibility of nature and the human good.

In light of this neo-Thomist/Lubacian debate, Part 2 turns to some distinctive contributions of Lonergan and subsequent developers of his thought. In light of a contemporary tendency to diminish rationality, chapter 3 focuses on the erotic roots of the intellectual desire of the concrete subject – the pure, unrestricted desire to know – on which Lonergan bases his account of the natural desire to see God. Though he encouraged the preservation of the theoretical wisdom of metaphysical terms and relations, he also challenged theologians to integrate them within the framework of concrete religious experience and the call for ongoing affective, intellectual, moral, and religious conversion. I thus note his shift in emphasis from an intellectual proof for God's existence in the tradition of natural theology to the variety of ways the question of God arises in the intellectual, moral, and religious dimensions of our concrete lives. Chapter 4 shows how Lonergan speaks to the legitimate Lubacian emphasis on the concrete and historical, on the one hand, and the Thomist call to affirm a more substantive account of nature, on the other hand. Lonergan's account of nature in scholastic terms and in his more dynamic and scientifically influenced account of emergent probability – along with his key explanatory terms of vertical finality and obediential potency – offers a reconciling voice to the debate. This substantive account of "nature" both preserves the gratuity of the supernatural order and creates the space for the role of intellectual and moral self-transcendence in rational deliberation about the natural, penultimate goods of social, cultural, and political life. In light of this shift from intellectual desire to a more holistic account of the concrete subject, chapter 5 focuses on Lonergan's later emphasis on the centrality of love. The chapter presents a non-extrinsicist account of the relationship between the natural and the supernatural – an account that preserves the language that has been privileged in the tradition (metaphysical), but transposes it into terms revelatory of the interpersonal experience of being-in-love (intentionality analysis, phenomenology) within a Trinitarian context. After establishing the Trinitarian roots of the human desire for the supernatural, the chapter treats the interpenetration of loving and erotic subjectivity.

Part 3 shifts the inquiry to a more substantive engagement with socially mediated desire. Can the integration of the innate drive for self-transcendence (Lonergan) and mimetic desire (Girard) shed light on the human desire for God as it is manifested in the concrete subject? Chapter 6 constructs a connection between the theme of socially mediated desire and concrete models of holiness. In light of Doran's integrative model, the chapter brings into conversation Lonergan's category of "incarnate meaning" and René Girard's theory of mimetic desire as a means of developing an account of the saints as "living texts" with the power to elicit human desire for God. It also highlights a distinctive feature of a Girardian account of sanctity – humility and resistance to scapegoating, which will pave the way for a discussion of the metaphysics of holiness and the habit of charity in the following chapter. Hence, chapter 7 examines the Trinitarian roots of a theologically grounded phenomenology of the graced life. If the previous chapter borders on the descriptive, this chapter's return to the four-point Trinitarian hypothesis helps to establish a more explanatory account of holiness. With particular attention to sanctifying grace and the habit of charity – two supernatural realities that make possible the kind of humble love and nonviolent resistance so integral to Girard's expression of Christian holiness – the chapter offers two specific examples of the human desire for God in a secular age: Thérèse of Lisieux and Etty Hillesum. If concrete subjectivity also reveals the biases that infect human desire for God in our fallen condition, then chapter 8 focuses on the task of mitigating the persistent witness of idolatry. This chapter considers more fully the vagaries of desire and the persistent temptation to worship at the altars of false and deviated transcendence. Mindful that theology "mediates between a cultural matrix and the significance and role of religion in that matrix,"[31] this chapter focuses on the phenomenon of consumerism, and argues that consumerism ought to be considered, at its extremes, a "sacralization to be resisted," a distortion of desire, a misdirected religious love.

PART 1

De Lubac, *Ressourcement*, and Neo-Thomism

1 De Lubac's Lament: Loss of the Supernatural

De Lubac's *Surnaturel* was "an intentional body blow to the neoscholastic understandings of reason and grace, as well as to neoscholastic conceptions of philosophy and theology and the relation between them."[1] Its publication constituted a "cultural event nearly as important as the publication of Martin Heidegger's *Being and Time* (1927) or Ludwig Wittgenstein's *Philosophical Investigations* (1953).[2] Beginning with *Surnaturel* (1949) along with a modified essay, "The Mystery of the Supernatural," published shortly thereafter in the same year, and continuing with *The Mystery of the Supernatural* (1965) and *Augustinianism and Modern Theology* (1965), Henri de Lubac sought to refute the doctrine of "pure nature" as developed by sixteenth- and seventeenth-century neo-scholastic commentators.[3]

The aim of this chapter is to communicate the heart or animating force of de Lubac's reflections on the natural desire to see God. Though this book is primarily systematic-theological, I want in the following pages to treat the natural and the supernatural with some attention to de Lubac's social, political, and ecclesiastical milieu. No doubt the historian will feel short-changed, as will the theologian. The systematic-theological issues raised here will receive more sustained attention later in my treatment of Thomist-Lubacian tensions and my retrieval of Lonergan's theological contribution. Here, I aim to show that de Lubac was principally concerned with identifying some of the decaying theological and political roots that underlay the disintegration of a sense of the authentically sacred in modern life.

The French Social and Political Context

De Lubac's particular stance on natural desire does not, in Lawrence Feingold's view, have intrinsic implications for his other works on ecclesiology, scripture, atheism, and so on. In other words, he does not hold that de Lubac's "particular interpretation of the natural desire to see God represents the key that unifies his theological work, without which it cannot stand."[4] Feingold means to suggest that his own trenchant critique of de Lubac on nature and grace – which is summarized in the next chapter – ought not indicate a widespread dismissal of the French Jesuit's contributions to the life of the Church.

One does not have to agree with de Lubac on all the fine details to accept the deeper implications of his work. In this book, after all, I attempt to retrieve the heart of de Lubac's project, but often differ in terms of the explanatory resources employed. At the same time, I question whether Feingold understates some of the interconnecting threads of de Lubac's work: "Most of de Lubac's other writing, which in a sense works out the thesis of *Surnaturel* in relation to ecclesiology, exegesis, inter-religious dialogue, and secular social and scientific thought, is of a similar character."[5] Even if overstated, Milbank is correct to point out a certain kind of organizing impetus to de Lubac's work. De Lubac's intellectual concerns with pure nature, the separation of the natural and the supernatural, impoverished religious education, and a rationalist theological culture require an acquaintance with the bitter political and ecclesiastical struggles that shaped his life into the 1950s.

In his essay on the disappearance of the sacred, de Lubac makes a connection between a dualistic understanding of nature and the supernatural and the abstract rationalism of theology (both discussed below) and the sociocultural and political environment of 1940s France. Such dualism and rationalism will not sustain in an age dominated by powerful totalitarian movements. The privileging of abstract propositions tied to ancient controversies and presented in a fragmentary way simply cannot communicate the internal fullness and radiance of the Catholic tradition. "Is a theory," de Lubac asks, "that tends to separate the supernatural from nature a suitable instrument for penetrating the whole of reality and life of the authentically sacred?"[6]

De Lubac's ongoing treatment of the relationship between the natural and the supernatural must be read in connection with his other great works of the time, including *Catholicism* and *The Drama of Atheistic Humanism*. De Lubac's concerns – and the larger issues at stake over the *nouvelle théologie* – were not, as much as they may read at first glance, "narrow, Church-internal controversies over esoteric issues."[7] In fact, de Lubac attempted to recover the redemptive role of theology in the world.

One problem had to do with poor religious instruction. De Lubac identifies a distinctive contrast between a mature grasp of secular knowledge and a puerile grasp of religious faith. The latter has "remained that of a child, wholly elementary, rudimentary, a mixture of childish imagination, poorly assimilated abstract notions, scraps of vague and disconnected teachings gathered by chance from existence."[8] The failure to foster a mature and intelligent grasp of faith often results in its abandonment. Even scholars have foregone a deep engagement with biblical texts, relegating it to a domain for a few specialists. The Bible became a "source for rationalist objections to which the apologist had to respond."[9] It was no longer studied seriously as a religious text – a reservoir of the sacred – and instead became a source for thin apologetics.

To grasp the impoverished religious educational scene requires acquaintance with the social and political situation of late nineteenth- and early twentieth-century France.[10] In broad strokes, the scene divided into supporters of the anti-clerical laicism of the Third Republic, on the one hand, and devotees of monarchy-nostalgic traditional Catholicism, on the other. The concrete political issue centered on the educational system. One side feared that Catholic schools were not fostering loyalty to the Republic, while the other charged the state-sponsored schools with perpetuating atheism and anti-Catholicism. The larger issue involved questions about the relationship between the Church and the world. Can one respect the autonomy of the secular without reducing the Church to a privatized ghetto? Several events indicate this tension. The Jesuits, for example, were banned from teaching in 1880. Religious instruction in public schools was made illegal in 1882. The Dreyfus affair (1894–1906) – a case involving the false accusation of a young military officer of Jewish descent – fuelled largely Catholic anti-Semitic, pro-army sympathies over and against anti-clerical republicanism.

In this wake, the movement known as *Action française* emerged. Led by Charles Maurras (1868–1952), *Action française* dedicated itself to both opposing anti-clerical republicanism and restoring the monarchy. This political movement was based on a naturalistic conception of human nature, but regarded religion as an important social

16 The Givenness of Desire

control. Even though Maurras was himself an agnostic, many Catholics believed that his denial of the supernatural "did not prevent his conception of the natural order from being both accurate and indeed in harmony with Catholic social teaching."[11] After France was defeated and occupied by the Nazis in 1940, the Vichy state of Marshal Pétain, with its motto of "Work, Family and Country," replaced the Third Republic with a new national revolution. Vichy's appeal to traditional values endeared the regime to many Catholics, including many bishops, especially those who had supported *Action française*.[12] Vichy brought in "a train of miseries, horrors and, for Christians, spiritual perils."[13] Pétain's Vichy regime inflicted "five long years of oppressive fascism, anti-Semitic legislation, and other forms of collaboration with Nazi Germany."[14] Particularly painful was the widespread support that many Catholics gave to *Action française* in the 1930s and Pétain's Vichy regime during World War II. Out of seventy-six thousand Jews deported from France to Germany during this period, only twenty-five hundred survived.

De Lubac's reflections on the convenient alliance with Catholicism of the founder of positivism, Auguste Comte (1798–1857), echoes his judgment of the Vichy regime's "extrinsicist" use of Catholicism. In *The Drama of Atheist Humanism* (1944), he writes:

> They pay homage to Catholicism; but, in varying degrees and often without being clearly aware of it, their purpose is to rid it more effectually of the Christian spirit. They stress the elements of superstition that still subsist in a body so large as the Church and which it is so easy to exacerbate, especially in periods of unrest. It sometimes happens that churchmen, paying too little heed to the Gospel, let themselves be caught by this. Positivism is gaining ground as its founder repeatedly predicted, far less by any conquest over former "metaphysicians" or "revolutionaries" than by a slow and imperceptible dechristianization of a large number of Catholic souls. The "accommodations" and "alliances" favored by Comte have actually borne fruit. They were followed by a period of spontaneous assimilation, and the faith that used to be a living adherence to the Mystery of Christ then came to be no more than attachment to a social program, itself twisted and diverted from its purpose.[15]

De Lubac analyses this kind of extrinsicism that emerged in lived French Catholicism. Though he recognizes that part of the problem lies intellectually with the influence of Kant's rationalist account of religion, he also notes a kind of sentimental abuse of devotions. The haunting mysteries of religion experienced in the past have been outstripped by religiosity. The separation of "pure nature" from the supernatural discussed below must be corrected by a view of religion that informs and penetrates everything.[16]

De Lubac resisted the temptation to support the Vichy regime, and also resisted the Nazis.[17] During the Nazi occupation of France, he co-edited a clandestine journal dedicated to elucidating "the incompatibility between Christianity and Nazism."[18] He often masked his critique in academic lectures on theological topics. In a 1941 letter to his superiors, he expressed his concern that Catholics did not recognize the threat of the Nazi regime because of extensive Vichy censorship and propaganda. Vichy's appeal to traditional values created the conditions for a kind of state worship in this so-called providential time for France. De Lubac offered strong spiritual and theological resistance to both the Vichy regime and the Nazi empire. He even had to leave Lyon for six months under a pseudonym. As Komonchak reminds us, "anyone who may at times feel lost in the massive erudition of *Surnaturel* might be fortified by the knowledge that it was in such circumstances that de Lubac used his exiles to make it ready for publication."[19]

To his superiors, he outlined the "war of conquest" being waged by the spread of Nazism.[20] This anti-Christian regime, he wrote, is in the process of imposing pagan teaching, systematically de-Christianizing the youth. And the economic, political, and cultural collaboration is rendering France defenseless against the "Hitlerian virus." The danger is that "one lets oneself fall asleep through the silences imposed" and then be "formed by the propaganda." The French were being led towards a "cult of the state that is contrary to Catholic doctrine."[21] And anti-Semitism was growing among the Catholic elite, even infecting the houses of religious orders. De Lubac expressed his wishes:

> I do not expect or desire any activity of the political order, any possible "crusade" from our spiritual leaders. What I would simply like is for them to be more fully informed so that they might better give knowledge of the danger to those who are uninformed, that they might be better even in encouraging our faith and in helping us save our souls; so that the impression that Catholicism is abdicating in the face of the terrible upheaval of the world may not gradually enter consciences.[22]

Three Centuries of Neo-scholasticism: Separation of Nature and Grace

Another internal cause of the loss of the feeling of the sacred involves de Lubac's indictment of the legacy of three centuries of neo-scholasticism that created a gulf between nature and the supernatural. For de Lubac, this was not simply a matter of theory, but perhaps more powerfully a habit of thought. In his judgment, the French sociocultural and political situation outlined above was inseparable from the natural-supernatural separation. So many Catholics uncritically accommodated the "fascist neo-paganism" of Vichy because the natural and the supernatural realms were formed into "two hermetically sealed departments," unequipped with the religious resources for political and cultural resistance.[23]

This wholly modern conception of nature and grace was formulated as a response to certain errors, such as Baianism and Jansenism (discussed below), which tended to confuse or even collapse the two orders. De Lubac's response in this early essay – characteristic of his response throughout his later works on this theme – is to return, in part, to the Fathers of the Church. As the Fathers emphasized, the human being was created in the image of God, endowed with reason, freedom, and immortality. The human being was destined to love eternally in God. Just as he continually returns his readers to the Fathers, de Lubac also reorients them to the actual texts of Aquinas himself. For St Thomas, there is "in human nature as such, because it is spiritual, a desire, a natural appetite, a sign of an ontological ordination, which could not remain ever unsatisfied without the work of the Creator having failed and which could be satisfied in no way but through the very vision of God, face to face."[24] This doctrine was part of "the unanimous Tradition, for fifteen centuries," according to de Lubac, and is captured by "this famous explanation of Saint Augustine, which should be taken in its reflexive and ontological sense: 'Lord, you have made us for yourself, and our heart is restless until it rests in you.'"[25]

A grasp of de Lubac's concern requires some acquaintance with his uncovering of two inadequate and diverging lines of interpretation that emerged in the sixteenth century, what might be called the "Thomistic consensus" versus the Baianist-Jansenist position.

The Thomistic Consensus: The Silver Age of Scholasticism

Shortly after joining the Jesuits in 1913, de Lubac was drafted as an infantryman in World War I. He suffered a serious head injury and returned to the Jesuits in 1916. Since religious orders were banned at the time from teaching on French soil, de Lubac remained on British soil until 1926. It was in England that he was encouraged by his professor, Joseph Huby, to compare selected texts of Thomas Aquinas with the same texts of the Dominican commentator Thomas de Vio, known as Cajetan. De Lubac discovered what he judged a "radical misunderstanding of Thomas by Cajetan," who had "corrupted authentic Thomism by introducing the destructive idea of pure nature into his discussion of the human desire for God, thereby inadvertently leading Catholic theology to infect Europe with an ideology of anti-religious secularism."[26]

The "Thomistic consensus" refers to a relatively consistent line of development associated with thinkers such as Cajetan, Sylvester of Ferrara, Medina, Báñez, Suárez, and John of St Thomas and continuing into the twentieth century with a notable thinker like Réginald Garrigou-Lagrange and today in the work of Lawrence Feingold, among others. This school of thought privileged the axiom that a "natural desire cannot be in vain." If the human desire for the beatific vision were natural, then God would seem obliged to offer it. De Lubac blamed Catejan as the root of the problem.

Even if Cajetan was at root, it was Francisco Suárez (1548–1617) who spread the key tenets of this consensus more effectively and systematically than any other thinker. In fact, twentieth-century *ressourcement* theologians often dub the Thomism they received "Suárezian Thomism." Developing the positions of earlier thinkers, Suárez argues that an innate appetite for the vision of God is untenable. The natural desire for God is not "innate," but "elicited," and "conditional."[27] His most important argument against the existence of an innate appetite for the vision of God involves the hypothetical possibility that God could create intellectual creatures without ordering them to beatific vision. This has become known as the possibility of a "state of pure nature" – the non-absurdity of a natural happiness for the intellectual creature that falls short of the vision of God. Suárez develops this position based on his understanding of *debitum naturae*, of what is due to nature. The gratuity of grace presupposes that there are things due to nature (rationality, union of body and soul, etc.) and other things due to a gratuity that exceeds the proportionality of nature (sanctifying grace, original justice, beatific vision, etc.). If our supernatural end is not due to our nature, then man could be created without being ordered to a supernatural end. There must then exist a "natural happiness corresponding to man's natural powers, in addition to his supernatural end."[28] For Suárez, natural happiness is certainly possible in the hypothetical state of pure nature, but is not even limited to this state: this capacity for natural beatitude exists in all human beings in the current economy of salvation. Grace after all does not destroy nature, but perfects it. Connatural beatitude then is truly possible for human nature and is the end for which intellectual creatures are naturally inclined. This connatural end includes the contemplation of God in creation, but not the beatific vision. Of course, it is also true that, in the present economy of salvation, this connatural end is only a final end in its own order and is ultimately subordinated and ordered to our supernatural end. Hence Aquinas considers happiness in our connatural end imperfect in comparison to that in our supernatural end, but it is still an authentic type of happiness that can be experienced in this life. The doctrine of limbo flows from this reasoning and claims that it is possible to experience natural happiness even after this life.[29] In his two treatments of limbo, Aquinas substantiates the possibility of natural happiness by his position that a lack of spiritual suffering exists in this state.[30]

In light of the axiom that "natural desire cannot be in vain," the sixteenth- and seventeenth-century Thomistic consensus holds, in sum, that the natural desire to see God exceeds the limits of what is due to nature. We are ordered by nature to a connatural end. The natural desire for God is not an innate desire, but elicited and conditional. Although this desire for God depends on our intellectual and volitional operations, the desire to know is not technically ordered to seeing God. That said, and this is important for the issues treated in this book, "the existence of this desire constitutes a powerful argument from fittingness, for the possibility of the vision of God, as well as for its actual offer."[31] I take up the theme of *convenientia* or fittingness later in this book.

Baius, Jansenius, and the State of Human Misery

The Thomistic consensus finds its counterpart in the teaching of two Flemish Louvain-trained thinkers, Michael Baius (1513–1589) and Cornelius Jansenius (1585–1638). In his work *De iustitia primi*, Baius argued that the "condition in which Adam was created was his natural condition and not a supernatural elevation."[32] He asserts that grace "has nothing to do with man in the state of innocence."[33] In this view of man's integrity, God could not have created the human person without destining him to the beatific vision. Thus Baius rejected the state of pure nature, in which the human person would have been ordained to a lesser end. This ordination to a lesser end would fail to do justice to the original integrity of man – an integrity that implies a unique destiny to the beatific vision. Since it is necessary and natural for the human person to reach beatitude, these gifts of sanctifying grace and original justice were also necessary and natural.[34] Through sin, however, Adam forfeited this state of integrity. The nature that remains after the fall is basically disordered desire. Baius offers a brutal account of the state of fallen man: every sin merits eternal punishment, and all works of unbelievers – even virtuous pagans – are sinful. Reacting to Renaissance theories that seemed to separate nature as too independent of a reality from grace, Baius sought to return to Augustine. It was reported that he read Augustine's corpus nine times and the works on grace seventy times. Ironically, with his collapsing of nature and grace, he ends up in a kind of Pelagianism.[35] He posits that real love is equated with observance of the law. With Baius, as de Lubac notes, we can no longer speak of "the relationship between God and man as a mystery of love; the whole thing has become a commercial transaction. Eternal life is offered to man on a basis of strict reward. Man demands, merits and claims; God provides the tool and pays the account, to the last penny."[36]

Baius deeply shaped the thought of Corenlius Jansenius, the forerunner to a movement that ended by deforming a rich French Catholic revival into one of the great crises in the history of the Church. Jansenius, along with the later thinker of a similar stripe, Antoine Arnauld (1612–1694), defended and developed the position of Baius. The Jansenist position, in sum, holds that the only possible beatitude for rational creatures is the vision of God. The human person thus has an innate appetite for this vision, though its realization is supernatural. Unequivocally rejecting the possibility of a state of pure nature, Jansenius argued that God must provide the creature with the means for reaching his final end, which is the beatific vision. Therefore, the innate desire for the beatific vision is absolute, and the frustration of such desire results only in a state of misery. The Jansenist argument from natural desire substantiates both the possibility of the vision of God and the impossibility of a state in which it would not be given.[37] Thus the vision of God would be considered something due to nature (*debitum naturae*) – a claim that seems to destroy the true gratuity of our supernatural end.[38]

De Lubac's "Natural Desire for the Supernatural"

In his key works on nature and grace, de Lubac treats the two diverging lines of interpretation that emerged in the sixteenth and seventeenth century, discussed above, which he calls "conservative Thomism in the sixteenth century"[39] and the "Baianist-Jansenist position."[40] Against Cajetan and the Thomistic consensus,[41] he was uncomfortable with the claim that human nature possesses two ends, natural and supernatural. This *duplex ordo* vision tended to create a divide in the human being and an impasse between philosophy and theology, ultimately treating the supernatural vocation as extrinsic to the natural end of the human person. This desire, which is not the result of actual or habitual grace, marks concrete nature as such. The concrete person "can achieve no genuine rest in a purely natural end."[42]

This overemphasis on a natural human end – an emphasis that is understandable in light of Jansenius's pessimistic resignation over the ruins of nature (which de Lubac also rejected) – was the result of a mistaken reading of Thomas Aquinas.[43] In the wake of this anthropological pessimism, the safeguarding of a natural end secured a more generous view of human nature, as exhibited in the doctrine of limbo, the legitimacy of the virtuous pagan, and the retaining of some ability to know the truth and to choose the good, even after the fall. But for de Lubac, this same hypothesis tended to separate nature and grace, and did so with disastrous consequences. With rhetorical flair, de Lubac invites us to consider that when Aquinas said, "Grace perfects nature," could he have foreseen that "what he said about the completion or perfecting of nature would be retained, while the grace which effects that completion would be left aside."[44] Or, take Aquinas's statement that "This immediate vision of God is guaranteed to us in Scripture." Surely, the angelic doctor "could not have supposed that one day people would attribute to him the idea of another vision of God, equally 'direct,' which could be obtained without reference to anything promised in scripture."[45] De Lubac poses a direct question to those who place so much stock in the modern hypothesis of pure nature: "Do you think that this hypothesis, as you present it, even were it basically sound, is really useful here?"[46]

There exists, then, for de Lubac, a "natural desire for the supernatural." Though the proponents of pure nature were attempting to safeguard the gratuity of grace, de Lubac argued that such a theory in fact marginalized the concrete religious vocation of the human person. As he writes, "For this desire is not some 'accident' in me." It does not result in a "possibly alterable" reality of "historical contingency whose effects are more or less transitory."[47] This desire results in our very membership in concrete humanity as it is in this historical order. This desire indicates a finality inscribed upon our very being – a nature that has no other genuine end "except that of 'seeing God.'"[48] In his writings on nature and grace, de Lubac envisioned the relationship between natural and supernatural as "anthropological unity" that situates the human person before God as "fully unified by grace, capable of being a partner in the Covenant in the integrity of a being that grace heals, renews, perfects in his nature."[49] He returns to an emphasis on the biblical image of the human being made in the "image" of God and to the paradoxical nature of the human spirit,[50] expressed succinctly in a 1932 letter to Maurice Blondel: "How can a conscious spirit be anything other than an absolute desire for God?"[51] De Lubac reiterates the absolute nature of this desire unequivocally in *Surnaturel* (1946).[52] Inspired by Blondel, he held that human intelligence – which involves human commitment and action – can arrive at some sense of the supernatural, revealing the paradoxical situation of the human person. As a *capax Dei*, the human person by nature desires the supernatural, but the fulfilment of this desire lies beyond nature. Hence, though we desire the supernatural end naturally, the means to attain this end remains utterly gratuitous; he explicitly maintains this dissociation.

De Lubac's positive argument for gratuity says that our innate desire for the beatific vision is the desire to receive this vision as a gift.[53] The only exigency of the human desire is "not to demand anything," but to "desire for a gift as a gift."[54] It is a desiring spirit that is essentially and ontologically humble: "The 'I who aspires' is not an 'I who requires.'" De Lubac's position on the gratuity of the supernatural develops from his treatment in *Surnaturel* (1946) to *The Mystery of the Supernatural* (1965). Whereas the earlier position tended to collapse the gratuity of the supernatural with the gratuity of creation as a "phantom of the imagination,"[55] the later position clarifies "two instances of gratuitousness,"[56] as I show in the next chapter. This desire of nature is not necessarily a deliberate, conscious act.[57]

Even if de Lubac modified his position, one cannot underestimate the centrality of "paradox" as a controlling theme in his work.[58] The Aristotelian principle of connaturality, noted in my presentation of Suárez, involved, for de Lubac, a rejection of paradox in favour of common sense.[59] This is an expression of the emergence of "extrinsicist thought patterns" in the scholastic tradition that de Lubac identified in his historical studies. In de Lubac's interpretation, Aquinas had relied too much on Aristotle for his understanding of nature. In a sense, Aquinas had difficulty cleanly integrating the "Aristotelian idea of a self-contained nature" and the "patristic understanding of image."[60] Still, the *imago Dei* teaching was important for St Thomas. De Lubac draws our attention to Aquinas's discussion of "trace" and "image" in natural beings in *Summa theologiae* I, q. 93. Natural beings are a distant reflection of God by way of "trace"; human beings resemble God by way of "image." Hence, De Lubac cites approvingly Gilson's claim that "Thomist nature is not Aristotelian nature."[61] This is not a self-enclosed nature. As the "image of God" theme suggests, human nature is intrinsically, but gratuitously, ordered to the supernatural. Throughout his writings, de Lubac expresses sympathy for Dominic Soto, a Dominican highly critical of Cajetan.[62] As Soto writes, "Aristotle knew nothing about the supernatural, and he would not have conceded that any matter has a natural inclination toward anything, unless it has the power and natural strengths to attain it; we, however, do concede that our nature is so sublime that it is inclined toward that end which we cannot obtain except through God's help."[63]

This separation of natural desire and the supernatural is in part due to Cajetan's account of "obediential potency." I examine this theme more thoroughly in the next chapter, as it continues to be a point of contention between Thomists and Lubacians. For now, it suffices to point out that de Lubac indicts Cajetan as an "unfaithful Thomist" in this regard. His particular teaching on obediential potency tended to naturalize the human being.[64] For Cajetan, our potency for God is only obediential. In one of its uses, "obediential potency" is the explanatory term associated with how miracles operate on nature. But for de Lubac, the relationship between the human spirit and the supernatural ought not to be characterized in terms of what is "abnormal" in the sense of a miracle;[65] for this characterization contributes to the sense that the supernatural is something super-added to an already enclosed nature. De Lubac prefers Thomas's principle that "the soul is naturally capable of grace." With little attention to paradox and mystery, neo-scholastic theology appeared, in de Lubac's estimation, like "a buildup of concepts by which the believer tries to make divine mystery less mysterious, and in some cases to eliminate it altogether."[66]

With an eye to history, de Lubac's pastoral concern is that those who intended to safeguard the supernatural by separating it conceptually from the natural ended up facilitating a vision of the human person during the Enlightenment that detoured into deism, agnosticism, and ultimately atheism.[67] Initially constructed to do important theological heavy-lifting, the development of a purely natural human domain "eventually gave rise to the space of the secular, free of religion and indeed of God."[68] De Lubac asked whether this thesis leads us to suppose a being similar to that so often presented by rationalist philosophies – both ancient and modern: a being sufficient to himself, and wishing to be so; a being who does not pray, who expects no graces, who relies on no Providence; a being who, depending on one's point of view, either wants only to continue as he is, or seeks to transcend himself, but in either case stands boldly before God – if he does not actually divinize himself – in a proud and jealous determination to be happy in himself and by his own powers.[69]

A presentation of nature and grace that envisions "pure nature" as the prolegomenon to the Gospel of Christ presents a dilemma: either the total renunciation of the self vis-à-vis grace or the renunciation of grace as superfluous to our lives in the real world. This leads to either an ineffective and culturally isolated ghetto Christianity or an Enlightenment theology that valorizes reason and rejects faith. It creates, in a counterintuitive manner, the conditions for an "ecumenical choir" of the Catholic proponents of "pure nature," Enlightenment deists and atheists, and Protestant defenders of "total depravity."[70] Their common song is that human nature does not incline the human person to supernatural union with God.[71]

Although he acknowledged a clear distinction between nature and the supernatural, de Lubac emphasizes

an intimate relation between them, an ordination, a finality. Nature was made for the supernatural, and, without having any right over it, nature is not explained without it. As a result, the whole natural order, not only in man but in the destiny of man, is already penetrated by something supernatural that shapes and attracts it. When it is absent, this absence is still a kind of presence.[72]

This language of presence and absence evokes the language of the "sacred" and "secular." Though a useful distinction as far as it goes, it is, de Lubac reminds his readers, in a sense an abstraction: "For in concrete reality, nothing is purely 'in itself'... all is sacred by destination and must therefore begin by being so through participation."[73] (The next chapter explores more thoroughly de Lubac's preference for discussing the natural desire for God with reference to "concrete nature" in the world-order, not hypothetically, but as it exists concretely.) The practical result of this dualism, for de Lubac, is that many have brushed aside the supernatural, placing it in a separate compartment. In the realm of pure nature, they set out "to organize the world, this world that was for them the only true real one, the only living one, the world of things and men, the world of nature and the world of business, the world of culture and that of the city."[74]

Even if de Lubac rightly lamented the loss of the sacred, it is fair to question if he overstated the root of the cause in the doctrine of pure nature. Scholars have urged a more complex diagnosis than the one he offered. As Mulcahy has argued, "French disaffection from the Catholic faith is more reasonably traced, not to the idea of pure nature, nor to scholasticism as such, but to other, more obvious factors."[75] These factors include the Church's alliance with royal absolutism, its neglect of the growing middle class, and its failure to resolve moral-theological questions raised by the Molinist controversy. Furthermore, history often shows that religiosity may wax and wane in response to various factors, including war, trade, legal development, technology, science, urbanization, and economic growth. In short, an "exclusively theological account of secularisation is surely simplistic."[76]

Impoverished Rationalism and a Return to Mystery

De Lubac also identifies the atmosphere and spirit of rationalism dominant in theological practice as an internal cause for the diminishing of the sacred. Hans Urs von Balthasar reflects grimly on the rationalism of his intellectual formation:

> My entire period of study in the Society was a grim struggle with the dreariness of theology, with what men had made out of the glory of revelation. I could not endure this presentation of the Word of God. I could have lashed out with the fury of Samson. I felt like tearing down, with Samson's strength, the whole temple and burying myself beneath the rubble.[77]

Referring to his training in Lyon, Balthasar expressed the consolation that "Henri de Lubac lived in the house. He showed us the way beyond the scholastic stuff to the Fathers of the Church and generously lent us all his own notes and extracts."[78]

It is difficult to grasp the significance of de Lubac's work, along with the Thomist-Lubacian tensions, without an acquaintance with Catholic theology in the early to middle twentieth century. Many of the thinkers considered in this book – de Lubac, Balthasar, and Lonergan, for example – received priestly and intellectual formation under a system shaped by a Suárezian-influenced neo-scholasticism.

On one level, Leo XIII's post–Vatican I encyclical *Aeterni Patris* (1879) shaped theological formation in this era. This encyclical launched a program "to implant the doctrine of Thomas Aquinas in the minds of students, and set forth clearly his solidity and excellence over others."[79] Leo called on universities to "illustrate and defend this doctrine, and use it for the refutation of prevailing errors."[80] He also penned a papal brief in 1892, *Gravissime Nos*, inviting the Jesuits to a genuine devotion to the work of Aquinas, which is relevant to the Jesuit formation of de Lubac, Daniélou, Balthasar, and Lonergan. It was not right, Leo's brief exhorted, to deviate from Aquinas "except in very rare cases."[81] The neo-scholastic theology manuals that shaped theological instruction from 1900 to 1960, however, rarely lived up to the ideal imagined by Leo in his promotion of the method and vision of Aquinas. This is due to the fact that the manuals were informed "less by Aquinas than by his Dominican confrere, Melchior Cano (d. 1560), and by Cano's posthumous work, *De locis theologicus* (1563)."[82] As Jared Wicks notes, dogmatic theologians of this style "were children of their positivist age, and so they tried above all to amass evidence from the sources to support the doctrine of divine instruction that they presented in carefully worded theses."[83] This theses-method gave "seminary theology an apologetic orientation in support of official Catholic teaching" and aimed "to supply elements of proof that showed that official doctrine in fact articulates positions given in the Bible and tradition."[84]

Connected to *Aeterni Patris* and the neo-scholastic manuals was the magisterium's condemnation of modernism, crystalized first in the Holy Office's July 1907 decree *Lamentabili sane exitu*, and then in Pope Pius X's (1835–1914) encyclical released two months later, *Pascendi dominici gregis*.[85] In short, concerns over modernism involved the worry that modern historical, scientific, and philosophical currents were infecting the Church's ability to faithfully transmit divine revelation and the truths of the faith. Beginning in 1910, all seminary professors were required to take an anti-modernist oath. Against the winds of historical consciousness, tradition, intuition, and experience, philosophical formation in Catholic seminaries revolved around the twenty-four Thomistic theses developed to uphold the notion of absolute and unchangeable truth. The history of Catholic theology in the twentieth century, then, is in part, the history of the attempted elimination of theological modernism.[86]

I referred above to de Lubac's designation of neo-scholasticism as "less a matter of theory" and more a "habit of thought." He captures this habit of thought in the following passage, worth quoting at length:

> Perhaps then we stroll about theology somewhat as if in a museum of which we are the curators, a museum where we have inventoried, arranged and labeled everything; we know how to define all the terms, we have an answer for all objections, we supply the desired distinctions at just the right moment. Everything is obscure for the secular, but for us, everything is clear, everything is explained. If there is still mystery at least we know exactly where it is to be placed, and we point to this precisely defined site. We are conscious of being specialists in knowing what common Christians do not, as the specialist in chemistry or in trigonometry knows what common students do not.
>
> Thus, for us, theology is a science a bit like the others, with this sole essential difference: its first principles were received through revelation instead of having been acquired through experience or through the work of reason. But this difference itself is, after all, extrinsic. How little mysterious, then, is this very word 'revelation' for us: God has spoken: What could be simpler? He said this and this and also this: that is clear. Consequently, one can deduce from this and this and also this. Scripture, Tradition are only points of departure: their contribution is at times judged to be a bit rudimentary, without anyone daring to say it too loudly. It is necessary to push "farther" than this revealed given. If doctrine increases in a way with the centuries, all is still explained wonderfully well: a major part faith, a minor part reason bring about a theological conclusion. The theologians lay in a stock of them, and they hand them over to the Magisterium, which will solemnly define those it judges appropriate according to the need. They are the proprietors of sacred doctrine. An elementary catechism teaches the rudiments, then there are more and more complex expositions at greater and greater depth, up to a large theological treatise, which comprises the science in its entirety.[87]

After capturing the spirit of a kind of dead rationalism at work, de Lubac follows up with a lament, not unlike Balthasar's cited previously: "Lord, Lord! There we have what men make of your Mystery! There we have how the best-intentioned and at times the most intelligent among them treat your Word! As if the revelation that, in your love, you have made of yourself were reduced in fact, as if it could be reduced to some series of statements."[88] He laments how little our treatises on God are rooted in the human experience of divine mystery. As Boersma argues, "The *ressourcement* project was not simply a protest against neo-Thomist intellectualism – though it was that, too. The purpose of the protest was to re-appropriate the mystery of being."[89] The shared sensibility among the diverse thinkers of the movement was a return to mystery – "to reconnect nature and the supernatural, so as to overcome the rupture between theology and life."[90]

Surnaturel amid Theological Tensions: Daniélou and Garrigou-Lagrange

I depart in this section from an exclusive focus on de Lubac, for the controversy around his work must be situated within the broader theological and ecclesiastical tensions in the 1940s. To offer a glimpse of this tension, I focus here on the public exchange between Jean Daniélou and Réginald Garrigou-Lagrange. Not only does this debate offer some context for the treatment of de Lubac, it also reveals differing visions of doing theology in the modern world. In the Daniélou/Garrigou-Lagrange exchange, one finds tension between openness to the categories of subjectivity, historicity, and culture (Daniélou), on the one hand, and reinsertion of a kind of rationalist scholastic metaphysics (Garrigou-Lagrange), on the other. Many years removed from this exchange it is plausible to say that both thinkers raised timely questions about theology in the modern world. In our post–*Fides et Ratio* era, the challenge of integrating subjectivity and history, while still remaining committed to theology's metaphysical range, remains.[91] This book is, in part, a response to that challenge.

Daniélou expressed his call for theological renewal in his 1946 "Les Orientations presents de la pensée religieuse."[92] Intended or not, Daniélou's article "had all the appearances of a manifesto and a call to action."[93] It was interpreted as a challenge to the Dominican journal *Revue Thomiste*, and a declaration of war on Thomism.[94] Daniélou was engaged in personal conversations with prominent French intellectuals: Maurice Merleau-Ponty, Gabriel Marcel, Jean-Paul Sartre, Simone de Beauvoir, among others.[95]

Daniélou casts this essay in light of the yearning for a living Christian thought that could adequately respond to ambitious forms of atheism that were calling into question the viability of Christianity as a whole. A perception of a rupture between theology and life was shown by the generation that gave birth to modernism.[96] Though he was critical of much of modernist content, Daniélou believed the emergence of modernist thinkers elucidated "the loss of the sense of God's transcendence by a rationalistic philosophy that treated God as just another object of thought."[97] Theological speculation severed from life commitment was on the precipice of the grave. The influential philosophical movements of the day, such as existentialism and Marxism, privileged commitment and action.[98]

In Daniélou's vision, contemporary theology could bridge the rupture between theology and life by (1) treating God as God, not as an object but as the Subject, *par excellence*; (2) entering into a new dialogue with contemporary intellectual developments – science, history, literature, and philosophy – and their reorientation of our understanding of space and time, of soul and society; and (3) functioning as a concrete attitude that engages the entire person, the inner light of an action where the whole of life is in play.[99]

In this essay, Daniélou notes a restored contact in contemporary religious thought with the essential sources, the Bible, the Fathers of the Church, and the liturgy. He recognizes the value of the historical-critical method, but also notes the challenge of treating the Bible as a "living nourishment for souls." The key is to continue the renewal of theology shaped by a retrieval of patristic sources. Daniélou notes the achievement of de Lubac's *Catholicism* in this regard. He emphasizes the attention to the vocation of the laity in the work of thinkers like Emmanuel Mounier, in the Catholic Action movements, in the new theology and spirituality of marriage, and finally in political activity.[100] Of the Vichy and Nazi challenges discussed above, Daniélou acknowledged that "the events of recent years have posed grave problems for numerous Christians, upon whom the duty of temporal engagement has imposed itself as an unavoidable requirement, and who have been reflecting on the meaning of that requirement."[101]

A new living theology also requires an enriching encounter with contemporary thought: "When a Nietzsche, a Dostoevsky, a Kierkegaard uncovers a human universe for us, when the material universe displays before our imaginations the depths of the history of the earth or spaces between the stars, theological thought is obliged to broaden itself to their measure."[102] Daniélou is attentive to historicity (Marxism, Darwin, Hegelian dialectic), subjectivity (Nietzsche, Sartre, de Beauvoir), and intersubjectivity ("the way each of our lives causes reverberations in the lives of others").[103] The Parisian theologian does not acquiesce to the positions of these particular thinkers just mentioned, but takes seriously the contemporary experiences and thought-forms from which they emerged. He counters these thinkers with Kierkegaard, Barth, Marcel, Scheler, and Teilhard de Chardin, even if some of their views on particular questions are questionable. Decadent neo-scholasticism, on the contrary, has little use for subjectivity, history, and intersubjectivity, moving in the world of essences. The "abysses" of Marxism and atheistic existentialism enable us to see that the "Christian mystery" makes possible a lived encounter of fullness – a vision communicated, for Daniélou, by Irenaeus, Augustine, Teilhard, and Kierkegaard, among others.[104] Existentialism, after all, emerged with Kierkegaard's reaction against the way theology of his time rationalized the Christian mystery: "Against a theology that treats God as an object, he affirms this mystery of a personal God, hidden among the shadows where no light can break its way in, who only reveals himself through love."[105] In an ecumenical manner, Daniélou notes how the converging views of Losski, Barth, Casel, Otto, Scheler, and Marcel might illuminate a "phenomenological path" to the irreducibility of mystery, in contrast to the "chaining together of concepts" in the manner of "Aristotelian logic or Hegelian dialectic."[106] Though this method is "incomplete," it is nonetheless "precious for its ability to reveal the originality of religious categories against the reductionism that is the basis for sociological and psychoanalytical interpretations of religion."[107]

Réginald Garrigou-Lagrange (1877–1964), the prominent Dominican professor at the Angelicum in Rome, published a scathing response to Daniélou's piece entitled "La nouvelle théologie, va-t-elle?"[108] Garrigou-Lagrange's answer to the question of where the "new theology" is heading was unequivocal – modernism. Explicitly critical of Henri Bouillard and Maurice Blondel, this essay attempted to show how the "new theologians" were, in the anti-modernist words of Pius X, perverting "the eternal concept of truth."[109] There had been a transition, Garrigou-Lagrange lamented, from truth understood as the "adequation of intellect and reality" to truth as "the agreement of mind and life."[110] This emphasis on the philosophy of action – an attack, of course, on Blondel – mistakably equates truth with process and becoming, draining it of immutability and eternity. When Blondel proposed this idea in 1906, "he did not foresee," suggests Garrigou-Lagrange, "all of the consequences for the faith. He himself would be perhaps terrified, or at least very troubled."[111]

In contrast to Daniélou, Garrigou-Lagrange worried about the deleterious effects of losing metaphysics in favour of psychological introspection, historical study, and religious experience. To ignore St Thomas on metaphysical questions offers a grave disadvantage. And to substitute metaphysics either for phenomenology or for a philosophy of becoming or action leaves a theologian on shaky ground. How can one affirm, for example, that "sanctifying grace is *essentially supernatural, gratuitous*, and not at all owed to human nature nor to angelic nature?" asks Garrigou-Lagrange.[112] It is crucial to distinguish between the light of intelligence and the light of revelation, the order of nature and the order of grace. Garrigou-Lagrange mentions in a critical manner de Lubac's recently published *Surnaturel*.

Garrigou-Lagrange also cites Daniélou's 1946 article "Present Orientations of Religious Thought," which stated that neo-Thomism was a guardrail but not an answer.[113] Garrigou-Lagrange responds by asking whether Leo XIII and Pius X were simply wrong in their advocacy of a Thomist renewal. Without solid foundations in Thomism, he suspects that this "New Theology" is heading down "the road of skepticism, fantasy and heresy"[114] and shares Pius XII's concern that the "New Theology" is in a constant state of flux. How can one secure the unchangeable dogmas of faith on such fluid foundations? For example, if the laws of evolution were theologically privileged, then the Incarnation, the mystical body, the universal Christ would simply be moments in the process of Evolution, based on a view of the constant progress of good from the beginning. This would seem to minimize or remove altogether the doctrine of the fall at the beginning of humanity.[115]

In sum, the "New Theology" returns to modernism because it accepts a position on truth intrinsic to modernism: truth understood not as the conformity of judgment to immutable laws, but as the conformity of intellect and life – the "conformity of judgment to the exigencies of action and to human life which is always evolving."[116] As Komonchak explains, "Garrigou-Lagrange's 'atomic bomb' had the effect of so frightening the Jesuit superiors in Rome that they refused to allow the indicted Jesuits to reply to it."[117]

In the midst of these controversies, de Lubac's *Surnaturel* was published: "When my book *Supernatural* appeared (1946), the cry for blood redoubled. It's true that, in it, I criticized certain complications of modern scholasticism. I proposed returning to the doctrine of St. Thomas [Aquinas], which was simpler, more profound, both more traditional and a better guide for us today."[118] When Pope Pius XII had the opportunity to address the delegates of the Jesuit order in Rome in the summer of 1946, he remarked that some have conjectured that the new theology's emphasis on constant development compromised the immutable dogmas of faith, as mentioned above. De Lubac, and several others who were indicted, wrote a letter – approved by their superiors – denying the formation of a new school of thought. In the letter they defended themselves from charges of doctrinal and subjective relativism, and suggested that many different theological schools could flourish in the Church.[119] As de Lubac would later reflect: "like all constituted bodies, certain groups of theologians don't like to have their habits disturbed. And, to boot, since I was living at the time at Fourvière, they created an imaginary beast called the "School of Fourvière" (as well as an imaginary 'New Theology') – of which I was supposedly the chief. The combat increased in violence."[120]

There is certainly evidence to support the suspicion that political differences played a role in the controversy over *nouvelle théologie*; staunch supporters of the Vichy government rejected the so-called proponents of this New Theology. Garrigou-Lagrange, OP and Charles Boyer, SJ[121] publicly opposed de Lubac and called for the superior general to issue a condemnation of the New Theology. Garrigou-Lagrange had long supported *Action française*, and his defense of Vichy had reached the point of accusing anyone who supported de Gaulle of mortal sin. He was close to the Vichy ambassador to the Holy See and had sent a "notorious dispatch in which he not only stated that the Vatican had no major objections to the Vichy anti-Jewish legislation but defended it by citations from St. Thomas, which de Lubac believes were contributed by 'Thomists,' either in Rome or in France."[122] As I explained previously, de Lubac, along with other theologians associated with the New Theology, had actively resisted the Nazis and the Vichy government. The philosopher Étienne Gilson observed, referring to Garrigou-Lagrange, "how peculiar it was that 'a master in theology belonging to the order of Saint Dominic … was able in conscience to sustain the notion that the 'best political regime' defended by Charles Maurras was the same as that taught by saint Thomas."[123] The steadfast opposition of Catholic *ressourcement* theologians to the Nazis is given scant attention compared to that of leading Protestant theologians. Yet *ressourcement* thought is "essentially a practical theology engaged in open, critical, and sometimes militant fashion with the most pressing issues of contemporary society."[124]

Even if de Lubac overstated the explanatory value of pure nature in his cultural diagnosis, it is still important to note that one cannot separate his critique of the neo-scholastic hypothesis of pure nature from his witness of political failure. The thrust of his work was, in part, to lead people back to the texts of Aquinas himself. He found the Thomism of the early twentieth century – the heir of Cajetan and Suárez – often "too rigid" and yet "not faithful enough to the Doctor it claims as its authority."[125] He witnessed Thomism employed as a support for *Action française*, Christian democracy, and neo-Marxism. De Lubac reflects, "I have more than once observed a 'Thomism' that was scarcely more than a tool in the hands of the government, the rallying point of a party, the password of a troop of ambitious careerists, or even the empty shell of a thoughtless conformity, the padlock closing the door to all understanding of the thought of others." "Even today," he adds (in 1975), "despite all the supervening changes, this still makes it difficult for me to be very loud in proclaiming that I am a Thomist."[126]

Pius XII's encyclical *Humani Generis* was published in August 1950.[127] The encyclical addressed "some false opinions threatening to undermine the foundations of Catholic doctrine." These principal trends included evolution, historicism, neglect of the magisterium, and so on. Pius also included existentialism and its focus on the "existence of individual things" and its neglect of "their immutable essences."[128] He decries a "contempt for terms and notions habitually used by scholastic theologians," which contempt leads to the "weakening" of "speculative theology."[129] The Church reiterates, on the contrary, its "authoritative approval to scholastic theology."[130] With particular significance to this book, Pius briefly mentions those theologians who "destroy the gratuity of the supernatural order, since God, they say, cannot create intellectual beings without ordering and calling them to the beatific vision."[131] Though it is tempting to identify de Lubac as the culprit, he himself tells a different story: "Far from containing any rebuke in my regard, the passage borrows a sentence from me to express the true doctrine. And it is no accident that it avoids all mention of that 'pure nature' so many established theologians wanted to canonize and accused me of not sufficiently appreciating."[132] Still, it is difficult to disagree with Hans Boersma that the encyclical seemed to target the Fourvière *ressourcement* scholars. It warned against a symbolic or spiritual exegesis of the scriptures (de Lubac and Daniélou). And it is difficult to imagine that the reference to theologians who "destroy the gratuity of the supernatural order" was not an allusion to de Lubac.[133] In the encyclical's wake, de Lubac did not teach or publish for several years.[134]

A Note on de Lubac's Theological Style

Prior to presenting one version of the neo-scholastic counternarrative in the next chapter, I will comment on de Lubac's theological style. De Lubac's own remarks on what animated his work, along with its shortcomings, certainly indicate a lack of concern with systematic rigour. And while de Lubac has identified in provocative ways important theological issues to address, there is plainly much systematic work yet to be done. As Mulcahy put it, de Lubac's treatment of "nature, grace, and their inter-relationship" has left us "with questions rather than systematic answers."[135]

In his own reflections, de Lubac urged people to recognize that most of what he has written was circumstantial and not crafted with technical precision. He did not receive specialized formation in systematic or historical theology and never had to complete a doctoral thesis. In other words, he maintained a distance, especially from 1950 onward, from scientific theology. Even de Lubac admits that it would difficult to isolate a clearly and coherently worked out synthesis in his work. That said, he did discern a "certain texture" that suggests a "certain unity":[136]

> Without claiming to open up new avenues of thought, I have sought rather, without any antiquarianism, to make known some of the great common areas of Catholic tradition. I wanted to make it loved, to show its ever-present fruitfulness. Such a task called more for a reading across the centuries than for critical application to specific points; it excluded any overly preferential attachment to one school, system, or definite age; it demanded more attention to the deep and permanent unity of the faith, to the mysterious relationship (which escapes so many specialized scholars) of all those who invoke the name of Christ, than to the multiple diversities of eras, milieu, personalities, and cultures. So I have never been tempted by any kind of 'return to the sources' that would scorn later developments and represent the history of Christian thought as a stream of decadences; the Latins have not pushed aside the Greeks for me; nor has Saint Augustine diverted me from St. Anselm or St. Thomas Aquinas; nor has the latter ever seemed to me either to make the twelve centuries that preceded him useless or to condemn his disciples to a failure to see and understand fully what has followed him.[137]

As Milbank notes, de Lubac does not contribute directly to a metaphysical or foundational theology. He offers rather a kind of "grammar" for

36   The Givenness of Desire

Christian understanding and practice. He affects his readers with a visionary spirit of renewal.[138]

A Different Kind of Lament: De Lubac after the Council

The focus of this chapter has been de Lubac's lament over the loss of the supernatural and the prevalent extrinsicism that marked pre- and post-war Catholicism in France. While his is the most germane lament in relation to the topic of this book, it was not his only lament. If de Lubac's vision was vindicated at the Second Vatican Council (and I believe it was), this same theologian expressed misgivings about some trends in the post–Vatican II era. If he had to defend himself as an innovator at one point in time, he suddenly became, in the view of some, the proponent of an outdated theology. De Lubac's later lament is captured in his 1969 lecture at Saint Louis University entitled "The Church in Crisis."[139]

De Lubac frames his address in the wake of the rapidity of development, the frenzy of violence and rebellion, and the widespread loss of meaning in technologically and scientifically advanced rational cultures, marked as they are by addiction, suicide, and distraction. And de Lubac detected – a point that disturbed him the most – the same kind of frenzy and rebellion in the Church:

> I stand in amazement at the good conscience of so many sons of the church who, never having accomplished anything exceptional in their own right, who have neither taken time to think nor ever really suffered, who do not even take the time to reflect, and yet who, each day, urged on by an unknown and unknowing crowd, become the accusers of their mothers and brothers. How frequently, when listening to them, I have thought how much more the church, the whole church, would be within its rights to complain about them.[140]

De Lubac's essay deserves searching scrutiny today, in terms of both what is dated and what endures. I simply highlight three enduring themes that are especially relevant to this book.

First, de Lubac identifies the separation between human reason and divine mystery. He notes the predominance of what he called "computer thinking," but what may also be called instrumental rationality or scientific-mathematical rationality. When intelligence is reduced to computer thinking, it becomes a principle of human oppression. What is missing when one narrowly focuses on the instrumental dimension of thinking is precisely contemplation. Without recourse to the contemplative dimension of the mind and a deeper appropriation of mystery, theology becomes, in de Lubac's words, "superficial," "crammed full of slogans borrowed from the advertising world," and an "escape into confrontation."[141] De Lubac recognized that he may be coming across as a reactionary or as outdated. But he believed, in the midst of such threats to unity, that the future of the Church – the very fruitfulness of its mission – was at stake.[142] Note de Lubac's worry: "It would seem that from all horizons of knowledge, starting with hermeneutic and stretching to the highest level of speculation, the progress made by the human spirit in recent years has been funneled together so as to turn us away from this love of Christ Jesus, this love from which St. Paul declared that nothing, absolutely nothing could ever separate him."[143] He adds that this split is foreign to the kind of witness we find in Teilhard de Chardin. The dissociation of the intellectual quest and the question of God is a theme that runs throughout this book.

Second, de Lubac notes a relegation of the love of Christ from the centre of history to the margins. The very idea has become for some a kind of cliché or passé notion. De Lubac speculates on some of the reasons: the reduction of the biblical text to its historical-critical meaning (Jesus is inaccessible to us), the relegation of religious love to sentimentality and childish immaturity (some forms of psychoanalysis), and the dismissal of the dogmatic statements of the early Church as outdated cultural expressions.[144] Later in the book I highlight Lonergan's reformulation of grace as being-in-love with God, which transforms, in his vision, human knowledge and action, and stands at the heart of the theologian's disposition and activity.

Third, in relation to the love of Christ, de Lubac finds recourse in the saints, living and dead. He highlights those who have "drunk at this source for the past twenty centuries":[145] Charles de Foucauld, Jules Monchanin, Madeleine Delbrêl, not to mention Origen, Bernard, Augustine, Aquinas, Möhler, and Newman.[146] After describing the profound simplicity and missionary zeal of the spirituality of Delbrêl, de Lubac comments: "There is nothing grand about so simple a gesture. Yet it will do more to maintain the cohesion of the church than so many opposite gestures which merely dig away at this very cohesion."[147] This book's later emphasis on concrete religious subjectivity – on disclosures of holiness as a concrete form of religious intellectuality – speaks to de Lubac's enduring concern.

Conclusion

This chapter attempted to illuminate the animating force behind de Lubac's reflections on the natural desire to see God, namely his lament over the disappearance of the sense of the sacred in contemporary life. I considered de Lubac's account of the relationship between the natural and the supernatural with significant attention to its meaningfulness in light of the social, political, and ecclesiastical milieu. The systematic-theological issues raised will receive rigorous attention in the next chapter; here my aim was to show that de Lubac was principally concerned with identifying some of the decaying theological and political foundations of a sense of the authentically sacred in modern life, symptoms of the decline of which included the horrors of the Vichy government and the Nazi regime. Against two diverging lines of thought – the Thomistic consensus and Baianism/Jansenism – de Lubac's account of the "natural desire for the supernatural" attempted to retrieve the Fathers and the authentic Aquinas as a corrective to the manifestation of the theory of pure nature in the religious extrinsicism of modern life. As the chapter indicated, de Lubac's position takes on heightened meaning when cast in light of the theological tensions churning during the postwar period in France, as exhibited in the Daniélou/Garrigou-Lagrange exchange and the controversy surrounding Pius XII's *Humani Generis*.

2 *Ressourcement* and Neo-Thomism: A Narrative under Scrutiny, a Dialogue Renewed

Although the precise meaning and impact of the Second Vatican Council remains a topic of dispute today, "no result of the council seems more secure that this conviction: that in the clash between neo-scholasticism and *ressourcement* theology, the latter had decisively won."[1] In terms of the previous chapter, one might say that in light of the Second Vatican Council and the pontificates that emerged thereafter, Henri de Lubac and Jean Daniélou were vindicated while the neo-Thomism of the Roman universities – Garrigou-Lagrange, Charles Boyer, etc. – was relegated to the dustbin of history.

This victory found expression, for example, in the widespread acceptance of Karl Rahner's theology of grace and his account of the "supernatural existential."[2] Consider also Walter Kasper's obituary for neo-scholasticism. Kasper writes, "There is no doubt that the outstanding event in the Catholic theology of our century is the surmounting of neo-scholasticism" and its aim "to establish a timeless, unified theology that would provide a norm for the universal church."[3] Kasper adds that it's "impossible to deny this attempt a certain grandeur. But in the long run a restoration was bound to fail."[4]

According to Oakes, however, recently "this same neo-scholasticism – which had been thought moribund these past four and a half decades, and whose obituary has been written so many times – has shown surprising signs of life."[5] A generation removed from Vatican II, certain scholars have investigated the work of Henri de Lubac and have questioned whether he misrepresented the Thomist tradition. An uncritical embrace of the developments associated with *ressourcement* has even, some suggest, contributed to the decline of vocations, religious apathy, secularism, and widespread dismissal of the Church's moral claims.

As one scholar notes, "Like a firefighter who does not know that the fire has spread far beyond one room and who inadvertently intensifies the fire elsewhere by redirecting the airflow, de Lubac's heroic effort to escape the implications of antecedent errors in certain critical respects served to amplify them."[6] Did not de Lubac's integration of nature and grace tend to collapse the two together, inscribing grace into nature? And did not this supernaturalizing of the natural diminish both the integrity of nature and the surprising, unmerited gift of grace?

The relationship between emerging forms of Thomism and the *ressourcement* tradition, however, has not been an altogether polemical affair.[7] They have at times exhibited similar aims as found, for example, in the *Ressourcement* Thomism project.[8] As William Murphy writes, "Catholic intellectual life has begun – and will need to continue – a more thoughtful encounter between these two overlapping streams of the tradition, a dialogue that … was unfortunately sidelined when Thomism was widely abandoned in the postwar years and even more in those following the council, at least partially due to a backlash against the official imposition of some aspects of it in the antimodernist era."[9] Even if we recognize that the very distinction between neo-Thomism and *nouvelle théologie* is sometimes problematic, the "underlying issues that these terms designate must be held in careful tension by any theology that calls itself Catholic."[10]

Although this book as whole might be understood as an attempt to integrate these overlapping streams, the more modest aim of this chapter is to capture some of the central tensions between the followers of de Lubac and contemporary neo-Thomists of various stripes on issues related to the natural desire to see God. Accordingly this chapter, first, describes several features of Lawrence Feingold's neo-scholastic counter-narrative as perhaps the most rigorous challenge to de Lubac's thesis; and second, highlights four key tensions: the relationship between natural and supernatural ends, pure nature versus concrete nature, obediential potency and the aesthetic compromise, and the intelligibility of nature and the human good. In doing so, I gather insights from many thinkers. It is important to note that I do not offer a full exposition of the thought of all these scholars. The aim is to present the main contours of the debate. These themes are important to my retrieval of Lonergan's thought in subsequent chapters.

Neo-scholastic Counter-narrative: Feingold's Challenge

Feingold's exhaustive study *The Natural Desire to See God According to St. Thomas Aquinas and His Interpreters* stands at the heart of this re-emergence. Other prominent representatives like Reinhard Hütter,

Steven Long, and Guy Mansini acknowledge their indebtedness to Feingold's work. Indeed, Feingold offers a thorough – though of course debatable – analysis of key texts from Aquinas, Scotus, Denis the Carthusian, Cajetan, Ferrariensis, de Soto, de Toledo, Medina, Báñez, Suárez, and Jansenius. And with his re-examination of this centuries-old conversation, he not only critiques de Lubac but challenges a presumed narrative and attempts to retell the story.

If de Lubac self-consciously exhibited a visionary style with a lack of systematic rigour, Feingold's work is both exegetical and systematic. Though my own constructive work in this book will articulate, at times, a different position from that of Feingold, one cannot underestimate Feingold's achievement in this book and his generosity as an interlocutor. More than Feingold, I integrate a historically conscious and concrete understanding of nature, along with phenomenological resources. Furthermore, I offer a different articulation of sanctifying grace, just to point out a few examples of where our positions may come into tension. That being said, my inquiry is still shaped significantly by Feingold's important questions and challenges.

As Reinhard Hütter notes, Feingold's revival of Thomas has characteristically drawn on "the historical reconstruction of the authentic Thomas behind the interpretive discourse of the once greatly esteemed but now equally widely despised Thomist commentarial tradition, a Thomas whose theology is properly foregrounded and again linked to its original *Sitz im Leben* in the contemplative tradition of Dominican spirituality." He also notes an increasing philosophical interest in Thomas: the historical embeddedness of philosophical discourse (Alasdair MacIntyre), in dialogue with analytic philosophy of religion (Eleonore Stump), and post-Wittgensteinian philosophy of language (Herbert McCabe, Fergus Kerr, David Burrell).[11]

Hütter is correct that Feingold's provocation largely ignores the advances just mentioned.[12] Rather, Feingold directly addresses the Thomist commentarial tradition that was so vehemently critiqued by de Lubac. And what makes Feingold's book so provocative is its form of discourse. In clear contrast to de Lubac's way of reading the commentators, Feingold chooses not to construct a historical hermeneutic. Rather, he engages the commentators by "reconstructing and thus entering their own way of conducting a speculative theological enquiry, a mimetic exercise reconstructing and thus continuing the commentators' discursive mimesis of Thomas."[13] Thus, Feingold displays, for Hütter, "a historical consciousness sui generis."[14]

In the last chapter, I highlighted de Lubac's deeper intent to bring to life the vibrancy of the Catholic tradition, to make it loved, and show its enduring fruitfulness. De Lubac's special impact on the *ressourcement* movement was to encourage the "reading and studying of the Patristic writers in a fresh way."[15] It is pertinent to point out that Feingold understands his own retrieval of the scholastic thinkers in a similar way – as a work of love, not an arch-reactionary retrieval of palaeothomism: "I have tried in this work to read the classical Thomistic tradition of the fifteenth through seventeenth centuries with the same love, benevolence, and understanding that de Lubac lavished on their forefathers in the Augustinian tradition."[16] Feingold's *ressourcement* of the silver age of Scholasticism aims to contribute to Catholic theology without diminishing the seismic impact of the Fathers and the golden age of Scholasticism.

Since this book is one of systematic and not historical theology, I am more interested in Feingold's systematic-theological proposal. A brief word on his pastoral concern, however, might illuminate his focus. Feingold believes that the classical Thomistic school that de Lubac most virulently opposed has, in fact, "the elements of a solution that provides a fine balance between the natural desire for the vision of God and the distinction of the natural and supernatural orders."[17] "The pastoral and spiritual solution to our crisis," contends Feingold, "cannot lie in weakening the distinction between nature and grace, or diminishing the coherence of the natural order, but only in rightly understanding how the Christian promise opens the horizon to what we already naturally desire in a dim and inefficacious way."[18] Feingold suggests, for example, that one of the pastoral challenges of our time is that so many tend to take heaven for granted. Heaven is due, many contend in popular consciousness, to our natural goodness. This naturalization of heaven demands a rekindling of "radical wonder at the inconceivable dimension of the gift of our supernatural vocation, which carries with it a true divinization, enabling man to enter into the divine friendship, into the spousal relation with the Holy Trinity, into the beatitude proper to God himself."[19] De Lubac's "natural desire for the supernatural" lends itself to exacerbating this pastoral challenge. Thus, it is crucial to preserve the notion that human beings have both natural and supernatural ends. The fact that human beings are not "intrinsically ordered by nature to the vision of God, but only by grace, better manifests the *humility* of the spiritual creature, whose nature is coherent and perfectly conceivable without the gift of the supernatural, to which it nevertheless stands uniquely open, and which alone will give it an absolutely perfect beatitude."[20]

Feingold offers several helpful services to scholars investigating these themes. First, he clarifies two fundamentally different interpretations of what Aquinas meant by natural desire. On the one hand, some interpret this natural desire as an innate appetite – the kind of appetite found in our lower nature, prior to any knowledge. This involves an innate tendency, inclination, or relation of will to its maximum and proper perfection prior to any knowledge. On the other hand, some interpret this natural desire as an elicited act of the will, following on natural knowledge of the good. The Thomist commentators understood the natural desire to see God as a "naturally elicited" and "conscious" desire that flows from knowledge of God's existence.[21] Feingold uses that latter strand in his critique of de Lubac, who by and large embodies the first.

The distinction between "innate appetite" and "elicited appetite" provides explanatory power to Aquinas's fluid identification of two mutually exclusive categories, but often without fixed terms.[22] The will has a natural appetite for its natural end, namely, universal good or happiness. In the presence of knowledge, however, the will also has "specific acts or movements of desire (elicited desire) toward the various goods that are apprehended by the intellect."[23] Knowledge of the goodness of the object can move the *unconscious potency* of the innate appetite to the *actual desiring* of the elicited appetite. Such knowledge draws out (elicits) an act of desire from the sensitive or rational appetite.

Second, Feingold identifies the chronology and substance of the key texts associated with Aquinas's teaching on the natural desire to see God.[24] His mature position appears in *Summa contra Gentiles* III, chapters 50–1, and from this time forward the argument is repeated in various contexts but without substantial change. Feingold carefully walks the reader through these key passages in *Summa contra Gentiles* III guided by the heuristic question: What kind of natural desire is operative?[25]

Feingold concludes, in sum: "It is not hard to see that all of St Thomas's texts on this subject show the existence of a *naturally elicited* desire of the will following upon knowledge."[26] He argues that, for Aquinas, the natural desire to see God is derived from "the dynamism of our natural desire to know." This natural desire to know leads to "the concrete desire to know the essence of the first cause." Hence, this natural desire to see God is a "naturally elicited desire of the will, which spontaneously seeks the perfection of the intellect." Once we grasp that God exists, we desire to know God's essence. This is based on the fact that we naturally want to know the ultimate causes of things, as stated above. Next, what makes this "natural" is the fact that, once we affirm the mystery and existence of God, we spontaneously wonder what God is and who God is. Finally, Aquinas does not specify whether the natural desire to see God is conditional or unconditional. For Feingold, it is "fairly easy to see," along with Báñez and Suárez, that for a person without the theological virtues of faith and hope, it is a conditional movement of the will.[27]

Third, Feingold recognizes that, in the midst of his own firm convictions, this subject matter is complicated and has evoked centuries of intense theological controversy. The challenge lies in harmonizing the dynamic reasoning of Aquinas with other key aspects of his teaching. For example, Aquinas often asserts that "the vision of God is an end too great for our will to desire, except through grace, since it exceeds all natural power of realization."[28] He normally uses this language in the context of defending the necessity of grace and the theological virtues. And grace and the theological virtues are necessary for us to desire our supernatural end. This begs the question, "In what sense then is the *natural* desire to see God a natural desire?"[29] In fact, though he states often that our supernatural end lies beyond the capacity of natural reason, his argument for the natural desire for God seems to provide at times "a strict demonstration of our supernatural end."[30] How can the principle – a natural desire cannot be in vain – apply to an object that exceeds what is due to nature? The positing of a natural desire to see God seems to imply that God is our natural end, and that anything lower – a connatural end, for example – would not suffice. Furthermore, Aquinas does not address, as Feingold points out, the relationship between the natural desire to see God and the theological virtue of hope.

Finally, at the end of his work, Feingold proposes a framework for understanding the human desire to see God. Though previous interpreters "have not usually distinguished these four states of our natural desire to know God," he is convinced that they are "waiting to be rediscovered and developed." "On the basis of this distinction," he contends, "we can more correctly analyze the relation between nature and grace, focusing on the transformation and *conversion* of this desire from the natural to the supernatural plane."[31] The following constitute the four states of the human desire for God.[32]

First, we possess an innate desire for our connatural end, that is, to know and love God through the mirror of creation. For Feingold, this follows from the very nature of our spiritual faculties. This is not an act, but simply the relation of the spiritual faculties to their proportionate end. This desire is innate and unconscious. It is important to note that, for Feingold, our natural end already involves a contemplation of God. It is not a nature disconnected from God.

Second, in the texts of Aquinas listed above, St Thomas demonstrates the existence of a "naturally elicited" desire for the vision of God's essence. Feingold infers that this desire is conditional without the aid of revelation and actual grace. The object of this natural desire is simply essential knowledge of the first cause. This requires prior knowledge of the existence of God. Hence, this desire is elicited and conscious.

Third, the elicited and conditional desire just described is transformed into an elicited and *unconditional* desire for the vision of God through knowledge of God's promise in revelation, together with the aid of actual grace. This desire reveals an act of theological hope – an act that presupposes the reality of faith. As Feingold writes, "The object of the desire based on Revelation is seeing the God who has revealed Himself as Father, Redeemer, spouse of the soul, and ineffable communion of three divine Persons, and who has promised that we shall see Him face to face if we correspond to His grace."[33] "On the basis of this Revelation," Feingold adds, "through the aid of actual grace, we can make acts of hope and charity. These acts then lead us to seek Baptism, by which we receive an abiding inclination directly for the vision of God, through the gift of sanctifying grace."[34]

Finally, the fourth state is a *supernatural habitual inclination* for the vision of God that results from sanctifying grace. This state consists of the theological virtues of hope and charity. This habitual inclination is present whenever a soul is in a state of grace. It is "independent of knowledge and thus *unconditional* and is based on the proportionality between grace and glory."[35] It is also innate and unconscious, but it underlies and shapes our conscious acts and desires. The innate inclination to our connatural end (first state) is "capable of transformation into a supernatural inclination to the vision of God through the reception of sanctifying grace, by which we are made mysteriously proportionate to a divine end."[36]

There is much to engage here. But for now it is pertinent to capture the heart of Feingold's claim – a claim that deserves both strong consideration and a critical response: "The natural desire to see God is not sufficient to naturally incline or order us to our supernatural end. For that purpose we need the supernatural virtue of charity which flows from sanctifying grace by which we are mysteriously made somehow proportionate to God, having become 'partakers in the divine nature.'"[37] In short, Feingold's challenge to us is to work out systematically the relationship between the natural desire to see God, the habit of charity, and sanctifying grace, which will be treated more explicitly in chapter 5.

Having summarized key features of Feingold's theological counter-proposal based in the neo-scholastic Thomistic consensus and written in opposition to de Lubac's "natural desire for the supernatural," I turn now to several issues that have emerged in the debate. The remainder of this chapter highlights four key tensions: between natural and supernatural ends, pure nature and concrete nature, obediential potency and the aesthetic compromise, and the intelligibility of nature and the human good. My aim is not to treat every thinker in full, but to offer the reader a sense of the main contours of the debate.

Natural and Supernatural Ends

A central question that permeates Lubacian-Thomist conversations deals with the relationship between natural and supernatural ends. Nicholas Healy has perceptively clarified some of "the terms of the question" that continue to divide de Lubac and neo-Thomists such as Feingold, Hütter, and Long.[38] Healy focuses on the neo-Thomist axiom that the innate desire of nature must be essentially proportionate to nature's power to achieve that desire. Healy notes a basic agreement between the Lubacians and the neo-Thomists on the twofold gift from God and hence the distinction between the natural and the supernatural orders. De Lubac distinguished the gift of creation and the gift of deification, that is, the ontological call to be transformed into a new creature. Pursuing the analogy of the gift, de Lubac clarifies the two distinct ways of declaring this twofold gratuity: first, "God has given me being," and second, "Upon this being he has given me, God has imprinted a supernatural finality; he has made to be heard within my nature a call to see him."[39] Whereas the first declarative statement expresses total contingence (natural being), the second communicates total gratuity (divine sonship). Noting a certain measure of common ground, Healy points us to Hütter's similar rendition: "the second gift necessarily presupposes the first gift (not in the chronological order, but in the logical as well as ontological orders) while the second gift is not necessarily entailed by the first." The second gift brings the first gift to a gratuitous, supernatural perfection and fulfilment. Hence, the second gift of supernatural orientation discloses the "ontological openness of creation for grace" without "canceling out the relative integrity of the connatural, proportionate end that is entailed" in the first gift of created nature.[40]

The key difference, as Healy notes, is how to think about human nature and the duality of ends implied in the twofold gift. De Lubac situates natural and supernatural beatitude in human nature itself as created in the image of God.[41] Human nature, in this frame, only has one final end, which is communion with God through beatific vision. However, de Lubac does not mean to imply that the beatific vision simply follows from the principles of nature. Rather, "God has freely inscribed in nature itself, prior to grace, a finality and a desire that goes beyond nature."[42] Neo-Thomists like Feingold, Hütter, and Long tend to reject the idea that human nature is created with a supernatural end. Although nature may be open to receiving a higher end, this supernatural end is given only with the second gift of deifying grace. With a Lubacian pushback, Healy suggests that the underlying premise is that the final end of nature must be proportionate to nature.[43] The key question then is whether both imperfect natural beatitude and supernatural beatitude are inscribed in nature itself from the first moment of creation (de Lubac), or whether our supernatural finality is later imprinted on our being first by sanctifying grace, a kind of super-addition giving us a new finality (Feingold). As Feingold observes, de Lubac's mature position on the twofold gratuity maintains that no other destiny is possible for concrete human beings in the actual order of the universe than an absolute natural desire to see God. Hence, for Feingold, the problem of gratuity in *Surnaturel* has simply been transferred under a different guise. Feingold continues to wonder what the phrase "supernatural finality imprinted on my being" means and, furthermore, how this qualifies as a double gratuity.[44]

It would also appear at first glance that there is a contradiction between the Lubacians and the neo-Thomists on the existence of a natural end relatively consistent in its own order. To some extent this is true. But, on Healy's account, both strands of thinking affirm the importance of positing some kind of a natural end. Tensions arise when we think about the natural end in relation to the supernatural end. Healy proposes that the natural order is relationally constituted from top to bottom. The relative closure of nature is, in fact, a deeper openness to God. The relative autonomy of nature, if one wants to use that phrase, is equated to creaturely dependence on God. Human beings have "an active readiness for God – one whose innate character is fully revealed" in the Son's assumption of human nature and in the fiat of Mary.[45] Healy credits de Lubac with, on the one hand, resisting the neo-scholastics' overemphasis on the claim that the innate desire of nature must be essentially proportionate to nature, and, on the other hand, deepening our thinking on the structure of nature as gift.[46] The structure of the gift – in light of creation and Incarnation – prioritizes the themes of receptivity and gratitude. If I am reading Healy correctly, the real issue of contention between Lubacians and neo-Thomists is not whether there is a relative integrity to nature, but whether nature itself is best understood under the aegis of receptivity and gift. "In other words, Christ reveals the nature of nature as receptive readiness for a surpassing gift."[47] This tension is germane to my full retrieval of Lonergan's positions in part 2 of this work.

Another way of parsing this tension between natural and supernatural ends involves the doctrine of limbo. Recall Suárez's claim (discussed last chapter) that in the present economy a natural happiness can be experienced in this life and even in the afterlife in the state of limbo. De Lubac disagrees. Since this natural desire for the supernatural is an absolute desire, then this desire "cannot be permanently frustrated without an essential suffering."[48] He identifies any state less than supernatural life as equivalent to the pain of the damned. And yet he does not say that the innocent suffer due to punishment.[49] Still, de Lubac asks, "Does natural beatitude mean contentment in a natural end truly attained and possessed, which can give the being a completely stable and positive satisfaction ...?" Attempting to rest in this imperfect end, one would experience only "anxious joy," "always poeticizing reality by dreaming," and calling upon "an indifferent and silent heaven." De Lubac actually prefers Gregory of Nyssa's approach of "eternal incompleteness" – the continual desiring of a God who is forever sought.[50] Real advance, real development in the life of the "uncalled" constitutes "at least the beginnings of possession" and a certain kind of delight.[51] Nevertheless, de Lubac as a whole seems to imply that natural happiness is a kind of anxious, melancholic state, akin to Dante's limbo: "Down there ... / there were no wails but just the sound of sighs / rising and trembling through the timeless air, / the sounds of sighs of untormented grief / burdening these groups, diverse and teeming, / made up of men and women and of infants ... 'In this alone we suffer: / cut off from hope; we live on in desire.'"[52] And in this light a "good and just God could hardly frustrate me, unless I, through my own fault, turn away from him by choice."[53]

Scholars dispute de Lubac's interpretation, retrieving Aquinas's two ways of answering this question about human beings who die without being baptized.[54] Thomas's earlier position suggested that infants in limbo are not afflicted with suffering, but live according to a kind of Stoic ethic through a virtuous moderation of desire. His later position says that those in limbo do not desire the vision of God "because they have no idea of God under this formality."[55] If the natural desire to see God, properly speaking, is elicited and conditional (as Feingold believes), then those without knowledge of revelation will not suffer.[56] Both solutions can stand together, if one maintains the clear distinction between the "species of the natural end" and the "species of the supernatural end."[57] Aquinas's account of the lack of spiritual suffering in limbo, according to Feingold, is fundamentally incompatible with de Lubac's interpretation. Since de Lubac holds that the natural desire to see God is "the most absolute of all desires, he cannot admit that it could be frustrated or unfulfilled without causing an essential suffering."[58]

If it seems difficult to escape this logic, Edward Oakes pushes back in a couple of ways. First, this way of stating the case seems to suggest (even though Feingold does not make this explicit connection) that limbo was offered as a defence of a naturally elicited desire for God. Limbo, in fact, was introduced to "get around Augustine's teaching that unbaptized infants go directly to hell."[59] Pelagius, of course, denied original sin and hence had to navigate the embedded practice of infant baptism in the early church. Mindful of the connection in John 3:5 of the necessity of baptism and the kingdom of God, Pelagius distinguished between the "kingdom of God" (which required baptism)[60] and "eternal life," which unbaptized infants enjoy by virtue of having immortal souls.[61] In response this Pelagian logic, Augustine argued that such babies are condemned to eternal death, for they have not received the remission of original sin and remain in solidarity with the sin of Adam. The justice of God demands nothing more.[62]

Second, although limbo makes some logical sense if one grants the legitimacy of two real human ends, Oakes points out that there has been a significant development in the twentieth century. From the documents of Vatican II through the writings of Benedict XVI, the consistent line of argument seems to be that, in reality, there is only one end for rational creatures – a supernatural end. This is captured, for example, in *Gaudium et Spes* 22, a passage that reverberated throughout John Paul II's papacy:

> The truth is that only in the mystery of the incarnate Word does the mystery of man take on light ... For by His incarnation the Son of God has united Himself in some fashion with every man ... All this holds true not only for Christians, but for all men of good will in whose hearts grace works in an unseen way. For, since Christ died for all men, and since the ultimate vocation of man is in fact one, and divine, we ought to believe that the Holy Spirit in a manner known only to God offers to every man the possibility of being associated with this paschal mystery.[63]

Of course, these contemporary documents do not minimize the necessity of baptism for salvation. How then do they reconcile the existence of one supernatural end and the necessity of baptism? Perhaps the answer lies in a turn to concrete subjectivity. This particular paradox is resolved, as Oakes notes, by resort to the principle of solidarity, indicating that our concrete lives are inextricably intertwined with the lives of others.[64] Many traditional accounts of sin, salvation, and limbo stress solidarity with Adam more than solidarity with Christ. Hence, many have perhaps examined this issue "through the wrong end of the telescope."[65] How might our views be changed "if priority were restored to our solidarity with Christ," or more accurately with "Christ's solidarity with us?"[66]

This principle of solidarity constitutes the heart of Benedict XVI's response in his encyclical *Spe Salvi*, which positively endorses de Lubac's *Catholicism*, especially his demonstration that salvation has always been considered a social reality.[67] In light of our social nature, and in the context of the enduring Christian belief in communion between the living and the dead, Benedict writes, "Our lives are involved with one another, through innumerable interactions they are linked together. No one lives alone. No one sins alone. No one is saved alone."[68] In the midst of our interconnecting lives, our prayer for one another is not "extraneous to that person, something external, not even after death." We must not limit our hope to asking, "How can I save myself?" but also, "What can I do in order that others may be saved and that for them too the star of hope may rise?" If recent Catholic teaching on limbo constitutes a kind of doctrinal development, one may ask whether this development is also a vindication of de Lubac's critique of pure nature and an affirmation of the single human end in the concrete order of the universe, which includes the present economy of salvation.

Pure Nature and Concrete Historical Nature

"It appears that both de Lubac and Balthasar perhaps breathed too deeply of the suspicion toward abstraction popular in the 1950s amongst a wide variety of both scholastic and non-scholastic authors."[69] This speculation of Steven Long captures the second tension between contemporary Thomists and the Lubacians that I wish to highlight in this chapter, the emphasis on concreteness.

One of the systematic issues at play in de Lubac's critique of the "pure nature" is the unity of the world order in relation to the unity and integrity of the divine plan. De Lubac continually returns to concrete, historic nature as distinct from a hypothetical, abstract nature. The doctrine of pure nature speculates about what we would be in a purely natural universe. Humanity as it is cannot be equated with a hypothetical nature "not called" to the vision of God.

De Lubac acknowledged many times that the state of pure nature could hypothetically exist, but in reality it is not a meaningful category. In this state, the human person "would have his rational ambitions limited to some lower, purely human, beatitude."[70] Therefore, it is more pressing to concentrate on the drama of the human person within the concrete world order. Though this natural desire for the supernatural is not always explicitly recognized, it is also not some mere accident in us. It is the result of belonging to humanity as it is in the concrete – humanity-as-called. "My finality," contends de Lubac, "is inscribed upon my very being as it has been put into this universe by God. And, by God's will, I now have no other genuine end, no end really assigned to my nature or presented for my free acceptance under any guise, except that of 'seeing God.'"[71] The vision of God refers not just to a possible or most fitting end, but an end really inscribed in the depths of our nature. Though it is the intent of the pure nature theorists to maintain the gratuity of the supernatural by positing a different order of things with a different finality, this is inadequate because it does not do justice to the concrete nature in the real world order. In fact, a purely natural order with purely natural ends supposes, for de Lubac, "another humanity, a different human being, and thus a different 'me.'"[72] In sum, the question of gratuity can only be asked and answered in relation to our concrete humanity.

De Lubac acknowledges that his reference to the concrete over the abstract might lead his critics to suspect a kind of nominalism – that is, a position that privileged the individual in the concrete at the expense of assigning substantive reality to nature. Yet, he understands his emphasis on the concrete as a retrieval of past tradition – a tradition far more personalist and existential that can be discerned at first glance. The Fathers never imagined reasoning from a pure abstraction disconnected from our concrete natures. Rather, citing Maximus, they were concerned with "the nature of the humble human being that we are."[73]

Even if de Lubac's work is wrought with a lack of systematic precision, it still played an essential role in achieving a more adequate consensus on "the unity of nature and grace in the single plan of God, according to the mind of him who repents not and has no second thoughts."[74] With explicit attention to Cajetan and Suárez, de Lubac points out what he judges to be a radical extrinsicism associated with the theory of pure nature. This framework presupposes the possibility that supernatural beatitude could be given "in addition to the essential, wholly natural, happiness that is desired, postulated, required, and won by nature."[75] This would seem to imply that "the ultimate destination of the universe has been changed in the course of time, without this fact making any change in the structure of the universe or the essence of the beings who constitute it; supposing that God had not willed to make himself seen, or even that to see him were utterly impossible, everything that goes to make up the universe and man would still be exactly the same."[76] Consistent with a metaphysically informed claim that God has no afterthoughts, de Lubac writes: "If God really destines man to see him, one can understand his not actually admitting him to that vision from the first, but there can be no understanding the idea that he only destines him to it from a given moment of his life or of world history."[77] De Lubac argues that "God is in no way governed by 'prototypes.' There is no idea within him prior to his Word. He has no other 'form,' no other 'reason for things' than that Word, that unique Word, begotten by him."[78] God's mind is not a "kind of reservoir in which all the combinations of the possible preexist, as it were, before the real and 'claim existence in proportion to their perfections,' competing among themselves until the one which is best triumphs over all the rest."[79] De Lubac has captured and critiqued in an undifferentiated way what Lonergan refers to as a static essentialist view of the universe, to be discussed at greater length in chapter 4.

Hans Urs von Balthasar reinforces this same Lubacian line of reasoning.[80] Balthasar acknowledges that pure-nature theorists often have ready-made answers to difficult theological questions. When answered with reference to pure nature, Balthasar opines, such conclusions are inadequate, since they offer a system of pure nature that is a "hollow phantom of the real, existing world order."[81] The practitioners of pure nature suggest the possibility of accounting for the essence of worldly structures in terms of purely natural and purely isolatable relationships.[82] "For where do we get the right to understand these intraworldly structures as if they were disengaged from transcendence?"[83] How can one drain marriage, to draw on Balthasar's example, from "its *concrete* relation to God and to the Last Things?" "The only end we know in our *de facto* world," writes Balthasar, "is our supernatural one. So how can we so blithely maintain that the world possesses a self-sufficient, *definitive* ground of fulfillment apart from this end?"[84]

For Balthasar, a more adequate theological approach operates within the concrete, complex order of this world. In the concrete world order, grace has already been given. Hence, theology must reverently acknowledge our unworthiness to receive such a gift. In this view, the "nature" that grace presupposes is createdness as such.[85] Balthasar posits a "formal concept of nature," which is a minimal concept that is expressed most adequately in the analogy of being. Created being by definition is created, dependent, and non-divine, on the one hand, but also cannot be totally dissimilar to its Creator, on the other hand. With Barth as his interlocutor, Balthasar acknowledges that being God and being creature reveal, of course, an utter dissimilarity. At the same time, in the very contrast itself we can also consider, under a different accent, *being* God and *being* creature – an accent that reveals some kind of similarity in being.[86] Nature defined as creatureliness ensures, for Balthasar, that grace is grace and is not collapsed into nature. Formal nature serves as an authentic presupposition for the incarnation of the Word. The ambiguity must remain as we consider concrete subjects within the concrete world order. Nature functions as a kind of "servant concept" to "protect the concept of grace and, in that function, has a legitimate place."[87] Accordingly, we include elements that have "already been affected by the *de facto* ordering of nature toward its supernatural destiny," among them "man's original state, his fall from grace, God's redemption and the awaited transformation of the universe at the end of time."[88] In this light, nature as it exists in the concrete order of things has one, single, supernatural end. There is "no slice of 'pure nature' in this world."[89] Balthasar's Lubacian reading privileges the concrete. Part of the lure of concreteness is that it resists a clear demarcation of philosophy and theology. Theology is not simply a superstructure grafted on to philosophy. They form, instead, a kind of symbiosis. Though the formal object of philosophy is the creaturely world as such, it is not cleanly isolatable, because creation as it actually exists is affected by grace and sin.[90]

In light of de Lubac's and Balthasar's emphasis on concrete nature, it is pertinent to note a lack of systematic precision in general and a fluid use of the term "nature" in particular. In response, Feingold has argued that this distinction between abstract and concrete nature is incompatible with the Aristotelian-Thomistic tradition. Feingold questions the very distinction between "abstract" and "concrete" as it pertains to nature. "For St. Thomas," Feingold writes, "a nature is necessarily the same in all the individuals that participate in that nature. It is the *individual* that is historical and concrete, and not the nature or essence itself."[91] A particular human person has individuated matter and accidental forms, which are not accounted for by human nature as such. But one cannot, in the Aristotelian-Thomist world of discourse, turn "abstract nature" into something concrete.

Feingold argues that a significant divergence exists between this line of reasoning and Aquinas. For Aquinas, in Feingold's reading, our intrinsic supernatural finality is "the result of an *accidental* form (sanctifying grace), given through *Baptism* and justification."[92] For de Lubac, our supernatural finality is, as noted above, essential to our concrete nature as created in the image and likeness of God. Critical of de Lubac, Feingold argues that if indeed a supernatural finality has been imprinted on our concrete nature, elevating our natural desire for God to a desire for the supernatural, then it necessarily involves the reception of sanctifying grace and hence a reception of a supernatural element.[93] Feingold has raised an important question and in many ways offers a viable critique of de Lubac. I return to the relationship between the desire for God and sanctifying grace in chapter 4.

Similar to Feingold, Steven Long orients his reader to the fallacy of concrete nature. Long argues that "nature is not merely a negative concept, a sort of empty theological Newtonian space" providing a vacuole for grace; rather, nature has "an ontological density and proportionate end."[94] Contemporary Roman Catholic theology, he observes, has tended to dissolve the structure of human nature into a limit concept.[95] This de Lubac-Balthasar theological frame privileges concrete nature as it exists within a vocational narrative, attentive to graced, fallen, and redeemed humanity. In doing so, it diminishes the proportionate natural end as unintelligible in its own right. Long acknowledges that the human *subject*, of course, is concrete. Although the subject has a nature, the concrete subject in the world is either more or less than its nature, depending on whether we consider concretely the way evil impedes or frustrates human nature.[96] Still, for Long, even if one recognizes the concreteness of human subjectivity, one ought not to dismiss the rich ontological density of human nature. Human nature is not simply a limit concept, but rather something created by God.[97]

> Human nature is a real principle in the human person, and its species is derived, not from the ultimate supernatural end of beatific vision, but from its proportionate natural end. Nothing in this, however, is to suggest that the natural end in its proper integrity and completeness may be attained apart from grace in the actually existing providential order. Nor can the ultimate supernatural end be attained by one who rejects the impress of the divine wisdom in the natural law and its dominion over his actions.[98]

For Long, nature has a theonomic character. This ontologically dense account of the intelligibility of nature constitutes a limited participation in the eternal law. Long's larger concern with de Lubac's and Balthasar's rejection of an ontologically dense account of nature involves an "antinomian rejection" of the magisterium's authoritative teaching in matters of faith and morals.[99] Moral experience does not involve a direct connection to the supernatural beatific vision without regard for created goods. In our moral lives, we do not simply face non-being, on the one hand, and the beatific vision, on the other hand. Rather, for Long, the "grammar of our assent to God weaves into its fundament all those subordinate natural teleologies that are further ordered in and by grace." The moral theology of marital fidelity exhibits this interlocking set of teleologies. Spousal relations constitute a natural human good. They also represent a sacramentally blessed natural good. "There is not hope," writes Long, "of seeking God through *infidelity* to one's spouse, because this does not merely violate the subordinated natural teleology but also – since that teleology *itself* is further ordered and elevated in grace – it contravenes supernatural charity."[100]

In the subsequent chapters of this book, I take seriously Feingold's and Long's call for a richer, more ontologically dense account of nature. For now, I want to highlight David Braine's recognition of de Lubac's philosophical informality. Though just as critical in some respects as Feingold and Long, Braine encourages a softer, more sympathetic reading of de Lubac's claim about concreteness. Braine claims that "the supernatural finality with which de Lubac is concerned is the end which man has according to the order of providence in which the whole of creation is actually set, the plan actually chosen by God and operative in religion as it is."[101] De Lubac's references to "concrete, historic human nature" and a supernatural finality "imprinted" or "inscribed" on human nature would be better served and more accurate with reference to the language of persons and personhood. Braine affirms de Lubac's instinct to return to existential and personalist categories. Such a return would inch us away from the "excessive naturalism and essentialism" expressed in the Thomistic tradition from Cajetan through Suárez and John of St Thomas to Garrigou-Lagrange.[102]

The tension between de Lubac and Feingold/Long prompts us to ask whether "pure nature" and "concrete nature" are our only options. Anticipating my retrieval of Lonergan in the chapters to come, I suggest that, while Lonergan believed pure nature was a marginal theorem, he strongly affirmed the speculative power of the category of nature. Thus it is fitting to turn to the work of Jean-Pierre Torell for a third way – the way of integral nature.[103]

The expression *natura pura*, as Torrell notes, cannot be found in the works of Aquinas. Thomas does use the term *pura naturalia*. He does not give this term a technical meaning, but it is clear that he distinguishes this from *gratuita*, the goods of grace. Torrell advises, given the term's complicated fate, translating *in statu naturalium* not as "in the state of pure nature," as is sometimes the case, and instead speaking of man's "natural powers alone."[104] It is clear in Thomas that this phrase is not the equivalent of pure nature in its sixteenth-century coinage, for it is only thought to be a temporary state as persons wait for God to elevate the creature by sanctifying grace. The term does, however, preserve the gratuity of grace and provides the concept of nature with a certain autonomy in relation to grace.[105] But Torrell notes that the term "integral nature" does much of the same work, and is more helpful in its explanatory power. Occurring forty-nine times in the works of Thomas, the state of "integral nature" designates the state of Adam before the fall. This state includes the privileges with which God endowed Adam at the moment of his creation, but abstracted from sanctifying grace. Integral nature preserves both the gratuity of grace and the autonomy of the natural order.[106]

Part of *natura integra's* explanatory power is the inclusion of its correlative term, *natura corrupta*. In the corrupted state, human nature is not altogether corrupted by sin, so as to lose all natural goods. Torrell's inventory shows that "the loss of the state of innocence did not return the first man to a chimerical state of pure nature, which he had never known."[107] Rather, the human condition that remained after sin is that of a human person who from the first instance had God as the ultimate end. The human person was capable of knowing and loving God at the supernatural level, called to live in beatific communion. The deprivation of the possibility of attaining this end leaves the human being in a sorrowful state of frustration. Aquinas insisted that Adam was created from the beginning with the reception of grace and hence "did not live for a second under a regime of pure nature."[108]

Obediential Potency and the Aesthetic Compromise

In a letter to de Lubac, Étienne Gilson expressed his opinion on the deficiency of the term "obediential potency."[109] This term, Gilson reflects, mainly refers to miracles, "where nothing in matter either prepares for, expects, or makes the phenomenon possible."[110] "Nobody will ever be able to capture, in a phrase," opines Gilson, "the synchronous, but not identically-related, natural and supernatural character of this natural desire to see God."[111] De Lubac, on the whole, concurs with Gilson, even if he carves out a space for the use of the term. De Lubac especially questions Cajetan's use of "obediential potency," which he finds wholly alien to Aquinas's. Obediential potency was often connected to the possibility of miracles occurring. Affirming obediential potency should not imply, for de Lubac, that human beings possess a purely natural finality, and then are only fitted to receive a supernatural finality beyond or against nature by a miraculous intervention. Rather, for Thomas, "it is precisely because the ultimate finality of this human nature is supernatural that it can receive sanctifying grace."[112] There is both an "obediential potency" and a certain "natural order" to the reception of grace. In the case of miracles, there is no such natural order.[113] In other words, as I said in chapter 1, the relationship between the human spirit and the supernatural, for de Lubac, ought not be characterized in terms of what is "abnormal" in the sense that a miracle is abnormal.[114] This characterization contributed to the sense that the supernatural was something super-added to an already enclosed nature. In order to preserve the more fitting use of the term, de Lubac suggests that the "passive potentiality" that marks "human nature in relation to that supernatural gift" can be called "specific obediential potency."[115]

It is important to distinguish *obediential potency in general* and the more specific *obediential potency proper to human nature*. In terms of obediential potency in general, the theologians of the thirteenth century meant the creature's capacity to receive a perfection directly from God, beyond the order of natural causes. In other words, the natural laws of the created order do not limit the Creator. This is exemplified by the biblical account of miracles where the winds and sea obey him.[116] As a clarification by contrast, obediential potency in general is distinguished from natural passive potency. Whereas "natural passive potency" refers to our passive receptivity to be moved by secondary causes, "obediential potency" refers to the passive receptivity to be moved directly by God.[117]

Specific obediential potency, however, refers to the fact that spiritual creatures – angels and humans – have transcendent obediential potencies that are unique to them.[118] This is the capacity "to receive supernatural perfections without losing one's nature and identity."[119] For Feingold, the principle of non-repugnance or non-contradiction should not be disregarded as only negative. It also implies astonishing possibilities – that of a spiritual creature who maintains its essential nature or personal identity while at the same time being called from natural to supernatural likeness.[120] In a related manner, Nicholas Healy highlights de Lubac's tentative support for a minimal use of the language of obediential potency. In the economy of salvation, God has placed a natural basis in human nature for the call to our supernatural end. In other words, at the heart of created nature there is a kind of receptive readiness, which he also calls specific obediential potency, except that de Lubac is not satisfied by the ability of the term "passive non-repugnance" to capture this dynamic pattern.[121]

For many neo-Thomists, obediential potency reveals a *convenientia* for the beatific vision. This natural desire constitutes "a powerful argument from fittingness, first for the possibility of the beatific vision of God, as well as for its actual offer."[122] This emphasis on fittingness or *convenientia* constitutes what Milbank calls the Thomist "aesthetic compromise."[123] Arguments from fittingness are in part aesthetic arguments. In Feingold's argument from fittingness, for example, the natural desire for God disproportionately exceeds the limits of what is due to nature. Hence, it cannot furnish a "strict demonstration of the possibility of the beatific vision (and certainly not its actual offer), although it does prove that *perfect* beatitude for the intellectual creature can only lie in the vision of God."[124]

Milbank notes the possibility of both consonance and incompatibility between Thomist and Lubacian thought. Is there a clear difference between the Thomist aesthetic compromise and de Lubac's thesis? There is much consonance, Milbank suggests, if one understands the *convenientia* of human nature for supernatural elevation as intrinsically participating in divine wisdom. This view envisions human nature as teleologically drawn to the beatific vision without claiming that human nature elicits it. On the other hand, if *convenientia* is presented in a more extrinsic manner, then incompatibility abounds. A conflicting view of the aesthetic compromise would communicate "an already replete human nature" lending itself to "a further end and purpose added on to it by God – as if, for example, a railway carriage turned out to be an ideal home for gypsies after the closure of the branch line, and a ruling government proclaimed that this had always been secretly envisaged by the earlier government that built railways in the first place."[125] In this interpretation, the Thomist aesthetic compromise finds itself in disagreement with the *nouvelle théologie*.

The Intelligibility of Nature and the Human Good

As I mentioned in the previous chapter, the debate over pure nature and the natural desire for God involves more than just quibbling over academic subtleties. De Lubac believed the hypothesis of pure nature constituted a "cancerous growth on the tree of theological development"[126] – a development with deleterious implications for our social, cultural, and political life. Granting legitimacy to a purely natural end created the conditions, in John Milbank's interpretation of de Lubac, for a "conception of individual and social self-sustaining in terms of the logic of survival and preservation of material well-being and freedom."[127] The logic of self-sufficiency ended up trumping the *telos* of flourishing. The autonomous self severed from morality, religious practice, and "mystical self loss," suggests Milbank, results in "joyless disciplinary programs for the maximizing of corporeal efficiency, and in the long run in nihilistic cults of individual and collective power."[128] The denial of "the natural desire for the supernatural" leads us to a situation where politics is just about politics and not about a holistic vision of human flourishing. Milbank's attempt to capture the larger implications of pure nature theory in a Lubacian vein here certainly raises more questions than it offers easy answers.

Feingold disputes this trajectory of thought. Naturalism, atheism, and secularism have come about not by neo-Thomism, but through "a denigration of the natural order and the power of natural reason" to know "the essences of natural things, natural law, and the existence of God."[129] Hence, for Feingold, fourteenth-century nominalism was the culprit, only to be augmented by the Protestant Reformation and carried further by Kant and philosophies that depend on his critique of reason.[130] Modern atheism, as exemplified by Sartre, for example, rejects both the connatural end and the supernatural end of human nature. The most fitting response, then, requires a "defense of the natural order (the *Logos* in nature) together with the supernatural, 'engaging the whole breadth of reason,' as we find eminently in the Thomistic tradition."[131] Though there is certainly truth to Feingold's account, an acknowledgment of the dialectical pattern evident in the emergence of atheism might complicate the neatness of his argument, lending a certain credence to Milbank's narrative. I suggest that the "pure nature" argument reflects something like the bracketing of the specifically religious in order to defend the God of religion.[132] This apologetic strategy asserts implicitly, as Michael Buckley argues, "the cognitive emptiness of the very reality one was attempting to support."[133] This dialectical unraveling is generated by omitting the particularity of religious life and experience in favour of natural philosophy – in this case the doctrine of pure nature. Again, even if de Lubac overstated the deleterious power of pure nature, it is plausible to explore further whether a dimension of the rise of extrinsicism resulted, in part, from this rather unintentional dialectical negation.

A similar tension can be detected in Steven Long's critique of David Schindler, a prominent thinker in the *ressourcement* tradition. According to Long – and this is an extension of his critique of de Lubac and Balthasar mentioned above – Schindler "seemingly thinks that natural truth and prudence offer to the mind in search of God no point of analogical reference or middle term that is distinct from supernatural revelation."[134] Rather, nature is constituted predominantly by its relation to the supernatural (de Lubac and Balthasar), which provides the basis for Christian discourse with the world. Schindler's insistence on emphasizing nature's orientation to the supernatural seems to depreciate, for Long, the intelligibility of nature itself. An ontologically dense account of nature, on the other hand, offers "genuine but limited wisdom regarding creation, providence, and moral life" that "might develop and contribute to man's public life." With his intellectual commitments, Schindler is "constrained to judge political, legal, social, and cultural order with too little aid from natural truth and prudence."[135] For Schindler, the privileging of an intelligible natural order tends to valorize *autonomy* over *created receptivity* in social life. Understanding human dignity merely in terms of intelligence and freedom easily slips, in Schindler's view, into an understanding of the human person as autonomously independent from God. Can such an image do justice to the ground of human dignity, which is a positive, constitutive relation to God received as gift?[136]

Though Long rightly calls for a more robust retrieval of "nature," the potential reach of his position may be stunted by a kind of "Christian epistemic superiority."[137] Authentic social cohesion, for Long, requires agreement on the speculative truths of natural law and a recognition that the Church is "our tutor in the natural law."[138] Though these truths are knowable apart from revelation, their "*full* existential appropriation and application requires advertence to truths only accessible through revelation."[139]

I take seriously Long's critique of the Lubacian position as presenting too anorexic an account of nature. My development of Lonergan's rich and dynamic account of nature in subsequent chapters might be understood in parallel with Long's project of retrieving the intelligibility of nature. That said, I agree with Bushlack that the natural intelligibility of human nature can be safeguarded "without recourse to the chimerical state of pure nature and without adverting to a form of Christian epistemic superiority with regard to natural law reasoning."[140] For Bushlack, Long's proposal lacks a measure of epistemic humility. Bushlack's alternative requires both a commitment to the human mind's capacity to know the truth and the "requisite humility demanded of one's pilgrim status in this world." The cultivation of "epistemological humility" and "intellectual solidarity" creates spaces for reasoning together with all people of good will about moral truth in pursuit of the common good.[141] Still, a more substantive account of integral nature not only preserves the gratuity of the supernatural order, but also creates more "conceptual breathing room for recognizing a public space for Christian engagement in rational deliberation about the natural, penultimate goods of the political community."[142] Furthermore, my own retrieval of Lonergan's thought later in this book provides of way of integrating, and not opposing, autonomy and receptivity.

Conclusion

This chapter highlighted some of the central tensions between the followers of de Lubac and contemporary neo-Thomists of various stripes, on issues related to the natural desire to see God. In light of these tensions, I will highlight in summary fashion four sets of questions that emerged.

First, what human operations are at work in our natural desire to see God? Are they primarily associated with the intellect or the will? And is this human desire simply *natural* or *naturally elicited* and *conditional* as Feingold argued?

Second, do human beings have both natural and supernatural ends? If so, are they intrinsically related or relationally constituted? And in what sense can we say that our natural end corresponds to a proportionate human happiness, apart from our supernatural end? What place does an explanatory term like "obediential potency" have in a contemporary systematic-theological presentation of the human desire to see God, cast as it is in metaphysical discourse? Is it more adequate to turn to the phenomenological language of gift and receptivity? Is our orientation to God more a question of fittingness or do we have by our very nature an innate orientation to the beatific vision?

Third, how might we navigate the tension between "pure nature" and "concrete nature"? Is "integral nature" a more potent explanatory term? How might this conversation look when nature is understood in more concrete terms – as suggested by de Lubac and Balthasar – but in a way that offers a less anorexic, more substantive and ontologically dense account, called for by many Thomists?

Finally, in light of de Lubac's connection between the theory of pure nature and its implications for religious extrinsicism and political resistance (or lack thereof), what is the relationship between the intelligibility of nature and the human good? Can a more substantive account of integral nature not only preserve the gratuity of the supernatural order, but also create space for a substantive engagement in intelligent deliberation about the natural, penultimate goods of the political community, including the resources for cultural and political resistance? What is the relationship between substantive human goods and supernatural goods, and how might we avoid an extrinsicism in this regard?

In light of these tensions and questions, the next few chapters retrieve key aspects of Lonergan's thought, mindful both of Lubacians' legitimate concern with the concrete and historical and of many Thomists' equally pressing concern for a more substantive account of nature.

PART 2

A Lonergan Retrieval: Pure Nature to Concrete Subject

3 The Erotic Roots of Intellectual Desire

Part 2 of the book explores Lonergan's distinctive contributions to the debate explored above. This chapter focuses on the question of what human operations are at work in our natural desire to see God. Are they primarily associated with the intellect or the will? For Lonergan, the natural desire to see God is rooted in intellectual desire – the pure, unrestricted desire to know, which constitutes the focus of this chapter. How Lonergan's position relates to Feingold's claim that this human desire is "naturally elicited" and "conditional" will be treated in the next chapter.

Although it is understandable that the current debates over the natural desire for God take this kind of desire for granted, human rationality's intrinsic orientation to transcendence is no longer self-evident. Does not human desire, many conjecture, include more than the human subject on an intellectual quest asking and answering questions – as central as this is to human experience? Indeed, postmodern thinkers have challenged us to prioritize the *other* or *what is otherwise*. The fields of hermeneutics and sociology of knowledge have illuminated the contingent, historical, and socially constructed dimensions of human knowledge and the plurality and ambiguity that accompany such fluidity.[1] There is something profoundly true about this – a reality that will be acknowledged in Part 3 of this book, which explores other-mediated and socially mediated desire. Still, even if Lonergan contextualized the human desire to know more broadly within the multidimensional experience of the life-world, he never diminished this human desire to know the truth, and the rich nobility that accompanies this desire. Lonergan's thought addresses in a distinctive way the challenge to engage the "whole breadth of reason and not to deny its grandeur."[2]

Analogy and Dialectic: Two Theological Trajectories

It is useful to situate this discussion of the relationship between intellectual desire and divine transcendence within the two major conceptual frameworks that often frame systematic-theological tensions: the analogical and the dialectical. My aim is simply to outline the basic trajectory of these two distinct but not unrelated theological languages.[3] Lonergan's account of the eros of the human mind falls within the analogical tradition – a tradition that nevertheless includes, as I note below, a dialectical moment.

The analogical framework prioritizes a "language of ordered relationships articulating similarity-in-difference."[4] Or as the oft-cited Fourth Lateran Council put it: within every similarity there is an ever-greater dissimilarity. Mindful of the goodness of the created order, analogical thinking emphasizes creaturely participation in meaning, truth, goodness, and love, which is the very meaning, truth, goodness, and love of the One who created the universe. Though it privileges the goodness of the human quest, a constitutive dimension of analogical thinking is also that of dissimilarity or negation. Hence, God is good, but not in the same way that creatures are good. God is the source of goodness, but to regard God as just another good in the great chain of goods would be to lose the ineffable core of the mystery of God. The moment of dissimilarity – the negative dialectic within the analogy – negates "any slackening of the sense of radical mystery, any grasp of control of the event and the similarities in difference" of God, self, and the world.[5] Analogical language surely focuses on experiences like trust, wonder, and giftedness, revealing a sense of harmony between human beings and the whole of reality. That said, when analogical theologies "lose that sense for the negative, that dialectical sense within analogy itself, they produce not a believable harmony among various likenesses in all reality but the theological equivalent of 'cheap grace': boredom, sterility and an atheological vision of a deadening univocity."[6] Perhaps one finds this tendency in the worst of the neo-scholastic manualist tradition described in chapter 1. This kind of conceptualism exhibits a capitulation to "the clear and distinct, the all-too-ordered and certain, the deadening, undisclosive and untransformative world of the dead analogies."[7] It is committed to certitude and not understanding, to univocity and not unity-in-difference.

The dialectical theological linguistic framework suggests, on the other hand, that the "participatory trust in similarities and continuities of the analogical language traditions" cannot account for "the rupture at the heart of human pretension, guilt and sin."[8] A core dimension of this theological style is to develop a theoretical framework that mitigates the temptation to find any easy continuity between Christianity and culture. At its extreme, this trend tends to negate any possibility of a positive point of contact between God and humanity, and emphasizes instead the "irrevocably, dialectical reality of God's revealed Word in Jesus Christ."[9]

Thomas Joseph White offers a helpful dichotomy that illuminates the dialectical and analogical traditions as they relate to the question of a natural point of contact between God and human beings.[10] For White, Karl Barth's position offers a "radical vision of the extrinsic transcendence of grace to nature" correlated to a "disavowal of any predisposition or potential inclination in human nature for the gift of divine life."[11] One cannot find in human nature a "natural point of contact" for grace to elevate; grace is required to create the conditions for its own reception. This Barthian position distrusts attempts by Thomists "to demonstrate a natural openness to God by way of philosophical assent through metaphysical analysis of created being and through a corresponding reflection on the natural final end of man as made in some real way for the contemplation and love of God."[12] De Lubac, on the other hand, as we discussed in the last two chapters, argues, more in the analogical tradition, for a natural inclination towards the supernatural that is inscribed in the human spirit from its creation. "We are always and everywhere," writes White, "animated by a latent natural desire for the gratuitous gift of supernatural beatitude, the vision of God."[13] Unlike Barth's rejection of a natural point of contact, de Lubac finds in the natural capacities of the human person an innate, inherent inclination towards divine life, even though paradoxically one cannot achieve this on one's own.[14] White affirms that the Barthians and Lubacians are both safeguarding important truths. Whereas the Barthians aim to "uphold the transcendence and gratuity of grace vis-à-vis all natural dispositions or inclinations," Lubacians wish to preserve "the deeply congruent rapport of nature's inner aspirations and the teleological promptings of grace, sealed within one concrete economic providence of God with respect to spiritual creatures."[15] In light of their respective emphases – gratuity of salvation vis-à-vis human effort (Barth) and the restless heart yearning for healing and elevating grace (de Lubac) – White suggests the need for harmonization, which he finds in "recourse to a certain kind of *philosophical* reading of Aquinas regarding

68   The Givenness of Desire

the final end of man."[16] In a related way, this book finds recourse in the thought of Lonergan.

The Diminishment of Intellectual Desire

Having just established a broad analogical-dialectical framework, I turn now to a trend that tends to diminish the analogical power of intellectual desire – a trend largely dialectical in character. For heuristic purposes, I focus the conversation on Girardian scholar James Alison and his critique of the natural desire to see God in light of mimetic theory. Alison's *The Joy of Being Wrong* and *Raising Abel* represent a fundamental rethinking of theological anthropology, Christology, and soteriology in light of Girard's groundbreaking contribution.

In Alison's "anthropology of conversion," the dimension of being human that most requires transformation is mimetic desire, and especially the violent expression of this desire that emerges ubiquitously in the human life-world.[17] In many ways, Alison communicates – in light of the analogical/dialectical discussion above – a more dialectical reading of human desire.

> This anthropological understanding links an understanding of the mimetic nature of desire with an understanding of the violent nature of desire, the resolution of that violence in the form of victimage, and eventually, the overcoming of the pattern of desire in question by a pattern of desire that is a rupture from, and yet in continuity with, the old pattern.[18]

Any account of human desire requires, then, a reckoning with rivalistic desire, the resolution of this tension in scapegoating, and the arduous task of reorienting our patterns of desire in non-violent ways. I attempt to do justice to a Girardian account of the dark side of mimetic desire later in the book; here I focus on Alison's account of natural desire, and especially on the natural desire for God.

Alison contrasts an "anthropology of grasping" with an "anthropology of self-giving." The anthropology of grasping perpetuates the romantic lie and the ongoing illusion of autonomy. It is rooted in what Girard calls "metaphysical desire" – the deviated desire to absorb the mediator of our desire into ourselves, especially the other's imagined autonomy and uniqueness. The anthropology of self-giving, on the other hand, corresponds to another kind of desire – "an anterior desire" identified with the "creative love of God" and manifested "only as self-giving."¹⁹ Grace is not lived by human beings who grasp the other. Alison extends his contrast of the "anthropology of grasping" and the "anthropology of self-giving" by considering more explicitly the themes of "self-transcendence" and "grace." In this vein, he identifies what he understands as a problem with both "intrinsicist" and "extrinsicist" accounts of the relationship between nature and grace. He considers the problem to be not with the theology of grace itself but with a corresponding anthropology of reception: "The dilemma between grace as somehow 'owed' to a human and grace as somehow 'already imbued in the human' shows that the discussion is taking place entirely within an anthropology of grasping and appropriating and is not focusing on the necessary gratuity of the transformation into gratuitous receivers of what remains lived in gratuity."²⁰ He relates this kind of grasping and appropriating to theologies that focus on universal human self-transcendence and prefers, instead, a theology that prioritizes the gratuity of God made present in concrete human historical circumstances.

In this light, Alison is understandably ambivalent about affirming a natural desire for God, which we can only talk about, he suggests, if we first prioritize a God who forms us in purely non-rivalistic, self-giving desire. Without this foundation, our construction of desire remains within the dynamic of appropriation and exclusion. Alison recognizes a natural desire for being, but this is largely an idolatrous desire for being. In practice, we desire obstacles to God because we desire by grasping and not by receiving. It is only in the transformation of our receptivity that our desire becomes an authentic "desire from and for God and is discovered to be such not as something plastered over our distorted desires, but as the real sense behind even those distorted desires, as something anterior to them."²¹ This is a return to our original way of being in the world as gift and not as acquisition – as something to be recovered.

Although human desire is, for Alison, intrinsically good, he still emphasizes its idolatrous temptations. Thus, he is critical of transcendental anthropologies that tend to pre-pardon "idolatry without transforming the idolater, without giving him or her the chance of a real restructuring of heart."²² Here, his theological anthropology emphasizes not so much the critical choice between theism and atheism, but between the God of Life and the gods of idolatry. The nature-grace debates discussed in Part 1 are marred on both sides by a kind of residual rationalism. They tended to present a "rosy" view of human nature as a kind of a "neutral intellectual feat" and depended on a "rationalist apologetics" that constructed "an intellectual scaffolding" in order to permit access to "the reality of God prior to the material proper to revelation."[23]

Many of Alison's statements require both further examination and serious consideration. This book as whole attempts to do justice to his account of distorted desire, the need for conversion and the re-envisioning of reception, and the persistent temptation to idolatry (see chapters 5 and 8). I will offer a more complex theology of religious love, grace, and receptivity in subsequent chapters. While Alison's suspicions about erecting intellectual scaffolding that permits us access to God prior to revelation are warranted, it is still plausible to ask whether there are others ways to interpret the human desire for being – ways that cannot be reduced to residual rationalism or a neutral intellectual feat.

Beyond the "Erotic Cemetery": Critical Realism and the Challenge of Intellectual Conversion

A substantive response to this plausible concern for residual rationalism and intellectual neutrality requires attention to the erotic roots of intellectual desire, the dimension of being human on which Lonergan builds his account of the natural desire for God. Accordingly, I frame Lonergan's contribution to a recovery of the eros of the mind with a few images from the work of the phenomenologist Jean-Luc Marion. It is not possible here to identify the variety of issues that would need to be worked out in a conversation with Lonergan and Marion. As I noted in the introduction, Lonergan deeply appreciated the phenomenological project, and one can detect the clear influence of phenomenology in the development of his thought.

Here I limit my framing to Marion's call for the need to restore the erotic roots of human knowing.[24] Marion's *The Erotic Phenomenon* attempts to rethink the human person and the relationship of the human person to the other in terms of the "erotic reduction."[25] The field of philosophy is, in Marion's words, an "erotic cemetery."[26] He laments the loss of philosophy as the love of wisdom. Many contemporary visions of knowing, in his estimation, are impoverished by ideology – a knowledge that sacrifices everything to power. The ubiquity of ideology demonstrates that the human person does not automatically "love the truth" in practice and often "sacrifices it for a lie, provided this lie assures him power."[27] By a forgetfulness of love and a corresponding loss of the erotics of wisdom, the wider culture is condemned to "feed on the scraps" of the "desperate sentimentalism of popular prose," the "frustrated pornography of the idol industry," and the "boastful asphyxiation" of "self-actualization."[28] Marion identifies the loss of erotic rationality with the influence of Descartes.[29] With modernity's emphasis on the primacy of thinking, love is relegated to the margins and reduced to a "passion." The modern subject is "defined by the exercise of rationality exclusively appropriate to objects and to beings," exemplified by Descartes's *"Ego cogito, ego sum,"* who principally thinks through the "ordering and measuring of objects."[30] Within this horizon, our erotic events are considered "incalculable and disordered accidents" that are "happily marginalized," and indeed can "do damage to the clear exercise" of the primacy of our thinking. For Marion, however, we are primordially oriented to the world by the erotic. Descartes's shocking and "monstrously mistaken description" points to the "erotic blindness of metaphysics."[31] Marion finds it necessary then to prioritize erotic meditations over metaphysical meditations – starting not with doubt but with "the fact that I *love* even before being."[32] For Marion, we desire to know for the pleasure of knowing – "perhaps the most exciting, the most durable, and the purest of the pleasures that is possible for us to experience in this life."[33]

Lonergan would reject the idea of substituting "erotic meditations" for "metaphysical meditations," at least in the way that he himself defines metaphysics, which is certainly not Cartesian. But his thought deeply affirms the heart of Marion's challenge, which is to recover the eros, the desire, the pleasure that constitutes the undertow of human knowing that precedes the actual content of knowing. To use Marion's language, erotic meditations lead to metaphysical meditations. Or to put it in Lonergan's own technical language: cognitional theory (What am I doing when I am knowing?) leads to epistemology (Why is doing that knowing?), which in turn brings us to metaphysics (What am I knowing when I am performing these activities?). In terms of the larger concerns of the nature-grace question, this a specifically Lonergan-influenced way of affirming the Toulouse Dominican Gilbert Narcisse's suggestion that "the problem is not only the relations of nature and grace, nor the natural desire for the supernatural, but above all that of being, of the consistency that we accord it and correlatively of the epistemological possibilities of attaining it in its ultimate meaning."[34] It is unhelpful to "multiply hermeneutical worlds or ways of doing theology" if we inadequately treat the desire to know and the ability to attain being. "For without being," Narcisse writes, "grace vanishes, and we risk falling into a kind of intellectual activism, as the mystics say about overly hurried disciples."[35]

Building on this conversation with Alison and Marion, let me suggest that Lonergan offers a larger picture of self-transcendence that integrates the eros of the human spirit and the gratuitous, gift-like realities prioritized by Alison. This chapter mainly focuses on the intellectual dimension. Subsequent chapters will examine other key dimensions of his holistic vision of self-transcendence: love, gift, intersubjectivity, among other themes.

Since I highlighted Narcisse's defence of being above, it is pertinent to point the reader to Lonergan's fuller philosophical system without, of course, having the space to explain it at length here. The epistemological correlates to the cognitional acts of experience, understanding, and judging are empirical, normative, and absolute objectivity. The metaphysical correlates are potency (material causality), form (formal causality), and act (existence). This cognitional-epistemological-metaphysical framework constitutes, in a nutshell, what Lonergan calls the integral heuristic structure of proportionate being.

Lonergan's critical realism is based on the fundamental "desire to know" as explained by Aristotle in the *Metaphysics*. Building on Aristotle, Aquinas provided a deeply penetrating theory of the nature of the human intellect. In his early work on Aquinas, Lonergan captures this complexity:

> Hence the light of the intellect, insight into phantasm, acts of defining thought, reflective reasoning and understanding, acts of judgment are above all psychological facts. The inner word of definition is the expression of an insight into phantasm, and the insight is the goal towards which the wonder of inquiry tends. The inner word of judgment is the expression of a reflective act of understanding, and that reflective act is the goal towards which critical wonder tends. The former answers the question, *Quid sit?* The latter answers the question, *An sit?*[36]

In *Insight*, Lonergan integrated what he discovered in Aquinas into a complex theory of human knowing – an explanatory theory that he situated within a differentiated account of the world process called "emergent probability." Human beings are endowed with the light and drive of intelligent inquiry, manifested through the asking and answering of questions. This drive is guided by the self-corrective process of knowing. Human beings possess a dynamically structured consciousness –

an awareness immanent in a dynamic pattern of cognitional acts. While some philosophers conceive of knowing in terms of perception, Lonergan conceives of knowing in terms of heuristic structure, in which different kinds of questions initiate sets of operations on different levels of conscious intentionality. Knowing is not simply a matter of deducing propositions, but of intelligent discovery made possible by the spirit of inquiry. This spirit of inquiry is the "prior and enveloping drive that carries cognitional process from sense and imagination to understanding, from understanding to judgment, from judgment to the complete context of correct judgments that is named knowledge."[37]

In order to appreciate the rich nobility of intellectual desire, one must grasp the limitations of a naive realist position that identifies knowing with "taking a good look" at the "already-out-there-now-real."[38] Often, we think of consciousness as "in here" and being or the real as "out there." This split is apparent, for instance, in Descartes's *res cogitans* and *res extensa*. Lonergan, however, overcomes this split by including conscious being as part of being. In chapter 11 of *Insight*, he challenges his readers to "an attentiveness of conscious operations" or a "heightening of consciousness." After all, such an epistemology is not abstractly verified, but affirmed only through performance. Each person must ask, "Am I a knower?" Insofar as one performs these activities, and verifies in judgment that one is performing these activities, one is a knower on its way to further knowing.[39] This is a crucial move. Because if one affirms that one is a concrete and intelligible unity-identity-whole, characterized by the acts of sensing, perceiving, imagining, inquiring, understanding, formulating, reflecting, grasping the unconditioned, and affirming, one is in fact transforming this conditioned into a virtually unconditioned. And because being is identified with correct judgments, and we have correctly judged that we in fact perform these activities, then conscious being is part of being.

Lonergan's critical realism, then, affirms an Aristotelian account of consciousness-as-experience, which roots knowledge not in confrontation but in identity: "the sense in act is the sensible in act, and in the case of immaterial beings that which understands is identical with that which is understood."[40] With knowledge as identity, "it is not too difficult to conceive consciousness as experience strictly so called, which is in the operating subject on the side of the subject, and through which the operating subject is rendered present to itself under the formality of the experienced."[41] Perhaps Walker Percy's account of "knowledge by identity" – which he is expressing to critique the reduction of knowing to a biological need – might illuminate Lonergan's insight here:

> For it will be knowledge, not in the sense of possessing "facts" but in the Thomist and existential sense of identification of knower with the object known. Is it not possible that this startling semantic insight, that by the word I *have* the thing, fix it, and rescue it from the flux of Becoming around me, might not confirm and illuminate the mysterious Thomist notion of the interior word, of knowing something by becoming something? That the "basic need of symbolization" is nothing more or less than the first ascent in the hierarchy of knowledge, the eminently "natural" and so all the more astonishing instrument by which I transform the sensory content and appropriate it for the stuff of my ideas, and therefore the activity of knowing cannot be evaluated according to the "degree to which it fills a biological need," nor according to the "degree to which the symbol is articulated," but by nothing short of Truth itself.[42]

The example of Augustine's intellectual conversion in book 7 of the *Confessions* can also illuminate the distinctiveness of critical realism. Though Augustine's conversion transcends the intellectual, it would be inadequate to ignore the painful intellectual questions that plagued his quest. He experienced a real ontological dilemma of reasoning about God. Is God merely a supreme being? If so, then where is God? Can God be divided up so there is less God here and more God there? Can God be accounted for in spatial terms? Augustine reflects, "Whatever was not stretched out in space, or diffused or compacted or inflated or possessed of some such qualities, or at least capable of possessing them, I judged to be nothing at all."[43] Extending this reasoning to God, he adds: "Hence, I thought that even you, Life of my life, were a vast reality spread throughout space in every direction."[44] The key to bringing his intellectual restlessness to rest involved an intellectual conversion: the transition from thinking about the real in terms of *spatial bodies* to the real in terms of *intelligibility*, which is a spiritual reality not intrinsically conditioned by space and time. In book 7, Augustine turns inward: "I proceeded further and came to the power of discursive reason, to which the data of our senses are referred to for judgment ... And then my mind attained to *That Which Is* ... Then indeed did I perceive your invisible reality through created things."[45] (This intellectual conversion was not the end of Augustine's restlessness; in chapter 5, I turn to the religious and moral dimensions of his conversion.)

In light of Lonergan's account of the complexity of the knowing process, I focus now on the fact that the kind of human knowing on which Lonergan grounds his account of the natural desire for God is rooted in a desire more erotic than is indicated by Alison's critique of neutral, residual rationality. In fact, Lonergan refers to the desire to know – discussed above – as the "eros of the mind." Lonergan's identification of the erotic roots of knowing might be interpreted as an affirmation of Alison's critique that a desire for being embodies a distorted anthropology of grasping. After all, in his influential account of eros and agape, Anders Nygren represents eros as humanity's longing for God – a longing manifested in acquisitive desire and egocentric love.[46] While it is certainly true that eros longs for God in Lonergan's account, it is not fully adequate to identify this longing as solely acquisitive and egocentric. In Lonergan's account egoism, for example, distorts the pure desire to know. Egoism dismisses the "further pertinent questions" that would lead one to question one's own selfish acts. The "cool schemer, the shrewd calculator, the hardheaded seeker" employ intelligence as an instrument for selfish purposes. Lonergan writes, "The egoist's uneasy conscience is his awareness of his sin against the light."[47] This experience of inner conflict is precipitated by both the eros of the mind to ask and answer further relevant questions and the fact that the egoist refuses to grant licence to this erotic drive by declining to consider further relevant questions. To state it more positively, it is precisely concrete faithfulness to the eros of the mind that helps us overcome the dramatic, individual, group, and anti-theoretical biases that infect our minds and, by extension, human culture more broadly.

When considering the knowing process, Lonergan does not have in mind a dry rationality. As mentioned above, he characterizes the intellectual dynamism as the "eros of the mind" – a desire that yearns for the "ecstasy of insight" and that parallels the way sexual climax brings sexual eros to rest. The experience of insight releases the tension of inquiry. The dramatic example he offers is that of Archimedes' discovery of the principles of hydrostatics. Lying in a bathtub, Archimedes experienced a "peculiarly uninhibited exultation" and ran into the streets proclaiming "Eureka!" Lonergan highlights both his "outburst of delight" and the antecedent desire that fueled it:

Deep within us all, emergent when the noise of other appetites is filled, there is a drive to know, to understand, to see why, to discover the reason, to find the cause, to explain. Just what is wanted has many names. In what

76   The Givenness of Desire

precisely it consists is a matter of dispute. But the fact of inquiry is beyond all doubt.[48]

Lonergan does not identify human knowing first and foremost with arid concepts. In fact, Lonergan's epistemological "enemy" is precisely what he terms "conceptualism." A conceptualist account of knowing stresses universal concepts and propositions, over the prior acts of inquiry and insight. Lonergan emphasizes, however, the erotic roots of the pure desire to know. The fact of inquiry

> can absorb a man. It can keep him for hours, day after day, year after year, in the narrow prison of his study or laboratory. It can send him on dangerous voyages of exploration. It can withdraw him from other interests, other pursuits, other pleasures, other achievements. It can fill his waking thoughts, hide him from the world of ordinary affairs, invade the very fabric of his dreams. It can demand endless sacrifices that are made without regret though there is only the hope, never a certain promise, of success. What better symbol could one find for this obscure, exigent, imperious drive, than a man, naked, running, excitedly crying, "I've got it"?[49]

Lonergan's later distinction between the "categorial" and the "transcendental" modes of intending help illuminate this distinction between concepts and this eros of the human spirit.[50] This distinction relates to the worry of many *ressourcement* theologians about the conceptualism that shaped theological training in the first half of the twentieth century. Recall the emphasis placed on the memorization of propositions. "Categorial," in Lonergan's usage, denotes the use of categories as determinations. They are needed "to put determinate questions and give determinate answers." But they also have a limited denotation and vary with cultural variations, whether the classification associated with Totemism or the Aristotelian categories or the achievements of modern physics, the periodic table of the chemist or the evolutionary tree of the biologist. The transcendental, on the other hand, are "comprehensive in connotation, unrestricted in denotation, invariant over cultural change." The transcendentals are the "radical intending that moves us from ignorance to knowledge." They are unrestricted in the sense that answers are never complete and are always open to further questions. They are comprehensive in the sense that they "intend the unknown whole or totality of which our answers reveal only part." Formation in the early-to-mid-twentieth-century neo-scholastic mode tended to prefer categories at the expense of understanding and the pursuit of further questions.

This radical transcendental intending of the eros of the human spirit articulated by Lonergan can also be experienced as a kind of transcultural call to be faithful to the transcendental precepts – precepts that correspond to the four levels of conscious intentionality: be attentive, be intelligent, be rational, be responsible, and, in anticipation of chapters 5 and 6, be loving.[51] With an eye to history, Lonergan suggests that a failure to follow the precepts results in a basic form of alienation in the person, but also compromises and distorts social and cultural progress, resulting in cumulative decline.[52] Lonergan extends this ecstatic account of knowing into his analogical framing of his theology of God: "Our subject has been the act of insight or understanding, and God is the unrestricted act of understanding, the eternal rapture glimpsed in every Archimedean cry of 'Eureka.'"[53]

Eros of the Mind I: Natural Theology

In light of this analysis of the eros of the mind and the richness of human knowing, I turn to several ways this erotic spirit shapes Lonergan's theological presentation. The first has to do with Lonergan's natural theology. This treatment does not attempt to exhaust every nuance of Lonergan's proof for the existence of God, but just to show the importance of the high nobility of intellectual desire as it shapes Lonergan's intellectual project – a richness that is no longer evident in many strands of modern theology.

Natural theology finds a multitude of objectors in the modern world. On the one hand, those inspired by Kant would suggest that real knowledge of God is not possible due to the limits of ontological reasoning by the a priori concepts of the human mind. On the other hand, the heirs of Luther might object that real philosophical knowledge of God is thwarted due to the fallen human mind and distorted will. God-claims set apart from the revelation of God in Christ are by their nature pretentious and idolatrous.[54]

Natural theology in Lonergan's Thomist-inspired system is not meant to indicate a "discipline that would attempt to construct an understanding of God in separation from Christian theology so as to judge the latter according to the criteria of knowledge of the former."[55] Rather, it is, as Thomas Joseph White notes, a discipline "that inquires into the distinctly natural or intrinsic capacity of the human mind to come to some real knowledge of the existence and nature of God by philosophical means, even though this knowledge is mediate and analogical."[56]

David Bentley Hart has recently revisited with a kind of interreligious consciousness the connection between the mystery of human consciousness and the mystery of God.[57] Hart's aim is largely one of clarification. He is responding in part to the rhetoric of the so-called New Atheists, who tend to exhibit a rather thin and even caricatured understanding of what many of the world's great religious traditions – Judaism, Christianity, Islam, Vedantic and Bhaktic Hinduism – mean when they employ the term "God." There is, he contends, a lack of appreciation for the "sophisticated and self-critical philosophical and contemplative schools" present in the history of such traditions.[58] In fact, Hart highlights "the moments when our experience of the world awakens us to the strangeness – the utter fortuity and pure givenness – of existence."[59] "No less wonderful than the being of things," he writes, "is our consciousness of them: our ability to know the world, to possess a continuous subjective awareness of reality, to mirror the unity of being in the unity of private cognizance, to contemplate the world and ourselves, to assume each moment of experience into a fuller comprehension of the whole, and to relate ourselves to the world through acts of judgment and will."[60]

In light of Hart's recovery of this kind of intellectual tradition as more than a dry, rationalist mode of discourse, let me highlight some salient points about Lonergan's position in *Insight*. Lonergan's argument for the existence of God is conditioned by his grasp of emergent probability in general and by his shift to human knowing as a scheme of recurrence in the concretely operating universe that is both emergent and hierarchically structured. The argument in syllogistic form states: "If the real is completely intelligible, God exists. But the real is completely intelligible. Therefore, God exists."[61] The crucial identification of being with the real, and of the real with intelligibility rather than with bodily aggregates is grounded in the human capacity to transcend biologically extroverted consciousness, described above. The intelligent conception and reasonable affirmation of this one contingent fact about being implies that being is not only intelligible, but completely intelligible. If in a judgment we affirm that something that exists or occurs is intelligible, then it is reasonable to conclude that everything that "is" is intelligible. Since there is no such thing as a brute fact, one may argue to a general transcendent knowledge that not only explains every contingent fact, but also understands itself as the ultimate explanation.

Otherwise, being would not be completely intelligible. But it is incoherent to affirm that the intelligibility of the whole is a mere matter of fact, rather than the result of an intelligent principle.

The analogical correlate to this erotic, unrestricted desire to know is God conceived as an unrestricted act of understanding – God as the source of being that understands everything about everything. "God is an act, the content of which is the idea of being."[62] When human subjects reach a virtually unconditioned, they do so because there are no further relevant questions. One who knows everything about everything would also understand why there are no further questions. In this regard, Lonergan speaks of primary and secondary components of the unrestricted act, whose content is the idea of being. The primary component of the idea of being is the self-understanding of the unrestricted act of understanding. If such an act did not understand itself, then there would be something it did not understand. It understands its reasons for being (unlike us), and the reason is precisely to understand.[63] The secondary component is that the unrestricted act understands everything about everything.

Hart notes that Lonergan's "complicated and ingenious" treatment of God as unrestricted intelligibility – an argument that is "powerful and evocative" and "inductively persuasive" – serves as an eminent example of the relationship between consciousness and the quest for God. "The essential truth to which Lonergan's argument points," writes Hart, "is that the very search for truth is implicitly a search for God." The mind's ascent "toward ever greater knowledge is, if only tacitly and secretly and *contre coeur*, an ascent toward an ultimate encounter with limitless consciousness, limitless reason, a transcendent reality where being and knowledge are always already one and the same, and so inalienable from one another."[64] "To believe that being is inexhaustibly intelligible is to believe also – whether one wishes to acknowledge it or not – that reality emanates from an inexhaustible intelligence."[65]

Eros of the Mind II: The Emergence of the Question of God

In his essay "Theology in Its New Context" (1967) – an essay framed explicitly within John XXIII's call for *aggiornamento* – Lonergan offers a distinction between the abstract and the concrete, a distinction that would become crucial to his subsequent thinking on the question of God.[66] His burgeoning aim was to move theology from foundations in "the static to the dynamic, from the abstract to the concrete, from the universal to the historical totality of particulars, from invariable rules to intelligent adjustment and adaptation."⁶⁷ And the new foundation is the concrete subject operating under the exigencies of intellectual, moral, and religious conversion – an "ongoing process" that is "concrete and dynamic, personal, communal, and historical."⁶⁸ More will be said below about the concrete subject operating within an intellectual, moral, and religious horizon and its relationship to the question of God.

Lonergan shifts the emphasis from an intellectual proof for God's existence in the tradition of natural theology to an emphasis on the variety of ways *the question of God* arises in the intellectual, moral, and religious dimensions of our concrete lives. That is, he emphasized the human call to self-transcendence and the way acts of self-transcendence enable the *question of God* to emerge in one's conscious horizon. In the midst of our attempt to be attentive, intelligent, reasonable, and responsible, we may raise the following questions: "Does there or does there not necessarily exist a transcendent intelligent ground of the universe? Is that ground or are we the primary instance of moral consciousness? Are cosmogenesis, biological evolution, historical process basically cognate to us as moral beings or are they indifferent and so alien to us?"⁶⁹ Lonergan's point is that a commitment to intellectual rigour and moral authenticity allow for the question of God to enter the horizon of human knowledge, that is, of course, if its dynamism is not mutilated or abolished by ideology or other constrictions of the human spirit. And this question can also arise in light of being-in-love, a state that lies at the heart of religious experience in Lonergan's conception. Religious experience, of course, takes on many forms and is part of a variety of human cultures; these forms are often marked by aberration, as Girard has shown us, illuminating the "precariousness of the human achievement of authenticity." Still, for Lonergan, underneath "the many forms and prior to the many aberrations," there also exists "an unrestricted being in love, a mystery of love and awe, a being grasped by ultimate concern, a happiness that has a determinate content but no intellectually apprehended object." The question of God arises here when we ask, "With whom are we in love?" The question of God arises on different levels, but it does not follow, for Lonergan, that these are distinct and separate questions.⁷⁰

> The questions are distinct but they are also cumulative. The question of God is epistemological when we ask how the universe can be intelligible ... It is moral when we ask whether the universe has a moral ground and

so a moral goal. It finally is religious when we ask whether there is anyone for us to love with all our heart and all our soul and all our mind and all our strength.[71]

Lonergan then connects the question of God to the theme of "pure nature." It could be argued, he suggests, that the last question about love would not occur if the human person existed in the state of pure nature. "But man at present," he adds, "does not exist in the hypothetical state of affairs named pure nature."[72]

By including the realm of "religious love" in this discussion of the question of God, Lonergan is envisioning a more dynamic interplay between theology and philosophy. For him, the multiple ways that the question of God emerges are "cumulative" and "belong together."[73] He marginalizes, once again, the idea of "pure nature":

> One must not think that the question of God fundamentally is philosophic, that in the state of pure nature it would not extend into theological terrain, that accidentally in the present state of affairs it merely happens to move out of its proper sphere and touch on matters that are theological. The vast majority of mankind have been religious. One cannot claim that their religion has been based on some philosophy of God. One can easily argue that their religious concern arose out of their religious experience.[74]

Thus we should "put an end to the practice of isolating" these two disciplines – one of the implications of static essentialism noted in chapter 4. For Lonergan, "the world of the theologian" is not an "isolated sphere" cut off from human affairs. The static viewpoint, of course, leads to such isolation. By rejecting the static viewpoint, by conceiving theology as an ongoing process guided by method, "one puts an end to isolationism." The concern of the theologian, he adds, is not "just a set of propositions but a concrete religion as it has been lived, as it is being lived, and as it is to be lived."[75]

It is pertinent to note that Lonergan articulated his account of the dynamic interpenetration of intellectual, moral, and religious conversion with the example of Augustine explicitly in mind. Augustine's movement from restlessness to rest in the *Confessions* exhibits this dynamic interplay.[76] In Augustine's case, one cannot overlook, as I said above, the importance of his intellectual conversion described in book 7 of the *Confessions*. There I highlighted his experience of the ontological dilemma and the way the neo-Platonists helped him think about the real not in terms of bodies but in terms of intelligibility. That being said, this intellectual conversion was not the end of Augustine's restlessness. He was still caught in the grip of lust; he came to a more adequate conception of God, but could not figure out how to enjoy the presence of God. Augustine had a divided will incapable of doing the good. His moral conversion would only come about in the narrative of the *Confessions* with his religious conversion. Having surrendered his freedom in favour of enslavement, Augustine did not have the power to retrieve it on his own. Only with grace – a gratuitous encounter precisely exhibited in the "take and read" episode – was Augustine able to experience God in a holistic manner, intellectually, morally, and religiously.

Nowhere is this new way of situating the question of God within the horizon of intellectual, moral, and religious self-transcendence more apparent than in Lonergan's rethinking of his "proof" for the existence of God. Shortly after the publication of *Method in Theology* (1972), Lonergan delivered three lectures at Gonzaga University that are now published under the title "Philosophy of God, and Theology" (1972).[77] Lonergan's development in these lectures reveals a progressive acknowledgment of the deeply historical, sociological, and contextual dimensions of knowledge. For Lonergan, "what lies beyond one's horizon is simply outside the range of one's interests and knowledge: one knows nothing about and cares less. And what lies within one's horizon is in some measure, great or small, an object of interest and of knowledge."[78] Furthermore, any rigorous "proof," including a proof for the existence of God presupposes both "the erection of a system in which all terms and relations have an exact meaning" and "a horizon, a worldview, a differentiation of consciousness, that has unfolded under the conditions and circumstances of a particular culture and a particular historical development."[79] Reflecting on his earlier formulated "proof" for the existence of God in *Insight* (1957), Lonergan writes:

> The trouble with chapter 19 of *Insight*[80] was that it did not depart from the traditional line. It treated God's existence and attributes in a purely objective fashion. It made no effort to deal with the subject's religious horizon. It failed to acknowledge that the traditional viewpoint made sense only if one accepted first principles on the ground that they were intrinsically necessary, and if one added the assumption that there is one right culture so that differences in subjectivity are irrelevant.[81]

In these 1972 lectures, Lonergan argues not against this position in *Insight*, but that a "philosophy of God" ought to be situated within the discipline of systematic theology. Systematic theology affirms the relentless, even scientific, quest for understanding, while at the same time presuming the context of faith and the ongoing process of intellectual, moral, and religious self-transcendence. It is "only in the climate of religious experience," Lonergan wrote, "that philosophy of God flourishes."[82] The "static viewpoint" of "deductivist logic" critiqued by Lonergan in his repositioning of natural theology involves a one-sided emphasis on the logical control of meaning. Lonergan shares the concerns of de Lubac, Daniélou, and others about the dominance of rationalism in early-to-mid-twentieth-century theological formation, as noted in chapter 1.

Lonergan's shift in emphasis from "proof" to the religious experience wherein the question of God emerges reveals his shift from *logic* to *method*. To understand the human control of meaning as logic is to prioritize, for Lonergan, the "deductivist ideal." In this view, systems of thought are either true or false. Objectivity is considered "the fruit of immediate experience, of self-evident and necessary truths, and of rigorous inferences."[83] Lonergan's vision is to integrate the quest for understanding and truth that presumably lies at the root of logic within a methodical understanding of human inquiry. His methodical view emphasizes complex human subjectivity where objectivity is not viewed as self-evident but as "the fruit of authentic subjectivity, of being attentive, intelligent, reasonable, and responsible." Lonergan captures this syllogistic style of theology as follows: "What God has revealed is true. God has revealed the mysteries of faith. Therefore the mysteries of faith are true."[84] Such an exaggerated and simplistic view of objectivity "insisted on true propositions" and neglected the human subject, along with the complex conditions required for advancing towards the truth.[85]

This shift from logic to method has implications for how one imagines the theological task. When deductivist logic prevails, theology is imagined only as "the science of God and of all things in their relation to God."[86] Lonergan, of course, does not want to relinquish the "scientific" dimension of theology, nor does he want to thwart a wisdom perspective that relates in a holistic manner God and created reality. What a methodical viewpoint adds is attention to the relationship between religion and culture. Theology, in this frame, is "conceived as reflection on the significance and value of religion within a culture, and culture itself is conceived, not normatively as though in principle there was but one human culture, but empirically and so with a full recognition of the many different manners in which sets of meanings and of values have informed human ways of life."[87]

The shifting of emphasis from natural theology to the emergence of the question of God within one's conscious horizon is one thing; to presume the legitimacy of the question of God within contemporary culture shaped by modernity is another. As Lonergan indicated in his vision of theology in a new context, the connection between religion and culture is an essential domain of inquiry.[88]

Eros of the Mind III: The Challenge of Bias and the Human Good

If Lonergan's account of the eros of the mind does substantive speculative work in his theological understanding of the God-human relationship, it is also intimately tied to his account of human progress and attention to the other. One of the central issues associated with the postmodern critique is "the priority of the ethical, or concern for the other, as constitutive of philosophical reflection."[89] Does not Lonergan fall prey to the postmodern critique levelled at the modern subject's "disembodied intellect unencumbered by its historicity, unaware that experience is mediated through body and culture"?[90] Concrete subjectivity, as this book envisions, resists this claim. In fact, what Lonergan offers is a commitment to the concrete subject as knower, but a knower situated within the larger drama of human living. Furthermore, in anticipation of the next chapter, Lonergan's account of natural desire bears the self-critical resources for cultural and political resistance, and hence is exonerated from the deleterious effects of pure nature, suggested in the previous two chapters by the Lubacian diagnosis.

Lonergan's account of the dialectical tensions in the human subject and human communities helps clarify the demands of progress. Continuous growth seems rare. There are biases and breakdowns. Lonergan writes, "Just as insight can be desired, so too it can be unwanted. Besides the love of light, there can be a love of darkness."[91] In *Insight*, Lonergan discusses four types of bias: dramatic, individual, group, and general.[92] Dramatic bias pre-consciously affects the level of experience. Often because of their painful nature, a dramatically biased subject censors certain images from entering consciousness. Affecting the level of understanding, individual egoism refuses to entertain certain relevant questions. Although a particular group achieves common meaning, group bias causes group egoism, with its hindrances to intelligence and reasonableness. Finally, the most insidious form of bias, general bias, indicates an anti-theoretical orientation linked to a lack of concern for long-term results.

To reiterate what was said above in response to Alison's concern for an "anthropology of grasping," the inner conflict of the egoist is precipitated by both the eros of the mind to ask and answer further relevant questions and the fact that the egoist refuses to grant license to this erotic drive, declining to consider further relevant questions. Perhaps it is fitting to say something about group bias and general bias as well to reinforce the fact that faithfulness to eros of the mind does not represent a modern rationalist disconnected from the ethical imperatives of the other, but a concrete subject who concretely affects social and cultural life.

Group bias indicates the blind spots that develop within different socioeconomic groups. We have different classes, in part, because we have so many different tasks to be performed in the present social ordering. In one respect, it is intelligent and reasonable to divide up different tasks and set up cooperative schemes that will provide for basic and surplus needs within our social, religious, economic, and political communities. Commonsense or practical intelligence generates successive social orders with their need for new and more specialized tasks of commonsense knowing and doing. But power plays tend to call upon group loyalties to repress relevant questions that would generate new intelligent, reasonable, and responsible courses of action. Group egoism tends to provide excuses, rationalizations, and socially supported ideology. And group egoism is perhaps "more damaging that individual bias," for it finds "reinforcement from others and from shared theories and doctrines."[93] Group egoism creates the conditions, in Lonergan's terms, for a shorter cycle of decline. It infects society with "deep feelings of frustration, resentment, bitterness, and hatred."[94] The bright side of the shorter cycle of declines is that it "creates the principles for its own reversal."[95] Over time, group bias becomes a "grotesquely distorted reality," exposing the "concrete distortions" for "the inspection of the multitude."[96] Of course, such an exposure might lead to a variety of responses, including violent revolution or a truly progressive correction of the distortions and a corresponding plan for preventing future recurrence. But the point here is that openness to further questions and to insight has real bearing on progress and decline.

In addition to group bias, Lonergan also includes another kind of bias, general bias, which is responsible for a "longer cycle of decline." General bias extends its "legitimate concern for the concrete and the immediately practical into disregard of larger issues and indifference to long-term results."[97] The linking of group bias with general bias results in a deeper, more insidious decline. In this state, there is a "neglect of long-term solutions good for the whole of society," and consequently a neglect of "the kind of ideas that would reverse decline."[98] A failure to live up to the transcendental precepts to be attentive, intelligent, rational, and responsible produces objectively absurd situations, where mistaken solutions are deemed intelligent, reasonable, and good. As Lonergan writes, "Imperceptibly the corruption spreads from the harsh sphere of material advantage and power to the mass media, the stylish journals, the literary movements, the educational process, the reigning philosophies."[99] When this kind of deep and all-pervasive penetration occurs, then a "civilization in decline digs its own grave with a relentless consistency."[100] Just as self-transcendence promotes progress, its refusal leads to cumulative decline. Such social deterioration and cultural retreat lead, at its extreme, to a totalitarian situation, which identifies "reality" falsely with "the economic development, the military equipment, and the political dominance of the all-inclusive state."[101] The means of such a false metaphysical totalitarianism include "not merely every technique of indoctrination and propaganda, every tactic of economic and diplomatic pressure, every device for breaking down the moral conscience and the secret affects of civilized man, but also the terrorism of a political police, of prisons and torture, of concentration camps, of transported or extirpated minorities, and of total war."[102] Though Lonergan did not experience the challenge of actively resisting the Nazis, as de Lubac did, the horrors of history significantly shaped his intellectual endeavours.

Conclusion

This chapter focused on the kind of desire on which Lonergan bases his account of the natural desire to see God. Rooted in the pure, detached, unrestricted desire to know, Lonergan's account of knowledge resists identifying the knowing of being with an act of idolatry. Noting the complexity of Lonergan's critical realism, along with the passionate eros of the spirit, the chapter captured several ways in which this account of intellectual desire continues to shape a contemporary analogical style of theological judgments in terms of natural theology, a shift to the "question of God," and the human good. Having established his account of the erotic roots of intellectual desire, I turn now to Lonergan's distinctive contribution to the neo-Thomist-Lubacian debate on the natural desire to see God.

4 Concretely Operating Nature: Lonergan on the Natural Desire to See God

I highlighted, in chapter 2, several tensions operative in conversations between the Lubacian and neo-Thomist positions on nature and the natural desire for God. This chapter begins to develop some of Lonergan's contributions to the debate over the natural desire for God, building on his commitment to the intellectual desire of the concrete subject discussed in chapter 3, a topic that will be developed further in chapter 5.

These pages retrieve key aspects of Lonergan's thought, mindful on the one hand of the Lubacians' legitimate concern with the concrete and historical and on the other hand of the call of many Thomists to affirm a more substantive account of nature. In light of the eros of the mind of the concrete subject, Lonergan's account of nature in scholastic terms and in his more dynamic and scientifically influenced account of emergent probability responds to both of these challenges. This chapter responds to the issues highlighted in chapter 2 on the de Lubac–Thomist tensions. Nature, after all, doesn't come to grace first with deficiency, but as a plenitude. "In order to take account of this 'wounded nature' in its historical becoming of sin and death," as Gilbert Narcisse notes, "we must again start out from this original plenitude of being. It alone is capable of not substituting for the light of being and of grace, the twilight of the tragic human condition."[1] Lonergan's dynamic account of nature responds in a historically conscious way to this call to articulate the plenitude of being.

Lonergan did not comment on de Lubac often. His main concern with de Lubac's work, however, was its lack of systematic precision. He believed de Lubac was at times "mixed up" and found some of his solutions unsatisfactory. He refers to the articles de Lubac published in the 1930s as a series of learned articles about sixteenth-century theologians. The problem was with the republication of the same articles with an added epilogue as

Surnaturel. Lonergan writes, "The epilogue was a mistake! While de Lubac is a man of extraordinary erudition and also respected as a very holy man by people who have lived with him in his own Province, he is not a competent speculative thinker. At least I don't find that in him."[2]

There is much to affirm in de Lubac's vision. On the one hand, the animating force beneath de Lubac's claim ought to be embraced, but on the other hand, his presentation of the relevant systematic issues often falls short when considered from a speculative perspective. Lonergan's position can, I think, be reconciled with many aspects of de Lubac's. In what follows, I argue that Lonergan offers many systematic resources for addressing the heart of Henri de Lubac's project, which is an attunement to concrete human persons oriented to the supernatural in the world order, as it exists. At the same time, I respond both sympathetically and critically to several contemporary critiques of de Lubac, as expressed by Feingold and other neo-Thomists.

This chapter first outlines key features of Lonergan's uses of the terms "nature" and "natural" in his earlier writings, with specific attention to the theological question of the natural desire to see God. I respond in a nuanced way to Feingold's and Mansini's claims about "naturally elicited desire." In light of Lonergan's distinctive position on natural and elicited desire, I turn to his account of the twofold end of the human person – an account that resists a static-essentialist view of human finality. With this more dynamic opening in mind, I then examine Lonergan's concrete account of nature as emergent probability, which reflects some key features of contemporary conversations in science and religion. This explanation of emergent probability sets the stage for an account of the vocation of concrete human subjects to ongoing intellectual and moral self-transcendence and the construction of the human good. The human desire for ever-greater fulfilment in various human goods – according to the normative scale of values – makes room for a conversation about our transcendent orientation, on the one hand, and the gratuity of divinization, on the other hand. Finally, the chapter explains Lonergan's distinctive account of obediential potency and vertical finality within the concrete world order – an account that paves the way for an understanding of aesthetic fittingness in relation to our desire for God.

Nature I: Lonergan's Scholastic Context

Lonergan spent a significant amount of time in his early academic career coming to grips with the complexities of Thomas Aquinas's theology of grace. As he gratefully acknowledged, the years spent "reaching up to the mind of Aquinas" changed him profoundly.[3] He completed his doctoral dissertation on operative grace in the writings of Aquinas in 1940 and rewrote and published his investigation in *Theological Studies* in 1941 and 1942.[4] Both of these writings together now constitute volume 1 of the *Collected Works of Bernard Lonergan*. In 1946, Lonergan composed a treatise, *On Supernatural Being* (*De ente supernaturali*), now translated and published in volume 19 of the *Collected Works*. Throughout the 1940s he wrote a series of articles that treated the theme of nature and grace, culminating in his 1949 address before the Jesuit Philosophical Association, "The Natural Desire to See God" – an address given in the wake of Henri de Lubac's controversial study *Surnaturel*. Lonergan's lecture on the natural desire to see God prompted him to return to "The Supernatural Order" and insert a clarification of his position on this vexed question.[5]

Lonergan's first treatment of nature in the scholastic context concerns the explanatory role it plays in conversations about grace and freedom.[6] To state it in summary form, without nature, one is left only with a grace-sin dialectic. The category of "nature" made possible a more rigorous articulation of grace as both healing and elevating. Lonergan highlights what he calls the Augustinian disjunction: "the will of man is always free but not always good: either it is free from justice, and then it is evil; or it is liberated from sin, and then it is good."[7] In light of this grace-sin dialectic, Lonergan importantly points out that Augustine did not develop a speculative system of nature and grace. The theological terms employed were not the theoretical specialties of later university theology, but the familiar concepts of scripture. Rather, Augustine skilfully marshaled an array of texts and communicated certain truths about grace and freedom with masterful rhetoric.[8]

For Lonergan, Phillip the Chancellor's articulation of the "theorem of the supernatural" in the thirteenth century served as a watershed moment in the "blessed rage for order" that constituted university theology. No one doubted that grace was a free gift from God beyond the desert of the human person. The difficulty was to explain why everything was not grace. As Lonergan notes, Philip the Chancellor presented the theory of two orders, entitatively disproportionate: grace, faith, and charity, on the one hand, and nature, reason, and the natural love of God on the other. The pivotal moment was Philip the Chancellor's formulation of the idea of the supernatural habit. With his theorem of the supernatural, Philip did not posit simply the supernatural character of grace, but also the theoretical validity of a line of reference termed "nature."[9]

The explanatory import of the hypothetical construct of "nature" is illuminated in Aquinas's response to the question of whether human beings can wish or do good without grace (*Summa theologiae* 1-II, 109.3). Recall my discussion of Torrell's recommended use of "integral" rather than "pure" nature in chapter 2. Aquinas invites us to consider nature in two ways: the state of integrity prior to the fall and the state of corruption after the fall. For Aquinas, both states of human nature require the help of God as first mover, as creator, to wish or do the good. Yet, for Aquinas, human nature is not altogether corrupted by sin; even in this state, a person can work some particular good by virtue of his or her natural endowments. That being said, a person in this corrupted state does fall short of what he or she could do by nature in the state of integrity. For Aquinas, grace is, in fact, required in both the state of integrity and the state of corruption. Adam did not live in the realm of pure nature without grace. For Aquinas, grace is always required to wish and do the good of infused, supernatural virtue. Thus in the state of integral nature, the human person only needs a gratuitous strength superadded to natural strength in order to do and wish supernatural good. In the state of corrupt nature, however, the human person needed gratuitous strength to be healed and to carry out the works of supernatural virtue.

For Lonergan, the grace/sin dialectic is dismantled with the theoretical construct of human nature. This explanatory term enables us to affirm human nature as good in itself prior to original sin. In this state of integrity, the human person can exercise the good of acquired virtues and can wish and do the good proportionate to nature. Even in the fallen state, the human person is still capable of doing the good; in other words, this is not a doctrine of total corruption or total depravity. Avoiding the error of Pelagianism, Lonergan affirms, by way of his analysis of Aquinas, that the supernatural good of salvation requires that grace both heal and elevate.[10]

Thomas's concern is not with pure nature but with the intelligibility of this world order. Lonergan elucidates this in a response to a question about natural and supernatural beatitude.[11] He clarifies that the Thomist distinction is between perfect and imperfect beatitude, and that perfect beatitude is natural to God alone.[12] Participation in the beatific vision then is a participation in God's beatitude. In Thomist thinking, imperfect beatitude is "the beatitude of the philosophers, in which they understand the whole universe, in which they get Aristotle's metaphysics perfectly" – the "sort of beatitude that you can have in this life."[13] Scotus, in Lonergan's reading, changed the theological landscape with his emphasis on what was necessary in all possible worlds. But Aquinas was not talking about all possible worlds. He was concerned with the intelligibility of this world, with the order chosen freely by divine wisdom. Aquinas is also humbly aware that he does not possess divine wisdom, and hence he does not emphasize the question of all possible worlds. This world order consists of what God has done and not what God might or must do. The world order is contingent; the divine essence is the only necessary concrete intelligibility.[14]

Lonergan's position on the "pure nature" question makes sense in light of his Thomistic concern for intelligibility of this world, and not other possible worlds. As he stated in *Insight*, the "abstract metaphysics of all possible worlds is empty."[15] Regarding de Lubac's worry about "pure nature," Lonergan presents a nuanced response. He affirmed de Lubac's concern to point out that God created natures and that these natures are embedded in a concrete world order.[16] He believed, in accord with de Lubac's later position, that a world order without grace is a concrete possibility. Nevertheless, he suggested that the concrete possibility of pure nature is not "a central doctrine but merely a marginal theorem."[17]

The Natural Desire to See God

Even if Lonergan marginalizes "pure nature," he does emphasize the importance of integral "nature" and the theory of two entitatively disproportionate orders as a breakthrough into the world of theoretical theology, as I noted above. This explanatory distinction shapes his position on the natural desire to see God. In this sense, Lonergan's thought works in consonance with Torrell's suggestion (chapter 2) that it is more fruitful to work with "integral nature" than "pure nature" as we continue to engage these ongoing questions about nature and the natural desire for God.

Lonergan roots his position in the dynamism of the human mind, in the natural desire to know discussed at length in chapter 3. For Lonergan, the human desire to know is natural, insofar as the desires of the intellect are manifested in questions for meaning, truth, and value. It is transcendent, insofar as the adequate object is *ens*.[18] Although the natural fulfilment is limited by a proportionate object, our desire to know is unlimited and hence wants to know everything about everything – ultimately, being itself. When we affirm that God exists through our natural knowledge of God, we seek to understand this affirmation with the question, "What is God?" In this sense, we have a natural desire to know God. Still, the "best that natural reason can attain," according to Lonergan, "is the discovery of the paradox that the desire to understand arises naturally, that its object is the transcendental, *ens*, and that the proper fulfillment that naturally is attainable is restricted to the proportionate object of the intellect." This natural desire includes God and can only be fulfilled supernaturally in the beatific vision.[19]

Feingold's position on the natural desire for God is in tension with Lonergan's position as just outlined. The tension revolves around the terms "natural" and "elicited."[20] Joshua Brotherton helpfully points out the way that Lonergan's critique of Báñezian Thomism creates a certain tension with Feingold, whose position certainly bears the stamp of Báñez, among several other sixteenth- and seventeenth-century neo-scholastics. Feingold considers Báñez's work as part of a larger developing consensus, as I noted in chapters 1 and 2, that includes Medina and Suárez (both of whom served as spiritual directors to St Teresa of Ávila). These three thinkers, in Feingold's interpretation, are important because of their development of the positions of Cajetan and Sylvester of Ferrara. The principle importance of their interpretation involves the extension of the denial of an innate inclination for the vision of God, the affirmation of an elicited natural desire for the vision of God as a conditional desire, and finally that Aquinas's argument for the possibility of the beatific vision is ultimately an argument from fittingness and not a strict demonstration.[21]

Báñez rejects an innate appetite for the vision of God, but he, along with Suárez and others, affirms that this natural desire is rooted in the natural desire to know, which flows from the possession of the intellect and will. The natural desire for God spoken of by Aquinas, in his interpretation, is an elicited act. In other words, the desire to know the essence of the first cause is elicited upon knowledge of the existence of God.[22] For Báñez, this desire to see God does not presuppose supernatural knowledge, but only requires knowledge that God exists. In other words, this elicited desire does not reside in us from the beginning, but exists only once we possess knowledge of God's existence.[23] In sum, the natural desire for God is ordered by God as a consequence of rationality, but is not naturally ordered to its realization. This natural desire constitutes instead "a powerful argument from fittingness, first for the possibility of the beatific vision of God, as well as for its actual offer."[24]

A full consideration of Feingold's position on natural desire (we consider supernatural desire in chapter 5) requires attention to his account of two states of the natural desire for God. As I summarized in chapter 2, we have, first, a natural or "innate" desire for God – to know and love God through the mirror of creation. This expresses the very relation of our spiritual capacities to their proper ends, a kind of ontological inclination or orientation. This dimension is "innate" and "unconscious." Second, we have a "naturally elicited desire for the vision of God's essence." This naturally elicited desire is merely conditional without the aid of divine revelation and actual grace. This desire acts as a kind of mediator between the innate desire to know and love God through the mirror of creation and the supernatural acts and habitual inclinations associated with hope and charity. This constitutes, in part, Feingold's differentiated response to de Lubac's claims that we have a "natural desire for the supernatural" or an innate, absolute, unconditional desire for the vision of God.[25]

In his treatment, Lonergan explicitly argues that the desire is "natural" and not "elicited." The opposite of "natural," in Lonergan's system, is "elicited," not "supernatural." This desire is not elicited in an appetitive power, but is the very ordering of the natural tendency of the potency itself – an ordering of potency to act. Lonergan's claim for a "natural desire" excludes elicited acts, but at the same time is in no way meant to imply that the beatific vision is natural – that it is to be offered in accordance with the requirements of our nature.[26]

Even if Brotherton is correct in pointing out the Báñezian-influenced tension, perhaps greater justice could be done to Feingold's full position, especially his more constructive suggestions on the two states of the natural desire for God just highlighted. How different are the positions of Feingold and Lonergan really in this respect? The distinctiveness of Lonergan's position as a whole will emerge as this chapter unfolds; it is a position that cannot always be reconciled with Feingold's. Still, it is important to note that that Feingold identifies Lonergan's position on this particular issue principally with Feingold's own fittingness or *convenientia* position, along with Scheeben, Maritain, and Garrigou-Lagrange, and certainly not with the position of de Lubac. I will say more below about the fittingness position of Lonergan as it relates to the "aesthetic compromise." For now, it suffices to reiterate that Lonergan roots the natural desire to see God in the natural desire to know. Once we affirm the existence of God through our natural reason, we naturally ask about the essence of God. For Lonergan this discovery creates a paradox: our ability to attain this knowledge is disproportionate to our unrestricted desire. Only supernatural beatitude can fulfil this desire.[27]

Again, how different is this position really from Feingold's two states discussed in chapter 2? Guy Mansini correctly observes that Lonergan's position pushes in the direction of Feingold's.[28] Despite Lonergan's apparent denial of an elicited desire to see God, he nevertheless "slides quite unmistakably into a discussion of what can be nothing but an elicited desire to see God."[29] The following statement of Lonergan clearly implies an elicited desire: "The natural desire is to know what God is. That desire neither includes nor excludes the Blessed Trinity. It supposes knowledge that God is. It asks to know what God is."[30] The desire to know the essence of God is elicited by knowledge that God is. In this sense, Feingold helps to differentiate a key moment that Lonergan includes in his thinking but does not explicitly acknowledge as "elicited."

Mansini notes that Lonergan also comes close to Feingold in his suggestion that the natural desire and its fulfilment have the same material object, but not the same formal object. The object of the natural desire to know is the transcendental *ens*, as highlighted above; the fulfilling object is the supernatural (beatific vision). The natural desire for God is presented not "as a determinate object to which there is an innate inclination, but as simply included within the scope of an intellect whose adequate object is the transcendental *ens*." In other words, the "elicited desire to know God," as Mansini translates Lonergan's position in terms amenable to Feingold's, "is just a 'corollary' of a natural and transcendental desire to understand whatever there is."[31]

To substantiate Mansini's hunch, I offer a key distinction of Lonergan's from a work not cited by Feingold or Mansini, presumably because it did not appear in the *Collected Works of Lonergan* until 2007. In his excursus "The Natural Desire of the Intellect," Lonergan offers a distinction between the implicit and explicit objects of the intellect.[32] He reformulates his argument as follows: the human person possesses an innate desire to wonder that precedes intellectual knowledge and leads to it. This innate desire is manifested in questions for understanding (what is it?) and judgment (is it so?). This innate tendency to wonder is so extensive that it does not rest until it sees God in God's essence. Hence it contains *"implicitly in itself* that drive towards the vision of God" that Aquinas explains in particular passages in the *Summa contra Gentiles* and the *Summa theologiae*.[33]

In light of the expansive nature of the intellect's reach, Lonergan entertains an objection. The objection states that the object of the natural desire to see God through his essence is absolutely supernatural and hence involves a supernatural act. Lonergan responds to this objection as follows:

> The direct and explicit object of this natural desire is not to behold God in his essence; it is being. Since God as something to be seen in his essence falls within the formality of being, the consequence is that this natural desire does not rest until it beholds God in his essence. Yet this consequence reveals not an explicit but only an implicit object; and because this consequence is not an affirmation but a negation (namely, "it does not rest until ..."), it indicates an object that is not only implicit but also, in a way, indirect.[34]

Note that Lonergan's subtle distinction between implicit and explicit objects differentiates "a desire's object, technically understood, and a further 'object' or item that is included within the scope of a desire."[35] In this sense, the object of the desire to know, technically speaking, is being, while the desire for God's essence is connected only implicitly by extension, and only becomes explicit after one affirms the existence of God. Lonergan also clarifies the importance of not confusing this natural desire with a specifically supernatural act.

> Supernatural acts belong to a certain genus and are specified by their proper objects. But a universal tendency, whether of the intellect towards being or the will towards good, is not specifically supernatural. Nor can the supernaturality of such a tendency be deduced from the fact that being implicitly includes supernatural beings and good implicitly includes supernatural goods. All that can be deduced from the tendency is that the supernatural is not utterly impossible; and thus does Aquinas conclude to the possibility of the beatific vision in *Summa theologiae* I, q. 12, a. 1.[36]

Those with onto-theological radars – attentive to the failure to employ analogical thinking in favour of the univocity of being – may worry that this comes dangerously close to imaging God as the highest being among beings. Brian Himes offers an important clarification:

> One might say that because God's essence is subsistent being and we explicitly desire to know being, we therefore explicitly desire to know God's essence. However, to equate *ipsum esse* with the transcendental, *ens*, is naive and erroneous. God is not identical to all that exists. That

is pantheism. In explicitly desiring to know all that exists (*ens*), God is included in that universal set because he exists ('God as something to be seen in his essence falls within the formality of being'), but this does not mean that we explicitly and innately desire knowledge of God as being the fulfilment of our desire to know. Failing to make the distinction between the implicit and explicit object of the intellect is to commit the error of onto-theology that Martin Heidegger and Jean-Luc Marion react against. God is not simply a bigger and better being among other beings, even though he can be included in the set of 'things that exist.'[37]

As Lonergan clarifies, "To desire implicitly and indirectly the vision of God inasmuch as the intellect tends to being is one thing; but it is quite another thing to want to see God, for this would be a specifically supernatural act specified by an absolutely supernatural object."[38]

In sum, I want to highlight three consonances between Lonergan and Feingold. First, Lonergan's accent on the pure desire to know corresponds in some ways to Feingold's first state – the innate, ontological inclination to know the causes of things and by extension to know and love God in the mirror of creation. I would add, however, that Lonergan offers a much richer epistemology, as I outlined in chapter 3. Second, Lonergan's argument about asking "What is God?" based on knowledge of God's existence corresponds to Feingold's second state – the naturally *elicited* desire to see God. Third, Lonergan's accent on the paradox and disproportionate fulfilment corresponds to Feingold's emphasis that the beatific vision exceeds the limits of what is due to nature. Lonergan, then, does not ultimately fall into the trap of confusing innate desire and conscious desire as de Lubac may have done.[39]

Although I have highlighted certain parallels between Feingold and Lonergan to avoid unnecessary oppositions, I also do not intend to paper over differences.[40] If Feingold's account emphasizes our natural inclination to what is proportionate, Lonergan's concrete account of nature, in terms of emergent probability, bears the mark of "vertical finality" – which is to say, we are concretely oriented towards an end beyond the proportion of nature. Prior to explaining his account of nature as emergent probability, I first explain Lonergan's understanding of the twofold end of the human person, along with his critique of a static-essentialist view of nature.

98 The Givenness of Desire

Twofold End of the Human Person: Beyond Static Essentialism

Affirming both the natural desire to see God and the supernaturality of its fulfilment in the beatific vision raises a question about human ends. Does the human person have two ends, one natural and the other supernatural? In terms of the recurring debate over the *duplex ordo*, Lonergan affirms two ends for human persons: the human natural end is an imperfect and analogical knowledge of the divine essence, and the human supernatural end is the beatific vision – a perfect vision of the divine essence. In Thomistic fashion, Lonergan frames the human desire for ends in terms of "restlessness" and "rest." Rest is experienced when an end is attained. But, metaphysically speaking, one can speak of a variety of levels of perfection. For Lonergan, the perfection of the rest corresponds to the perfection of the end. Prior to elucidating these more or less perfect human ends, he importantly distinguishes human rest from the intrinsic immobility of God. Unlike the cessation of movement experienced in human rest, the intrinsic immobility of God is rooted in pure act, which does not involve passive potency. Pure act belongs primarily to the divine beatitude enjoyed by God and secondarily to the gift of divine beatitude offered supernaturally to creatures.[41]

The distinctiveness of Lonergan's argument as it relates to "nature" resides in his rejection of a particular way of framing the debate, namely, a static-essentialist view of the world order. Static essentialism, in Lonergan's view, conceives finite natures as prior to world orders. In this view, God – who by God's very essence knows all things – first sees the possibility of finite natures (men, horses, cows, cats) and only secondarily sees possible world orders. Finite natures, then, serve as the "ultimate element into which all else must be reduced."[42] It is the static-essentialist view that resides at the root of the two-storey conception of the universe associated with sixteenth- and seventeenth-century neo-scholasticism brought to light by de Lubac. The consequence is a two-part vision of the world order: "a *necessary* part which meets the exigencies of finite natures, and a *contingent part* that may or may not be present" – the latter of which is the realm where "God's free gifts over and above the exigencies of nature" is situated.[43] The two parts of the world order, in this view, are imagined as distinct and separate. Instead of envisioning, as Lonergan does, a "positive relation whereby the higher part subsumes the lower, retaining the intelligibility of the lower by perfecting it, there is simply the negative relation of non-contradiction."⁴⁴ The relationship between the supernatural and the natural is constituted merely by non-repugnance. The natural certainly does not resist the "excess" of the supernatural, but it is difficult to imagine within this frame a richer, more transformative, and vibrant relationship that might be detected in the mystics, for example. Within the static-essentialist view, our natural desire for God tends to find its satisfaction in the natural order. As a result, the beatific vision in the second part of the world order tends to take on the shape of a super-added gift. But, one wonders, in this static-essentialist account, whether it perfects in any intrinsic way a natural potency in the subject.

The essentialist view also has implications for a particular conception of the relationship between philosophy and theology, rejected in Balthasar's critique above, and the context out of which Lonergan was compelled to offer a fresh vision of doing theology within a new context. The essentialist view of the relationship suggests that philosophy deals with the necessary part by the light of natural reason, while theology deals with the contingent part of revelation.⁴⁵ As Stebbins notes, "The only relation between the two, in addition to that of non-contradiction, consists in the fact that theology borrows from philosophy its logical technique and various truths established on the basis of human reason."⁴⁶

In contrast to static essentialism, Lonergan's "open intellectualism" offers an account of unitary, dynamic cosmic world order that exists prior to finite natures. Within this frame, "God sees in his essence, first of all, the series of all possible world orders, each of which is complete down to its least historical detail," and only consequently "does God know their component parts such as his free gifts, finite natures, their properties, exigencies, and so on."⁴⁷ Christopher Malloy asks, in light of Lonergan's critique of static essentialism, "what is 'ordered' if 'order' is intelligibility first?"⁴⁸ "And if we ask this question," Malloy warns, "we run into the question of finality, since essence and finality are necessarily correlative."⁴⁹ A response to this helpful question requires more on Lonergan's understanding of "emergent probability," to be treated next, and also "vertical finality," which will be explained later in the chapter. In sum, finite natures are derivative possibilities in an intelligible world order where "lower natures are subordinate to higher natures, not merely extrinsically, but also intrinsically, as appears in chemical composition and in biological evolution."⁵⁰ For Lonergan, the natural and the supernatural are "intrinsically related parts of a single cosmic order."⁵¹

Nature II: Lonergan on Emergent Probability

Contemporary conversations about the natural and supernatural, especially the de Lubac-Thomist debates highlighted in a previous chapter, give little attention to ongoing science-religion conversations. A value of retrieving Lonergan's thought for this conversation is his integration of the wisdom of Thomistic metaphysics in a more contemporary cosmological vein. A fuller treatment of Lonergan's understanding of nature requires an account of his understanding of nature as emergent probability. Lonergan's emergent probability represents his transposition of Aquinas's account of contingent being into the terms of the complementarity of classical and statistical procedures in empirical science. Emergent probability yields, "not a universe whose laws could be theoretically deduced according to some iron necessity, but a universe of emergent probability open to the rhythms of limitation and transcendence, and constitutive of the dialectical tension between essential and effective human freedom."[52] Emergent probability offers a theoretical framework that does justice to the "actual world order in which things persist and things change, in which some things are universal or general and other things are particular or localized."[53] It does not just concentrate on fixed natures related by unchanging laws, but persists in the quest to understand the essences of things. Ultimately, the aim is "an ongoing discovery of the intelligible relationships governing the world order as it concretely exists, an order in which new things have various probabilities of emerging."[54]

Scientists employing the classical heuristic method intelligently anticipate an explanation of the way things relate to one another in terms of universal laws. Galileo's law of falling bodies and Newton's theory of gravitation were explanations formulated in invariant correlations among two or more changing variables. Galileo worked to understand the intelligibility of a free fall.[55] Confident that there was an intelligibility to be grasped, he took as his clue that some correlation could be found between the measurable aspects of the falling bodies. But in the process, he began to question the commonsense assumption that the weight of an object is the cause of falling bodies. Galileo focused on two measurable aspects of every free fall: distance and time. Through the process of gathering data and plotting measurements, he discovered a general rule: "the distance traversed is proportional to the time squared": a correlation between space and time. Classical laws such as the law of falling bodies are invariant, because such correlations and laws are abstracted from the particular times and places in which laws are verified. Classical laws are concerned not with the concrete and complex features of actual events but with the systematic laws that are relevant regardless of particularity. Such concreteness provides matter for statistical method.

Whereas classical method anticipates systematic regularity, statistical investigations anticipate the non-systematic character of large populations. Unlike classical scientists who abstract from concrete situations, statistical scientists analyse concrete and particular events in order to discover the ideal, possible, probable, and actual frequency of events.[56] Cynthia Crysdale offers an example of the contrast and complementarity of such investigations:

> The classical laws of biology explain what occurs when a sperm fertilizes an egg and conception takes place. In doing so, they delineate the conjugates that define conception. Without these conjugates it is impossible to determine fertility rates. But the biological definition and explanation of conception cannot, in and of themselves, determine fertility rates. In order to determine these, one must count and calculate, considering a range of variables, such as age, education, health, and frequency of intercourse, among couples within a certain geographic location.[57]

Statistical method, however, investigates the concrete details that are an empirical residue for classical method. Thus "frequency of intercourse" or the "health of the partners" may be helpful in determining the probability of conceiving a given child specifically, or fertility rates in general. But in determining fertility rates, classical laws are only helpful inasmuch as they explain what would happen under the ideal circumstances, approximated by scientists under laboratory conditions. Combinations of classical laws in the abstract begin, continue, or cease to function concretely in accord with statistical probabilities.[58]

For Lonergan, such a world process is open, and while it may be increasingly systematic through the successive realization of schemes of recurrence, it also admits breakdowns and blind alleys.[59] So far our analysis has left the intelligent nature of inquiry only implicit. Both classical and statistical investigations seek intelligibility, although they are asking different questions. The heuristic nature of human inquiry underlies both investigations. Emergent probability recognizes that there is immanent intelligibility or order or design by conceiving of classical and statistical heuristic methods as yielding a distinct yet unified intelligible account of the world process. There is, then, the intelligibility of "directionality" in the universe. This is to say that the universe as a whole has been continually evolving towards more complex and highly differentiated configurations over the past 13.7 billion years.[60] Systems and organisms have also been gradually evolving from simpler to more complex, but such an evolution is not always clear, smooth, and inevitable. Rather, it occurs by natural selection as entities and organisms undergo modifications in ongoing interaction with their environments. Still, this directionality happens with stops, starts, and significant reversals. Furthermore, directionality remains only a direction. It does not involve the strict control of a divine micromanager. Rather, similar to the language of emergent probability, "for any particular system or organism within a particular environmental context, there is an orientation toward a well-defined, limited range of proximate outcomes."[61] The possibility and probability of "outcomes are based on the conditions of the present time and the processes, regularities, relationships, and constraints to which it and its environment are subject."[62] Evolution – the continual emergence of more complex systems and organisms – does depend on the "decay and break-up of earlier systems and organisms," suggesting that "fragility and transience" are necessary in such a complex and open-ended universe.[63] It also involves a certain sense of randomness and chance. But such randomness and chance operate within the larger intelligible framework of the dynamic order just discussed.

In sum, Lonergan's concrete account of nature as emergent probability reflects some key insights from contemporary conversations in science and religion.[64] His thought expresses a "formational and functional unity and integrity of nature." The integrity of nature – a phrase highlighted in chapter 2, but reframed here with more attention to the natural sciences – includes an evolution towards complexity and life. This complexity involves "the critical roles of relationality, hierarchical organization, directionality, transience and fragility, and emergence."[65] Lonergan's account of the intelligibility of both classical laws and statistical laws, of regularity and chance, along with the relative autonomy of intelligent and free human persons to shape the world, contributes to this understanding. As I suggest later in the chapter, Lonergan's account of "vertical finality" expresses an understanding of the world process that is both emergent and hierarchically structured – a universe where the "supernatural" is both a gift and at the same time a real, and not extrinsic, part of the world process. Before exploring these terms, however, I turn to the relationship between this concrete account of nature and the human good.

The Intelligibility of Nature and the Human Good Revisited

Human knowing, in Lonergan's account of emergent probability, is intimately connected with the concrete, dynamic working out of the human good. In chapter 2, I highlighted the Thomist-Lubacian tension over the theme of nature and the building of the common good (Long, Schindler, Bushlack). In this section, I introduce some of the key components of Lonergan's account of the human good as a dimension of "nature" within the concrete world order. This serves as a way of responding to scholars who have argued for a more robust account of integral nature. An account of integral nature preserves the gratuity of the supernatural order, but also creates more room for rational deliberation among diverse people about the connection between intellectual and moral transcendence and the human good. As a way into the conversation, I first highlight the position of Peter Ryan, which is noteworthy for the way it reframes the question of the natural desire for God in terms of human goods. The terms Ryan employs resonate with Lonergan's emphasis on the human good.

Ryan argues that we "naturally seek neither the beatific vision itself nor perfect natural happiness."[66] Rejecting both de Lubac's natural desire for the beatific vision and Aquinas's claim about the human desire for perfect happiness, he reframes the conversation in terms of human goods. Though not uncritical of Rahner, he credits Rahner with showing that the views of the pure nature theorists and the Lubacians are untenable. He also credits Rahner with identifying that human nature is unconditionally oriented to ever-greater happiness, but not perfect happiness.[67] Such a framing requires an explanation of how the beatific vision is not simply an extrinsic addition. What do we desire naturally, if not the beatific vision, nor perfect happiness? The human person naturally desires ever-greater fulfilment in a variety of human goods, including life and health, truth, friendship, creative work and play, marriage and family, and so forth. Of course, we do not pursue all of these goods in every act, and often choose not to purse some of these goods: a monk decides against marriage, for example. Still, we are naturally drawn to these goods – an indication that a creator creates us, sustains us, and directs us to these goods.[68]

Natural religious desire seeks peace and friendship with God. For Ryan, "the natural human aptitude for friendship with God makes it possible for us to receive a greater-than-human good: a share in the divine nature" – divinization as a "dynamic principle ordered to the fullness of divine life, the beatific vision."[69] The beatific vision, in this framework, is not "a direct fulfillment of human *nature* but of human *persons* insofar as they share in *divine* nature."[70] What are the implications of this position in an era where catechetical instruction, parish formation, and evangelization have presupposed the restless heart? In Ryan's view, the focus on the beatific vision as the answer to the restless heart tends to diminish the role of human goods as essential to both present happiness and heavenly happiness. Conversely, he urges us to heed the intimate connection displayed in *Gaudium et Spes* 39 between earthly and eschatological goods:

> The expectation of a new earth must not weaken but rather stimulate our concern for cultivating this one. For here grows the body of a new human family, a body which even now is able to give some kind of foreshadowing of the new age. Hence, while earthly progress must be carefully distinguished from the growth of Christ's kingdom, to the extent that the former can contribute to the better ordering of human society, it is of vital concern to the Kingdom of God. For after we have ... nurtured on earth the values of human dignity, brotherhood and freedom, and indeed all the good fruits of our nature and enterprise, we will find them again, but freed of stain, burnished and transfigured, when Christ hands over to the Father: "a kingdom eternal and universal, a kingdom of truth and life, of holiness and grace, of justice, love and peace." On this earth that Kingdom is already present in mystery. When the Lord returns it will be brought into full flower.[71]

Lonergan's thought contains the resources for responding to Ryan's account of natural desire as a desire for ever-greater fulfilment in various human goods. Lonergan's historical account of nature as emergent probability is constituted in part by concrete human subjects called to ongoing intellectual and moral self-transcendence in a universe marked by emergent probability. This ongoing quest for the human good always takes place concretely, and, as we noted in chapter 3, it does so in the midst of decline, whether the lack of authenticity in an individual subject, the shorter cycle of decline brought about by group egoism, or the longer cycle of decline precipitated by a general, anti-theoretical bias.

In Lonergan's system, understanding nature requires attention to the concrete, dynamic working out of the human good. "The specific difference of human history," writes Lonergan, "is that among the probable possibilities is a sequence of operative insights by which men grasp possible schemes of recurrence and take the initiative in bringing about the material and social conditions that make these schemes concretely possible, probable, and actual."[72] In the language of the previous section, human persons become the executors of the emergent probability of human affairs. In other words, instead of being passively shaped by our environment, we can transform our environment as we commit to the arduous and ongoing task of self-development. This takes place through the intelligible, reasonable, and responsible working out of concrete possibilities and probabilities in a dynamic world order. In sum, Lonergan importantly highlights how human beings with the capacity for understanding and judgment, deliberation and action are, in part, "shapers" of history. Hence, the practical dimension of human intelligence and choice has consequences for the realization of the human good, or of human bias and decline. Lonergan's explanatory treatment of nature in terms of conscious historical subjectivity must be situated within his theological analysis of human history. First, as intelligent and reasonable, human beings yield the fruit of progress. Second, however, human bias causes unintelligent and unreasonable conduct, resulting in decline. Finally, there is the "redemptive process resulting from God's gift of his grace to individuals and from the manifestation of his love in Christ Jesus."[73]

Lonergan extends his understanding of concrete human subjects as "shapers" of history in his later development of a framework for the human good. The human good is constituted by the higher integration of natural processes, by human aesthetic-dramatic (psychic), intellectual, moral, and religious self-transcendence, and by the common meaning of communities committed to such self-transcendence. It is not my intention to elaborate in detail the structure of the human good within the dialectics of history. For Lonergan it involves, as a whole, an integration of (1) individuals and the realization of their potentialities; (2) cooperating groups; and (3) reflection on the purpose, end, *telos* of human operations and cooperation.[74] This heuristic framework offers a foundational language as we ask questions about the concrete human situation. Such questions capture the heart of what first motivated practical and political philosophy: What's the right way to live? What constitutes the good life? This reveals an appropriation of the ancient virtue tradition, but recast in terms not confined by a Greek classicist notion of culture, and more open to an empirical, dynamic account of culture as "the domain in which society reflects upon and appraises its way of life."[75] "Classicist culture," in Lonergan's account, refers to the assumption that there is "one culture" that is "both universal and permanent."[76] Attentive to the concrete, this book is more sympathetic to an empirical understanding of culture: a culture is the set of meanings and values that inform a way of life, and there are as many cultures as there are different ways of life.[77] An empirical understanding of culture recognizes the dynamism of culture and that cultures may be "in process of slow development or rapid dissolution."[78] In this light, what is normative is not culture itself, but the transcultural core of human nature that is the source and measure of every culture. In other words, culture is not the normative measure of human beings; rather, human beings in their authenticity are the normative measure of cultures. If Lonergan's account of the human good both affirms and transposes the ancient Greek concern about the priority of the question of the good life, it simultaneously rejects modernity's replacement of the normativity of virtue and the desire to know with the fundamental desire for self-preservation, as evident in Bacon, Hobbes, Locke, and Spinoza, just to name a few.[79] This repositioning recognizes Milbank's suggestion that pure nature declined into self-sufficiency and power politics, while at the same responding to the Thomist concern for a thicker account of nature.

A key dimension of Lonergan's explanatory framework for the human good is the "integral scale of values," developed more fully by Robert Doran and his contextualization of the scale within the matrix of a "set of distinct but related and currently distorted dialectics of the subject, culture, and community."[80] I cite at length Robert Doran's interpretation of this scale:

> From above, then, religious values condition the possibility of personal integrity; personal integrity conditions the possibility of authentic cultural values; at the reflexive level of culture, such integrity will promote an authentic superstructural collaboration that assumes responsibility for the integrity not only of scientific and scholarly disciplines, but even of everyday culture; cultural integrity at both levels conditions the possibility of a just social order; and the just social order conditions the possibility of the equitable distribution of vital goods. Conversely, problems in the effective and recurrent distribution of vital goods can be met only by a reversal of

distortions in the social order; the proportions of the needed reversal are set by the scope and range of the real or potential maldistribution; the social change demands a transformation at the everyday level of culture proportionate to the dimensions of the social problem; this transformation frequently depends on reflexive theoretical and scientific developments at the superstructural level; new cultural values at both levels call for proportionate changes at the level of personal integrity; and these depend for their emergence, sustenance, and consistency on the religious development of the person.[81]

Doran outlines here in heuristic fashion the complex relationship between religious, personal, cultural, social, and vital values. In fact, this five-scale level of values "can be best understood as an unpacking of the traditional nature-grace distinction."[82] Similar to the dynamism of nature as expressed in emergent probability and vertical finality (discussed below), the scale of values represents an interrelated, dynamic scheme whereby "vital needs are taken up by the higher-level operation of the social, the social into the cultural and the cultural into the personal."[83] Moreover, the personal realm is "open to a higher level of integration through the incorporation of schemes of operation (theological virtues/religious values) that order us to higher-level goals, that is, incorporation into the divine life itself."[84] This scale preserves the metaphysical structure of the higher and the lower in the human person, but also integrates more concretely the social, cultural, and historical dimensions of human existence.[85]

The introduction of key components of Lonergan's account of the human good as a dimension of nature responds in a distinctive way to scholars who have called for an ontologically dense account of integral nature. This particular account affirms the human desire for ever-greater fulfilment in various human goods as a sign of our transcendent orientation, and at the same time preserves the gratuity of the supernatural order.

Obediential Potency and Vertical Finality in the Concrete World Order

In light of the extended discussion of "nature" within a concrete framework, it is fitting to reinterpret the categories of finality and obediential potency through the prism of this account of the dynamic world order. Both terms are important to the neo-Thomist–de Lubac tension, as discussed in chapter 2. They constitute two essential themes in Lonergan's explanation of the natural desire for God wherein the natural order and the supernatural order are conceived as intrinsic parts of the concretely operating universe, indicative of a kind of analogical thinking prioritized in this book.

If static essentialism focuses on horizontal finality, emergently probability considers a variety of finalities – horizontal, vertical, and absolute – that more adequately captures the complexity of divine-human relationship. Avoiding the pitfalls of both mechanistic determinism and chaotic relativism, emergent probability accounts for a wise ordering of the universe, but an ordering that is fertile, dynamic, unpredictable, and at the same time constituted by intelligible and interrelated schemes of recurrence.

As a way of framing this section, I focus briefly on Christopher Malloy's suggested solution to the contestability of obediential potency. Malloy challenges those sympathetic to Lubacian critiques of Thomism to ask whether the category of specific obediential potency really implies a dualism or extrinsicism. Many theologians – de Lubac included – have offered this charge. Hopefully a grasp of the meaning, suggests Malloy, would at least mitigate attempts to uncritically caricature this explanatory term. But Malloy also recognizes the need to explain this reality in a way that avoids the loss of the dynamism of the divine-human encounter. He proposes a loose conception of Hegelian sublation as a possible way of explaining how grace builds on nature without destroying the intrinsic intelligibility of nature. What is the difference between a person in the state of nature and a person called and divinized, asks Malloy? As a way of responding to de Lubac, he emphasizes the overarching difference that God is drawing the called and divinized person to himself. This Hegelian sublation enables us to show, Malloy suggests, that the divine call affirms and expands the goodness of the natural life on a higher plane. "When God calls a man to himself in intimacy," writes Malloy, "he galvanizes all properly human dynamisms for an all-embracing end inclusive of every other licit and practicable end."[86] Malloy has offered a worthy, albeit tentative, proposal. I suggest that Lonergan's account of vertical finality and obediential potency in a concrete world order contains the explanatory resources for meeting Malloy's challenge.[87]

I first consider Lonergan's distinction between horizontal finality and vertical finality, and then connect it to his particular understanding of obediential potency. "Horizontal finality" refers to the abstract connection between nature, potency, and act. For example, animals by nature have the capacity to realize in act their potency for self-movement. Human beings by nature possess the capacity to realize in act their potency for intellectual knowledge. These two examples point to a certain correspondence in horizontal finality between the kinds of potencies and acts proper to the essence of the particular nature under consideration. Vertical finality, however, acknowledges the possibility in the concrete universe not only for horizontal unity but also for emergence. For Lonergan, the world process is both emergent and hierarchically structured into physical, chemical, biological, psychological, intelligent, rational, and volitional manifolds. Hierarchical structure means that "reality is organized in levels of complexity nested within one another."[88] The human body or any multicellular animal

> is composed of many organs, all working together and each composed of different types of structures. Each structure within an organ and within the body as a whole functions the way it does because of different types of cells (muscles, blood, nerve and brain, bone, heart, kidneys, etc.) of which it is composed. But each of those cells is itself a very complicated functioning unit in its own right, with many different components. Furthermore each of the tens of thousands of different molecules that make up cells or that cells produce has its own basic structure and special ways of interacting with other molecules. The type of interaction depends on the structure and the properties of various types of atoms that constitute the molecule, and particularly on the relationships among the atoms. If one magnifies one's investigation sufficiently, one eventually arrives at the stage of the fundamental particles, the protons, neutrons, and electrons.

This hierarchical structure manifests, at the same time, a profound relationality. Such constitutive relationships make things what they are as contributing aspects of the formal cause of each system, entity, and organism.[89]

In Lonergan's account of hierarchical structure and profound relationality, plants comprise the physical, chemical, and biological.[90] Animals comprise physical, chemical, biological, and psychological levels. Human beings comprise physical, chemical, biological, psychological, intelligent, rational, and volitional levels of being. For Lonergan, lower levels are not annihilated but rather sublated by the higher. Hence, in the instance of human beings, the biological and chemical levels are raised up, enriched, and unified by the overarching levels of intelligence, reason, and choice. Vertical finality denotes an emergent, upward-directed drive that gives lower beings the capacity to set the conditions for the emergence of higher beings. Vertical finality embraces science's dynamic perspective of the world. A static conception does not do justice to the emergence of new entities, structures, and processes. As Arthur Peacocke says, "The traditional notion of God *sustaining* the world in its general order and structure now has to be enriched by a dynamic and creative dimension – the model of God sustaining and giving continuous existence to a process which has a creativity built into it by God."[91]

The important insight for this conversation on the natural desire for God is the way Lonergan, in his explanatory account of the universe, preserves the distinction between nature and supernature, derived by analogy from the interactions among the gradations of being, and enables us to understand more clearly the absolute gratuity of grace. Accordingly, higher levels on the natural plane, if you will, are *relatively supernatural* to lower ones, that is, chemical compounds are relatively supernatural in relation to subatomic particles. By vertical finality there is an upward-directed dynamism from the lower to the higher. Lower levels set the conditions for the emergence of higher levels.

The second key term is obediential potency. Lonergan distinguished the human natural end and supernatural end in terms of their respective potencies. In metaphysical terms, the potency that corresponds to the natural end is a natural potency; the potency to the supernatural end is an obediential potency. While these potencies are distinguished, Lonergan emphasizes that they possess "the same formal object of knowledge," namely, the divine essence.[92] At the same time, they possess different ways of knowing this object. The knowing associated with natural potency is natural and analogical; the knowing associated with the supernatural end is supernatural and univocal.[93] Despite these important distinctions, Lonergan stresses that natural potency and obediential potency are, in reality, the same insofar as they are intrinsically one and the same potency. They differ, however, according to the causal agent proportionate to each respective actuation. A finite agent actuates a natural potency; an infinite agent actuates an obediential potency. This extrinsic difference gives rise, then, to the diversity of ends.[94] Within this framework, obediential potency is a passive potency, which means that no finite being can cause or produce absolutely supernatural realities. Since obediential potency can only be actuated by God, it constitutes the capacity for receiving, but not producing, an act. This explanatory term enables Lonergan to argue that the desire for the vision of God is "innate" rather than "elicited" while at the same time denying a natural exigency for grace.[95] This point provides a response to the Lonergan-Feingold tension noted above between natural and elicited desire.

In sum, this natural desire only reveals, for Lonergan, that there is an "obediential potency for this vision of God."[96] Vertical finality opens up an analogical possibility. Just as the lower can set the conditions for the emergence of the higher, the concrete plurality of human beings, analogously, have the obediential potency to receive the free self-communication of God. Grace does not annihilate our upward-directed drive to understand, judge, and choose, but fulfils such a drive with a disproportionate, absolutely supernatural reality. The supernatural is not extrinsic to but a really integral part of the concrete, evolutionary world process. In light of this integral vision, it is relevant to note that Lonergan's articulation of sublation in *Method in Theology* corresponds nicely to Malloy's intention, highlighted above. Lonergan mentions that he is using "sublation" in Rahner's and not Hegel's sense, to mean "that what sublates goes beyond what is sublated, introduces something new and distinct, puts everything on a new basis, yet so far from interfering with the sublated or destroying it, on the contrary needs it, includes it, preserves all its proper features and properties, and carries them forward to a fuller realization within a richer context." [97]

Obediential potency understood within a static-essentialist view, however, looks quite different. For Lonergan, the difference between natural and obediential potency is only extrinsic. Obediential potency is a kind of "amplification of the innate virtualities of finite nature."[98] As a higher dimension of being, "grace preserves and is conditioned by the lower grades that it subsumes. Hence, there is no obediential potency without a corresponding natural potency." But in the "bifurcated cosmic scheme" of static essentialism, finite natures have no innate inclination towards anything lying beyond their own proportion. Within this worldview, "obediential potency represents the mere 'non-repugnance' of any creature to God's action on it." In other words, natural and obediential potency are "no longer intrinsically linked: the former is necessary and determinate, the latter contingent and wholly indeterminate." The danger of this perspective – a perspective that seeks to maintain the transcendence of grace – is that it may unintentionally distort a more unified vision of nature and grace.

Lonergan's explanatory framework concerning the intelligibility of the world order helps to elucidate, as Raymond Maloney has argued, de Lubac's insistence on the human desire – the orientation of the mind – to the beatific vision.[99] Lonergan's framing of the issue in terms of the concrete world order – emergent probability, vertical finality, and obediential potency – responds to de Lubac's and Balthasar's emphasis on concrete, historic human nature. On one level, then, Lonergan's framework enables us to respond to Lubacian concerns, but still suggests that a "relentless insistence on 'natural desire for the supernatural'" is "at best an oxymoron, if not a contradiction in terms."[100]

Still, Maloney lends some credence to this conviction of de Lubac. If nature and, by extension, natural desire are a function of the world order, and if the world order has a supernatural character, then one might say that we are called to our supernatural end – the beatific vision – by our very concrete nature in this concrete world order.[101] With the emphasis on the priority of the world orders over natures highlighted above, it is reasonable to suggest that because we are ordered to a supernatural end, God has built into us an innate and natural tendency to see God. Lonergan's concrete account of the supernatural here is very similar to de Lubac's, as Mansini suggests: "I am what I am only because God has called me to himself."[102] Or framed in a distinct but complementary way, if we consider "the emergence of the supernatural, not according to classical and necessary laws, but according to statistical laws and schemes of probability, then one can retain the intelligibility de Lubac was reaching for while disowning any intrinsic and necessary ordination of natural to supernatural."[103]

The Aesthetic Compromise Revisited

In light of our discussion of complex intelligibility of the world order, it is fitting to return to Milbank's discussion (chapter 2) of the possibility of compatibility between the Thomist "aesthetic compromise" and de Lubac's "natural desire for the supernatural." To reiterate, consonance remains possible if one understands the *convenientia* of human nature for supernatural elevation as intrinsically participating in divine wisdom. This view envisions human nature as teleologically drawn to the beatific vision without claiming that human nature elicits it. Incompatibility abounds if *convenientia* is presented in a more extrinsic manner; recall Milbank's image of a railway carriage that turned out to be an ideal home for gypsies after the closure of the branch line.

In chapter 2, I highlighted Feingold's claim that the natural desire to see God does not provide a strict proof for the possibility of the beatific vision, but only an argument of fittingness. De Lubac, of course, suggests that the natural desire for God exhibits that the beatific vision is not fitting, but rather probable and actual. The relevant point here is that Feingold identifies Lonergan with the fittingness or *convenientia* position, along with Scheeben, Maritain, and Garrigou-Lagrange, and not with the position of de Lubac. Feingold's judgment seems largely correct, though this chapter has attempted to retrieve de Lubac's legitimate concerns and show how resources in Lonergan's thought can respond favourably and in a more systematic way.

Lonergan expresses his predilection for fittingness in both "The Natural Desire to See God" and his treatise "On the Supernatural Order" – a position that, in my estimation, passes Milbank's extrinsicist test. Earlier in this chapter, I highlighted Lonergan's claim that the best that natural reason can attain is the discovery of the paradox that the desire to understand arises naturally, but that the ultimate fulfilment of this natural desire is the beatific vision. To use the terms noted above, our natural potency reaches limits in its search for answers, and our understanding of this same desire as an obediential potency "capable of being actuated in some mysterious fashion by the divine essence itself, is dependent upon a prior revelation and a prior series of judgments of faith."[104] Hence, the beatific vision is an absolutely supernatural mystery known only through revelation. When one presupposes revelation and the fact of this vision, then one can find, says Lonergan, "arguments of fittingness to demonstrate its possibility in the case of man."[105] Lonergan situates his emphasis on fittingness in the context of his understanding of Thomas Aquinas. Aquinas wrote primarily as a theologian, he insists, and "in the absence of some positive evidence to the contrary we must believe that he was presupposing truths of the faith rather than prescinding from them." In terms of the knowability of the beatific vision, Lonergan suggests that Thomas did not "work out a concept of 'pure nature' and so wrote about what actually exists, not mere possibilities." To conclude, for example, that Aquinas held that the vision of God is naturally owed to human beings in *Summa Theologiae* 1, q. 12, a. 1 supposes that Thomas was speaking "more as a philosopher than a theologian" and fails to consider "his habitual way of adducing arguments of fittingness."[106] The fittingness of the natural desire for God and its fulfilment in the beatific vision aids us in "understanding how our supernatural end" is "the fulfillment of the innate tendency towards being that characterizes us as incarnate spirits."[107] Our supernatural end, in other words, is not something extrinsically tacked on to our nature. Lonergan's form of "aesthetic compromise" passes Milbank's extrinsicism test, especially when considered in the context of this chapter as a whole, which framed this desire within an account of the dynamic world order and the concretely operating subject – unconfined by static essentialism. In this sense, an emphasis on Lonergan's use of fittingness exonerates him, perhaps not from all of Mansini's concerns, but at least from the concern that Lonergan's position tends towards the Lubacian innate and absolute desire for the supernatural.[108]

Lonergan's argument from fittingness can also respond to Milbank's claim that the *convenientia* of human nature for supernatural elevation ought to be understood as intrinsically participating in divine wisdom. In his lecture on this theme, Lonergan identified fittingness as something that is intelligible and yet not necessary in terms of its essence or existence.[109] And in a theological context, what is fitting "cannot be perfectly understood by us in this life." The connection between the human desire for God and its fulfilment in the beatific vision is, at its core, a mystery – not because it is per se unintelligible, but "because of its excess of intelligibility."[110] Fittingness is rooted in the divine wisdom and recognizes that all things are possible with God, except that which contains a contradiction. Still, "since divine wisdom is coextensive with divine power, it is clear that all things possible are ordered in such a way that nothing in fact could exist without being consonant with divine wisdom and divine goodness." The natural, erotic desire for meaning, truth, and goodness fittingly corresponds to the beatific vision. It reveals the "excellence of order."[111] This thrust for self-transcendence is part of the good of the order of the universe, as expressed above in this chapter.

Conclusion

This chapter retrieved key aspects of Lonergan's thought with heightened awareness of both the Lubacian concern with preserving the concrete and historical and the Thomist concern with the need for a more substantive account of nature. In light of the eros of the mind of the concrete subject, Lonergan's account of nature in scholastic terms and in his more dynamic and scientifically influenced account of emergent probability responds to both concerns. His distinctive use of explanatory terms like "vertical finality" and "obediential potency" offered a reconciling voice to the debate. In terms of the natural-elicited question, I argued that, for Lonergan, the natural desire to see is a natural desire, but mainly a desire for an implicit object. Hence, though their positions cannot be fully reconciled, I pointed out much consonance with Feingold's insistence on the natural desire for God as a naturally elicited desire. Lonergan includes an elicited moment in his account of the natural desire to see God, even if he does not name it so. Furthermore, Lonergan's account of nature as emergent probability responds to the call for a more robust account of integral nature as more than a remainder concept. His account of nature not only preserved the gratuity of the supernatural order, but also created space for the role of intellectual and moral self-transcendence in rational deliberation about the human good. Finally, Lonergan's own discussion of fittingness contributed to the Thomist aesthetic compromise, as described by Milbank.

5 Being-in-Love and the Desire for the Supernatural: Erotic-Agapic Subjectivity

If the natural desire for meaning and truth, propelled by the erotic drive of the mind, orients us to desire God's essence, do we also possess a supernatural desire that orients us to the beatific vision, which is, as we noted in chapter 4, the ultimate fulfilment of our natural desire for God? What shape might this take if we acknowledge the shift in emphasis from a natural desire for God conceived within the categories of scholastic faculty psychology to the variety of ways *the question of God* arises in the intellectual, moral, and religious dimensions of our concrete lives? Does the very language of "supernatural desire" itself indicate an "extrinsicist" account of the relationship between the natural and the supernatural?

An extrinsicist account of nature and grace tends to depict the relationship between the natural and supernatural as if there were one set of desires "over here" hermetically sealed off from another set of desires "over there." The "supernatural" is presented as superimposed, as a kind of artificial superstructure or arbitrary imposition on the real or natural aspirations of the human spirit.[1] One of de Lubac's central concerns with an extrinsicist account of the supernatural is that has isolated the church into "ghettos that we have made our prisons."[2] How does the Church address all aspects of human personal, social, and historical life? The pastoral implications of an extrinsicist account of the supernatural tended in the direction of the private and the personal – a trend he sought to correct in his book *Catholicism*. Nevertheless, there is the challenge of formulating the relationship between the natural and supernatural in new ways – ways that constitute a more organic, more unified conception.[3]

One finds at the end of de Lubac's *The Mystery of the Supernatural* an explanation of the "the call of love." De Lubac privileges the recovery of interpersonal and spousal images: "Seeing face to face, speaking mouth to mouth, being in the presence of the bridegroom, drinking the life of beatitude from its fount."[4] Even if his formulation – "natural desire for the supernatural" (see chapter 1) comes uncomfortably close to collapsing the supernatural into the inner orientation of the desiring subject, he does nevertheless maintain that the supernatural is essential gift: "God could have refused to give himself to his creatures, just as he could have, and has, given himself."[5] The supernatural order is gratuitous by its very nature and can never be something simply owed to human beings. He recalls at the end of his study the utter gratuity of love – the "revelation of love – not merely of the love of God, but of God who is love."[6]

In light of de Lubac's concerns, the aim of this chapter is to present a non-extrinsicist account of the relationship between the natural and the supernatural – an account that preserves the language that has been privileged in the tradition (metaphysical), but transposes it into terms revelatory of the interpersonal experience of being in love (intentionality analysis, phenomenology).

To this end I respond to Lawrence Feingold's challenge to construct an alternative model that develops the relationship between the natural and the supernatural in a non-extrinsicist way, but that gives priority to the language of Aquinas, especially an account of the *supernatural habitual inclination* for the vision of God resulting from sanctifying grace. This analysis integrates the work of Lonergan and his contemporary interpreters in order to transpose the elevating habits of sanctifying grace and the habit of charity into the interpersonal language of being-in-love. And, in a related manner, the chapter draws on the Trinitarian four-point hypothesis, to envision this "supernatural being-in-love" as a graced participation in Trinitarian life. Finally, I explore, with Lonergan and Marion, a specific dimension of love – spousal love and the love of family vis-à-vis the love of God – in a way that both preserves the metaphysical control of meaning and transposes it with the phenomenological language of interiority and intersubjectivity. This chapter ultimately argues that the supernatural – understood within a Trinitarian framework and transposed into phenomenological terms – does not establish a *new end to human nature* (extrinsicism), but rather a *new relation to that same end* (elevating, inner unity). If the *natural desire* for meaning and truth orients one to desire God's essence, the supernatural gifts of sanctifying grace (being on the receiving end of God's unrestricted love) and the habit of charity (loving God in return with all our hearts and minds and souls and strength and loving our neighbour as ourselves) constitute a *new relation* – a habitual inclination – *to this same end*, the fullness of Trinitarian life. Sanctifying grace and the habit of charity – articulated in terms of being-in-love – are not extrinsic to, but permeate and shape, our most intimate loves.

The Extrinsicism of Supernatural Desire

Feingold's trenchant critique of de Lubac highlighted in an earlier chapter should not be read as an embrace of extrinsicism. "Contemporary critiques of extrinsicism," notes Feingold, "often frame their critique as a rejection of the two-story conception of nature and grace," where "the supernatural is envisioned as an extrinsic superstructure added on top of human nature."[7] This metaphor obscures the unique interrelation between the orders. In a clear rejection of extrinsicism, Feingold submits that the two orders cannot be sealed off from one another, since human nature has a specific obediential potency to receive the beatific vision.

Feingold's critique of de Lubac should also not imply a minimization of de Lubac's indispensable contribution to contemporary theology. Feingold believes that de Lubac identified a great pastoral problem – that the contemporary human person has lost a sense of the supernatural. De Lubac was correct, according to Feingold, in emphasizing the natural desire to see God, and the organic relationship between human natural aspirations and supernatural vocation. If de Lubac has rightly identified a key pastoral problem, and if indeed he is correct about the inadequacies of the extrinsicist two-storey model, a new model is needed to replace both the extrinsicist framework and de Lubac's own inadequate proposal.[8]

I pointed out in chapter 2 that Feingold offers an initial attempt to build such a vision. He substantiates his use of the term "supernatural desire" in selected texts from Aquinas, especially his commentary on 2 Cor. 5. In this commentary, Aquinas distinguishes between "natural" and "supernatural" desire: "God produces natural desires and supernatural desires in us: the natural, when he gives us a natural spirit suited to human nature," and "supernatural desires when he infuses in us the supernatural spirit, i.e., the Holy Spirit."[9] In light of Aquinas's distinction, Feingold identifies two states of supernatural desire, which it is useful to reiterate here: an elicited and unconditional desire for the vision of God made possible by knowledge of God's promise in Revelation, together with the assistance of actual grace; and the supernatural habitual inclination for the vision of God rooted in sanctifying grace. The second is more relevant to this chapter. This supernatural inclination consists in the theological virtues of hope and charity. The habitual inclination is present whenever a soul is in a state of grace. It is, according to Feingold, "independent of knowledge," a commonly held position in the tradition.[10] I suggest below that sanctifying grace – when understood as being in love with God in an unrestricted manner – may not be *known*, but it may be a state we are *conscious of* at the level of *experience*.

According to Feingold, a full flowering theology of nature and grace must account for the rich distinction and interpenetration of our natural and supernatural desires. As he comments, "The natural desire to see God is not sufficient to naturally incline or order us to our supernatural end. For that purpose we need the supernatural virtue of charity which flows from sanctifying grace by which we are mysteriously made somehow proportionate to God, having become 'partakers in the divine nature.'"[11] The natural desire to see God prompts us to recognize that "only the promise given to us in the Gospel to see God face to face will fully and perfectly satisfy the dynamism of the human intellect and will."[12]

Feingold's positing of distinct natural and supernatural desires might strike one initially as a derailment into an extrinsicist account of nature and grace. Closer attention to Feingold's presentation, however, reveals a deliberate attempt to avoid an extrinsicist account of natural and supernatural desire. Feingold refers, for example, to the four "states" of the natural desire for God, and the "transformation" and "conversion" of this desire. The "dynamism of the intellect and will" discloses our "fittingness for the supernatural end promised to us by Christ."[13] Feingold's reference to "states," along with his use of the language of "conversion," "transformation," and "fittingness," represent an attempt to avoid the often caricatured extrinsicist account.

Even if we grant that Feingold explicitly avoids extrinsicism, are there not other ways to envision the relationship between sanctifying grace and the human person? What transpositions might help us account for the shift from the scholastic language of natural human inclinations to the language of concrete subjectivity, which gives greater attention to concrete intellectual, moral, and religious self-transcendence, operating within the climate of religious experience and the level of interpersonal relations?

Sanctifying Grace and the Habit of Charity

In the course of his career, Lonergan ultimately identified sanctifying grace with the dynamic state of being in love with God in an unrestricted manner. As noted throughout this book, Lonergan envisioned in his later work a methodical theology that finds its starting point in intentionality analysis, with a focus on human self-transcendence, and not first on metaphysical terms and relations.

In his work *Grace and Freedom* (1941–2), for example, Lonergan employs the metaphysical category of habit to articulate the operative habitual grace that is called sanctifying grace. For Lonergan, habits are a human necessity. The frailty of the human condition suggests that we cannot reason ourselves into the right attitude before each act. Habits make action easier, and more agreeable. Deliberate vigilance will not sustain: "If only he puts his mind to it, the sinner can resist every temptation. But he cannot constantly be putting his mind to it."[14] Human beings cannot always be on, and hence it is inevitable that we find recourse in the spontaneous orientation of our wills. A life of flourishing rests on the kind of habitual orientation that shapes our desire – the desire that orients our inquiring, knowing, choosing, and loving. "The human will," as Lonergan notes, "does not swing back to a perfect equilibrium of indifference with every tick of the clock."[15] Present orientation tends to be determined by past operations, though not absolutely determined.

This "change-agent" is what Lonergan, following Aquinas, calls sanctifying grace. In the world of discourse informed by Aquinas, it is important to note that different kinds of graces are correlative terms: operative and cooperative grace, habitual and actual grace, and sanctifying and gratuitous grace. The kind of grace Lonergan has in mind is operative (God acts in us without us), habitual (abiding habit giving us new powers for acting), and sanctifying (it makes us holy and unites us with our ultimate end). The infusion of grace "constitutes a permanent change in the inclination or spontaneous orientation of the will: it plucks out the heart of stone that made the sinner a slave to sin; it implants a heart of flesh to initiate a new continuity in justice."[16] In Lonergan's technical language, it is the "remote proportionate principle of the operations by which we attain God as he is in himself."[17] Sanctifying grace is the root of charity, and charity is the kind of love that can only exist between friends; it makes us friends with God.[18]

In *Method in Theology*, Lonergan transposes this scholastic articulation of grace in the more intimate language of the state of "being in love with God in an unrestricted manner" and identifies this state with sanctifying grace.[19] As he says, the two are only notionally different. Lonergan writes, "Being in love with God, as experienced, is being in love in an unrestricted fashion."[20] Although all love involves self-surrender, this love is being in love without limits or conditions. Though this state does not result from human initiative, from our knowing and choosing, it is a conscious and dynamic state of love, joy, and peace, along with the other fruits of the Spirit. For Lonergan, this state is *conscious* without being *known*. In other words, it is a mysterious reality *experienced* but not necessarily grasped in *understanding* or affirmed in *judgment*. This unmeasured love is attractive, fascinating, awe-inspiring, and holy; it is a gift we are possessed by and grasped by. If the language of sanctifying grace speaks of a "permanent change in the inclination or spontaneous orientation of the will" in a more metaphysical fashion, this new language speaks of a "new horizon in which the love of God will transvalue our values and the eyes of that love will transform" our knowing.[21] Intentionality analysis, to connect the point to the two previous chapters, "brings into focus human nature in its spiritual dimensions by specifying the remote and proximate principles of self-transcendence (movement) and integration (rest). The human being is a being 'on the way,' a being in the constant tension of self-transcendence."[22] The ineffable, open-endedness of our capacity for self-transcendence "transposes the Scholastic concept of obediential potency" and is "transformed, enlarged, sublated by a love that is otherworldly, a love in search of meaning beyond the confines of this world."[23]

Lonergan's identification of sanctifying grace with being in love with God in an unrestricted manner prompts us to ask about the *habit of charity*, identified, as we just saw, in Lonergan's early treatments on grace. The Aristotelian framework on which a Thomistic theology of sanctifying grace was based required a distinction between sanctifying grace and the habit of charity. Sanctifying grace was considered entitative – rooted in the essence of the soul – while the habit of charity was accidental – rooted in the potency of the soul.[24] When one is attempting to transpose these distinctions from a metaphysical context to religious interiority, one must ask whether this distinction survives. It could be that sanctifying grace and the habit of charity appeal to the same reality in conscious experience. Lonergan even admitted that his identification of sanctifying grace and being in love with God represented an amalgamation of sanctifying grace and charity. Though there has been debate over its preservation, Robert Doran, following Aquinas, maintains the distinction in order to avoid a retreat into the "undifferentiated common sense about interiority," and for its systematic explanatory power in providing a "hypothetical understanding of how it can be true that we do indeed enjoy distinct created relations to each of the three uncreated divine persons as terms of these relations."[25] Doran argues, then, that the metaphysical distinction of sanctifying grace and the habit of charity ought to be transposed into the categories of being on the receiving end of God's unqualified and unconditional love (sanctifying grace) and loving God in return with all our hearts and minds and souls and strength and loving our neighbour as ourselves (habit of charity).[26]

The Four-Point Hypothesis: Trinitarian Structure of the Supernatural

Having just highlighted Doran's transposition of sanctifying grace and the habit of charity, I turn now to his account of these same supernatural realities in a more explicitly Trinitarian context. In the four-point hypothesis, Lonergan and Doran identify grace as a set of created participations in the supernatural life of God. Grace, in other words, possesses a distinctly Trinitarian structure. The four-point hypothesis identifies four absolutely supernatural ways of imitating God through a created participation in the divine relations. Guided by the logic of contingent predication, these "participations do not constitute a change in the divine relations themselves, but do create a real, albeit created, participation in the divine nature."[27]

Though there are four supernatural realities in Lonergan's schema, I limit my analysis here to the particular divine relations connected to created imitations and participations of sanctifying grace (active spiration) and the habit of charity (passive spiration). (I extend these categories in chapter 7 in my development of an explanatory theology of the saints.) Doran states his analogy clearly as follows:

> The starting point in unpacking that four-point hypothesis is the link between sanctifying grace and charity as created participations in, respectively, active spiration and passive spiration. From the standpoint

of religiously and interiorly differentiated consciousness, these created participations are (1) the recalled reception (*memoria*) of the gift of God's love (that is, of sanctifying grace as it affects consciousness) grounding a subsequent set of judgments of value (faith), as these together participate in active spiration and so set up a special relation to the indwelling Holy Spirit, and (2) a return of love (charity) participating in the Proceeding Love that is the Holy Spirit, which establishes a special relation to the indwelling Father and Son. Memory and Faith combine to imitate and participate in active spiration, and charity imitates and participates in passive spiration.[28]

First, the divine relation of active spiration connects to the created reality of sanctifying grace. In other words, sanctifying grace imitates and participates in the Father and the Son together as they "breathe" the Holy Spirit, and so bears a special relation to the uncreated Holy Spirit. Second, the divine relation of passive spiration connects to the created reality of the habit of charity. The habit of charity proceeds from the reception of sanctifying grace and participates in the "proceeding Love 'breathed' by and proceeding from the Father and the Son, and so bears a special inverse relation to the Father and the Son."[29] The habit of charity animates the return of good for evil in an abiding friendship with God.[30]

The Shift to Interpersonal Relations: New Relation to the Same End

Sanctifying grace and the habit of charity directly relate to this chapter's theme of supernatural desire, or, as I will rearticulate the matter below, the elevation of human desire to a new created (supernatural) relation to that end. Scholars have debated the question of how sanctifying grace ought to be articulated in a methodical theology, a theology grounded in the conscious operations and states of the existential subject. In a methodical vision, metaphysical terms and relations are not prioritized. But does this mean that such metaphysical terms should be discarded? Doran recommends against their dismissal. The metaphysical terms provide a fruitful and much-needed control of meaning, and hence Doran suggests a preservation and transposition of these terms into the language of interiority, as I noted above.[31]

For Doran, the key to this transposition is more explicit treatment of the level of interpersonal relations.[32] When marked with self-transcendence, this level includes the love of intimacy, devotion to the human community, the reception of God's love, and the return of love for God in charity.[33] The distinguishing character of this level is not the supernatural as opposed to the natural, but a concern with the "other" – with the presence of the beloved in the lover.[34] This interpersonal level makes possible the "conscious relation between the conscious subject and the other with whom the subject is in love."[35] This level of interpersonal relations is constituted by self-gift, the very handing over of one's central form to the determination of another in love.[36] One may even discern a fourth stage of meaning that sublates the conscious interiority of the subject more fully in the context of a community of loving persons.[37]

In light of this relational matrix, I propose that the supernatural does not offer us a new end, but a new relation to the same end, who is God.[38] In terms of final causality, the "supernatural cannot add a new end beyond what is already given naturally but must be a new mode of attainment of that goal."[39] Since grace perfects nature rather than replacing nature, it is more fitting to frame this in the language of relationality and continuity. In other words, human beings have a natural orientation to God as knowable and loveable with an unrestricted reach, as I claimed in chapter 4. The supernatural is not a new final cause then, but a new created relation to that end. In this instance, it is not simply a matter of the relationship between creature and creator. This is because, if the human person actually attains here God as God *in se*, then these new supernatural relations would be created participations in the internal relations of Trinitarian life.[40] This solution involves the rich interconnection between Trinitarian theology and the grace-nature distinction that I attempted to highlight above. This line of reasoning contributes to Feingold's challenge to account for the elevation of natural desire into a supernatural inclination to the vision of God through the reception of sanctifying grace. Lonergan, along with Doran's and Ormerod's developments, preserves the distinction between the natural and the supernatural, but also transposes this distinction into the context of interpersonal relations, which helps us avoid an extrinsicist account of natural and supernatural ends.

Metaphysical and Phenomenological Accounts of Love

I turn now to Doran's challenge to both preserve the metaphysical categories of sanctifying grace and the habit of charity and to situate them in the realm of the interpersonal. How might we think about spousal love and the love of family as infused love with God in a way that preserves the metaphysical control of meaning, but transposes in the phenomenological language of the interpersonal? Such a transposition offers resources for articulating the relationship between natural loves and supernatural loves in a more organic, less extrinsic way.

Metaphysics of Love: Vertical Finality and a Critique of Extrinsicism

In the previous chapter, I noted the importance of the explanatory term "vertical finality," which indicated, in the concrete universe, the potentiality not only for horizontal unity but also for emergence. "Vertical finality" denotes an emergent, upward-directed drive that gives lower beings the capacity to set the conditions for the emergence of higher beings. If the emphasis in chapter 4 was on the upward dynamism of intellectual operations, I now focus on the upward dynamism of love – from natural love to charity, the only virtue to remain in the beatific vision.

In his essay "Finality, Love, Marriage" (1949), Lonergan extends the term "vertical finality" to the theme of love. He notes this upward-directed dynamism of human love from the level of nature to the level of the beatific vision[41] and the transformation that happens when the heart is startled by a beauty and shifts the centre of desire out of the self to the other. This experience of eros prompts a yearning for the other. And, in the course of the relationship, a shift occurs from "the merely orgiastic tendencies of nature to the rational level of friendship with its enduring basis in the excellence of a good person." Hence, there is a "dispositive upward tendency from eros to friendship, and from friendship to a special order of charity."[42] Married life offers the matrix of conditions that shows this upward tendency from human to supernatural perfection – an upward movement to love of God and neighbour.[43] Marriage is a human friendship that embodies horizontal finality in the procreative process and vertical finality in its pointing to "our eternal embrace with God in the beatific vision."[44] Lonergan's account here comes close to Steven Long's argument in chapter 2 about marriage in the natural and supernatural orders, though Lonergan's use of vertical finality situates this dynamism within the concretely operating world order.

In *Insight*, Lonergan also discusses the role of charity in the concrete world process, but does so in this context with the problem of evil explicitly in mind. I bring this to light because it is an explicitly anti-extrinsicist argument. Charity, along with faith and hope, are considered the higher conjugate forms with which God meets the evils of sin and bias. While general transcendent knowledge is the knowledge of God that answers the basic questions raised by the question of being, special transcendent knowledge includes God's solution to the problem of evil.[45] Lonergan describes the general characteristics of the divine solution as follows:

> Thus any solution would be one; it would be universally accessible and permanent; it would be a harmonious continuation of the actual order of the universe; it would consist in some reversal of the priority of living over the knowledge needed to guide life and over the good will needed to follow knowledge; this reversal would be effected through conjugate forms that in some sense would transcend human nature, that would constitute a new and higher integration of human activity, that would pertain not to static system but to system on the move, that would be realized with man's apprehension and consent and in accord with the probabilities of world order.[46]

The point especially relevant to this inquiry into the natural and supernatural is Lonergan's claim that the solution would be a harmonious continuation of the actual order of the universe. This provides a way of recognizing the absolute supernaturality of grace, while at the same time avoiding a presentation of the supernatural as extrinsically added on to human nature. Here, charity is indeed envisioned as transcending human nature in some sense. But this kind of transcendence would constitute not a new desire or a new activity, but "a new and higher *integration* of human activity," and would be realized in accord with the probabilities of world order.[47] This new and higher integration is a harmonious continuation of the actual order of the universe willed by God.

It is this actual order of the universe – not some ideal of perfection divorced from the complexity of the world process – that is a "good and value chosen by God for the manifestation of the perfection of God."[48] Apart from the distortion of sin, then, the universe is in love with God. The person of good will – the person who wills concretely the good of the universe of emergent probability – is in love with God.[49] To love God and to affirm the good of the universe is then to embrace a universe shot through with contingency, a universe that operates according to probabilities. In the midst of all this complexity, Lonergan can say that the good of the universe "includes all the good that all persons in the universe are or enjoy or possess."[50]

The conjugate forms that Lonergan proposes are the supernatural virtues of faith, hope, and charity, which are part of the complex heuristic structure of the supernatural solution to the problem of evil, willed from all eternity by the one God within the one world order.[51] Lonergan identifies charity with the dialectical attitude of returning good for evil, self-sacrificing love, repentance, and joy:

> For it is love of God above all and in all, and love is joy. Its repentance and sorrow regard the past. Its present sacrifices look to the future. It is at one with the universe in being in love with God, and it shares its dynamic resilience and expectancy. As emergent probability, it ever rises above past achievement. As genetic process, it develops generic potentiality to its specific perfection. As dialectic, it overcomes evil both by meeting it with good and by using it to reinforce the good. But good will wills the order of the universe, and so it wills with that order's dynamic joy and zeal.[52]

The operation of charity in this one world order is not limited to a particular conclave in the world or a particular church as if it were extrinsic to the fact that all human beings have a natural desire for meaning, truth, goodness, and love. And the higher integration given by faith, hope, and charity elevates and transforms these natural desires in harmonious continuation of the actual order of the universe.[53] This is not to deny the centrality of Christ and his mystical body, the Church. Later in this chapter and in the next, more will be said about Christian particularity, created participation in the Trinitarian relations, and the possibility of the vestiges of the Trinity to be discerned inside and outside concrete ecclesial life. But Lonergan recognizes the presence of charity in a variety of walks of life. He does so, however, not in a naive fashion, but in a way that challenges us to discern the pitfalls of imperfect charity and the half-loves that constitute our actual concrete relations in the world.

Phenomenology of Love: Lonergan and Marion

Having offered a metaphysically oriented account of love, I turn now to Lonergan's later treatment of love, from *Method in Theology* (1972) on. Although Lonergan has established a helpful framework – a heuristic structure, if you will – I contend that a more sustained treatment of the interpersonal dimension of intimate family love requires the help of other thinkers who have explored these kinds of loves in a phenomenological way. In this section, I integrate selected themes from the work of Jean-Luc Marion (and by extension insights from Balthasar, Jean Vanier, and Wendell Berry) into the analysis. Scholars have noted the attention both thinkers devote to the priority of love and "the excess of the gift of God."[54]

The phenomenological tradition's focus on intersubjectivity aims to account for the other as a subject – a subject endowed with a rich inner life in a world mediated by meaning and motivated by value – rather than as a substance, to employ the scholastic terminology. There is indeed a thread of intersubjectivity and the interpersonal that runs throughout much of Lonergan's work. That said, Lonergan's heuristic framework could benefit from richer phenomenological descriptions of interpersonal love. Perhaps a central motif from the writings of Hans Urs von Balthasar – one of the key influences on Marion – will help initiate us into this mode and offer us a glimpse of the fundamental reordering of priorities, to be described below. For Balthasar, a child does not awaken into consciousness with the question of why there is something rather than nothing nor ask, with more existential urgency, "Why am I here?"[55] In interpersonal categories, Balthasar writes, "Its 'I' awakens in the experience of a 'Thou': in its mother's smile through which it learns that it is contained, affirmed and loved in a relationship which is incomprehensibly encompassing, already actual, sheltering and nourishing."[56] Balthasar continues:

> The body which it snuggles into, a soft, warm and nourishing kiss, is a kiss of love in which it can take shelter because it had been sheltered there *a priori*. The awakening of its consciousness is a late occurrence, in comparison with this basic mystery of unfathomable depth. It finally sees only what has always been, and can therefore only confirm it. A light which has been perpetually asleep awakens at some point into an alert and self-knowing light. But it awakens at the love of the Thou, as it has always slept in the womb and on the bosom of the Thou. The experience of being granted entrance into a sheltering and encompassing world is one which for all incipient, developing and mature consciousness cannot be superseded.[57]

It is within this interpersonal matrix – captured here by Balthasar – that Lonergan situates the role of multidimensional loves in human living. In his later writings, he envisions a movement in human living – a movement "from above downwards" – as the "transformation of falling in love" in its multiple forms – marriage, family, friendship, and civic.[58] Beyond these forms of human love, religious experience discloses a being in love with God in an unrestricted fashion. This is sanctifying grace in a metaphysical context. Whereas our unquenchable desire to know reveals our quest for self-transcendence, religious love fulfils this capacity, dismantling and abolishing "the horizon in which our knowing and choosing went on" and setting up "a new horizon in which the love of God will transvalue our values and the eyes of that love will transform that knowing."[59]

In terms of accounting for love as the fundamental horizon for human knowing and acting, it is relevant to note that both Lonergan and Marion turn to Blaise Pascal. For Lonergan, there is a kind of knowledge only possible through love. In his explanation of this love-knowledge, Lonergan draws on Pascal's dictum that "the heart has its reasons which reason does not know." Lonergan identifies reason with the three levels of cognitional activity – empirical, intellectual, and rational. He identifies the "heart's reasons" as "feelings that are intentional responses to values," and the "heart" as the subject operating on the "fourth, existential level of intentional consciousness and in the dynamic state of being in love."[60] In other words, in addition to factual knowledge, there is another kind of knowledge reached only by a person in love. Divine love neither results from nor is conditioned by human knowledge of God. Rather, it is a gift that precedes such knowledge and prompts the very cause of our seeking.[61] Lonergan cites Pascal's reflection in *Pensees* vii: "Take comfort, you would not be seeking me if you had not already found me." This gift orients us to transcendent mystery – a mystery to love with all one's heart, soul, mind, and strength.[62]

In similar fashion, Pascal provides Marion with the resources for thinking about the primacy of love in terms of a phenomenology of charity and not metaphysical proofs. To contextualize, Marion's work is animated in part by overcoming the kind of metaphysics that emerges in modernity – a thought-form that prioritizes epistemology and the thinking subject's knowing of being in the manner of Descartes and Kant. And for Pascal, thinking of God solely in terms of metaphysical proofs is an exercise in vanity. Thus, Pascal helps Marion articulate a phenomenological reduction rooted in charity. In *On Descartes' Metaphysical Prism*, Marion writes of Pascal that love does not dispense with knowing, but becomes the road to knowledge.[63] In the tradition of the saints, we should love in order to know; we can enter the truth by way of charity. Love, for Marion, functions as a "hermeneutical principle that opens onto a new world."[64] "To see the 'order of charity,' one has not so much to know a new object, as to know according to a new condition, loving."[65] In sum, one finds here in both Lonergan and Marion a kind of reversal of the axiom that "knowledge precedes love" – that you cannot love what you do not know. In terms of God's love in relation to human yearning, "love precedes knowledge," and the "very beginning of faith is due to God's grace."[66] Lonergan and Marion give priority to love and suggest that there is a desire and knowledge that only love can give.

Erotic Subjectivity and Divine Grace

I now focus on Marion's more sustained account of intimate love as a way of establishing a kind of supernatural desire for God that is rooted in sanctifying grace and the habit of charity. If Lonergan and Doran help us both preserve the natural-supernatural distinction in a non-extrinsicist way and transpose sanctifying grace and the habit of charity within an interpersonal, and ultimately Trinitarian, matrix, then Marion helps us penetrate in phenomenological fashion the relationship between the human love of intimacy and the love of God. This integration of Marion relates, in part, to Dadosky's attempt to expand Lonergan's patterns of experience to the sexual pattern. The sexual pattern of experience is closely related, Dadosky argues, to the biological pattern (desire for sexual gratification in a similar manner to water quenching our thirst or food meeting our need for sustenance), but also interpenetrates the aesthetic and dramatic patterns – patterns that embody spontaneity, play, and freedom. Human sexuality bears the capacity to mediate "the mystery of another person."[67] And a successful negotiation of the dialectic involves both a "commitment to a person in a way that brings about and furthers one's development and self-transcendence" and deepens one's commitment to ultimate transcendent value.[68] It is important to note that this chapter does not offer a full account of the nuances of *The Erotic Phenomenon*, but attends in a selective manner to some of Marion's overarching themes as a way of enriching a framework already established by Lonergan and Doran. Thus, I take the liberty of illuminating Marion's rather elusive style with some concrete examples from other writers. A fundamental point, however, to keep in mind is that the human capacity to love, for Marion, is ultimately made possible by finding ourselves "always and already loved" by God. Marion's phenomenological approach enables us to account for a more intrinsic relationship between human and divine love than a neatly partitioned extrinsicist account.

In *The Erotic Phenomenon*, Marion challenges us to rethink the question that matters most. He prioritizes erotic meditations. "I thus had to admit," he reflects, "that no question reached me more radically that that which asked me not, 'Am I thinking?' but 'Does anyone out there love me?' To be or not to be is no longer the question, but only 'Does anyone out there love me?'"[69] Rather than certitude in being, the radical question involves assurance in love. Hence, the questions that shape Marion's phenomenological analysis are: Am I loved by another? Can I love first? And, in a more declarative manner: You have loved me first.[70]

Desire to Be Loved

In terms of the first question – "Am I loved by another?" – one inquires into one's own "loveableness" and consequently one's worth. Marion treats this question in relation to our experience of space, time, and identity, along with the temptation to vanity that the question prompts. For the sake of my attempt to navigate this question in a way that enriches the priority of love affirmed by Lonergan in his later work, I offer an example from the life and work of Jean Vanier, the founder of the L'Arche communities for the severely mentally disabled. Vanier says that, upon entering L'Arche, they often blame themselves. "If I am not loved," they seem to say, "it is because I am not lovable, I am no good. I am evil."[71] When Vanier started living at L'Arche, he quickly realized that he was surrounded by men and women crying out, "Will you be my friend? Am I important to you? Do I have any value?"[72] While those who do not experience severe mental disabilities are able to mask over this fundamental need through a variety of defence mechanisms, Vanier notes that the rejected and institutionalized cannot hide the pain and loneliness of abandonment. At L'Arche, he witnesses tense, fearful, and angry bodies become relaxed, peaceful, and trusting. He offers the example of a woman named Jane who came to the community from the psychiatric hospital. Full of anger and pain, she would continually hit her head with her fist: "Over the ten years she has been with us, she has grown more peaceful. Her eyes are now bright with life. She still cannot speak or walk, but it is as if her flesh has in some way been transformed."[73] Vanier's life with the mentally disabled reveals that the most fundamental human question is not about *certitude in being*, but about *assurance in love*, and that an affirmative answer to this question significantly shapes the flourishing of our relationships, families, and communities.

Loving in the Flesh: Sexual Pattern of Experience

Although the question "Does anyone love me?" indicates the deep desire for love in the human condition, Marion challenges us to refocus the question in favour of one that does not presume love is reciprocal, and that leads us into the realm of charity: Can I love first? This recasting conditions us to think about self-emptying, of gift, and not simply of mutuality and reciprocity. In what follows, I concentrate more on sexual expressions of love that challenge us to advance towards the other and to see the other not as an object but as a person. In *The Erotic Phenomenon*, Marion offers a more personal signification of the other in the faithful performance of the oath in a deliberate distancing from the primacy of the ethical in Levinas's phenomenology of the face and the height of the other. According to Marion, we must indeed recognize the privilege of the face.[74] But our encounter "no longer depends here on a distance, nor on an ethical height," as it does with Levinas, but rather on intimacy with particularity. In this intimate encounter, the face of the other person is not saying to me "Thou shall not kill!"[75] In other words, this encounter does not disclose itself as a fundamentally ethical encounter concretizing a universal commandment. But in more deeply personal, intimate, and erotic language the other "says to me, in sighs or words, 'Here I am, come!'"[76] Marion's key claim is that when we love a person – when we make love in person – our experience is not ordered by an abstract universal ethic; rather, it is surrounded by and imbued with particularity – "mine and his or hers, since it is a question of me and of you and surely not of a universally obligating neighbor."[77] In the mutually erotic zone, each gives to the other in the flesh, thus transgressing the universal.

The theme of flesh is crucial for Marion's phenomenological rendering of conjugal sexual intimacy. Recognizing the formative nature of love, he says that each act of love is "inscribed forever in me and outlines me definitively." We do not love by proxy, but only in the flesh.[78] We do not have flesh, but are flesh. As bodies, we are flesh in the world. But not every encounter of nakedness with another is an encounter of the flesh. Medical nudity, for example, does not manifest me in the flesh.

It re-transforms me instead into "an object of examination, measurable under every angle, diagnosable like a physical machine, a chemical metabolism, an economic consumer, etc."[79] The denuding of *flesh*, for Marion, is opposed to the uncovering of the *object*. In erotic intimacy, provoking the desire of the other paradoxically consists most often in "showing that one does not show – for the flesh distinguishes itself from the body precisely in that it cannot and must not appear on an equal footing with objects, on the same stage as the things of the world."[80] Rather, it is to be faithful to a phenomenological principle: no flesh can appear simply as a body. That is, "if one understands this appearing in the simple sense of offering itself naked to the gaze, it is only fitting for a body and never for a flesh, precisely because that which gives the flesh its privilege – the capacity to feel and feel itself feeling – cannot appear directly under any light."[81] We often feel and experience other bodies in the daily happenings in the life-world. This experience is marked by our day-to-day encounter with others' bodies, but predominantly as resistance or impenetrability or unavailability. And this happens because of spatiality. To avoid misunderstanding, this is not a matter of "I in the flesh" attempting to encounter every other body as flesh. Rather, it is to set the stage for distinguishing how different it is to experience another as flesh. This fleshly encounter "feels that something *puts up no resistance to me*, and that, far from turning me back into myself and thus reducing me, this something withdraws, effaces itself and makes room for me, in short that this something opens itself, I know that I am dealing with flesh – or better, with a flesh other than my own, the flesh of an other."[82] To be flesh with another – whether the relationship between mother and child or an authentic sexual experience – is to experience the kind of sheltering that is fully human. "I can only free myself and become myself by touching another flesh, as one touches a land at port, because only another flesh can make room for me, welcome me, and not turn me away or resist me – that is, comply with my flesh and reveal it to me by providing it a place."[83]

Marion's distinction between *gazing at a body* and *feeling in the flesh* finds expression in the reflections of the agrarian poet, novelist, and essayist Wendell Berry. One of the boasts of our contemporary age, reflects Berry – from artists, psychologists, and therapists to anthropologists and pornographers – is that the bedroom door has been opened wide and now we see what sex really is.[84] Voyeurs, for Berry, in fact are "the most handicapped of all the sexual observers; they only know what they see."[85] True intimacy cannot be known by an outsider; it cannot be shown. In a fashion that illuminates Marion's point, Berry claims that the intimacy of the union itself cannot be observed: "One cannot enter into this intimacy and watch it at the same time, any more than the mind can think about itself while it thinks about something else."[86] It's not that sexual intimacy ought to be avoided as a subject of the imagination; Berry's point is that voyeurism often drains sex of its mystery and sanctity. After all, Homer, Shakespeare, the Bible, and Jane Austen have imaginatively depicted the intimacy and power of sexual love, while at the same time respecting its privacy and honouring its dignity. The best representations of sex make one aware "with profound sympathy, of the two lives, not just the two bodies that are involved; they make one aware also of the difficulty of full and open sexual consent between two people and of the history and the trust that are necessary to make possible that consent. Without such a history and trust, sex is brutal, no matter what species is involved."[87] The profoundest artistic expressions of sex help us imagine "the sweetness continuing on through the joys and difficulties of homemaking, the births and upbringing of children, the deaths of parents and friends – through disagreements, hardships, quarrels, aging, and death."[88] And this is precisely what Marion alerts us to: misdirected eroticization and the importance of oaths.

Marion recognizes the potential pitfalls associated with misdirected eroticization. Although erotic love individualizes us, it is not always directed to the person as person; the temptation to treat the other as an erotic object endures. The way to overcome this difficulty, for Marion, is to enter into an eroticization that is marked by freedom and not instinct or coercion, where not only flesh but access to the person is gained.

You Have Loved Me First: Human Oath and Divine Love

Marion concretizes this phenomenological vision with a reflection on fidelity – the kind of fidelity called for with the arrival of children. The priority of love – the call to make love in person – is nourished by fidelity, and fidelity is what allows the phenomenon to be seen. The erotic phenomenon in this richer sense demands long and deep faithfulness.[89] "I thus receive myself, in the end, from the other person. I receive from the other my ipseity, as I have already received my signification in his or her oath, my flesh in the eroticization of his or hers, and even my proper fidelity in the other's declaration 'You truly love me!'"[90] In this vein, Marion invokes the Levinasian third, as a possible witness to the oath of fidelity between the lovers. The child receives the gift of origin, but can never return it. The child can, however, embody the gift: "The child certainly reproduces the oath of the lovers on his face."[91] While the child may embody the oath of fidelity, he or she cannot ultimately assure the permanence of the oath; hence, Marion invokes God as the eternal witness.

For Marion, then, the lovers "accomplish their oath in the *adieu* – in the passage to God, who they summon as their final witness, their first witness, the one who never leaves and never lies."[92] Which leads us to the final formulation of the erotic reduction: "You loved me first."[93] In a way that complements Doran's transposition of sanctifying grace and the habit of charity, Marion says that our capacity to love is actually made possible by finding ourselves always and already loved.[94] In this erotic reduction, the lovers realize that "there has been another lover who has preceded me there and, from there, calls me there in silence."[95] Marion's invocation of a theological foundation for our "loveableness" resonates with and can be integrated into a systematic theology by way of Doran's formulation of sanctifying grace as being on the receiving end of God's unqualified and unconditional love. For Marion, the first lover is eternally God. We love God because God has loved us first. In fact, "God practices the logic of the erotic reduction as we do"; God loves "in the same way we do."[96] Marion immediately qualifies this with a note on the "infinite difference" that is also operative here:

> When God loves (and indeed he never ceases to love), he simply loves infinitely better than we do. He loves to perfection, without a fault, without an error, from beginning to end. He loves first and last. He loves like no one else. In the end, I not only discover that another was loving me before I loved, and thus that this other already played the lover before me, but above all I discover that this first lover, from the very beginning, is named God. God's highest transcendence, the only one that does not dishonor him, belongs not to power, nor to wisdom, nor even to infinity, but to love. For love alone is enough to put all infinity, all wisdom, and all power to work.[97]

Conclusion

This chapter attended to Feingold's challenge to develop an alternative model that develops the relationship between the natural and the supernatural in a non-extrinsicist way that still gives priority to the language of Aquinas, especially an account of the *supernatural habitual inclination* for the vision of God resulting from sanctifying grace. With Lonergan, and the developments of Doran and Ormerod, this chapter argued on the one hand for the ongoing relevance of Aquinas's language of the elevating habits of sanctifying grace and the habit of charity, and on the other hand for the need for these explanatory terms to be rearticulated in the interpersonal language of being-in-love. Situating these elevating habits within a Trinitiarian context equipped us with the resources to argue that the supernatural is not an abstract essence that hovers over the natural and descends to relate to our natural lives in a vague and extrinsic way; rather, "supernatural being-in-love" is a graced participation in the specific divine relations of Trinitarian life. Aiming to present a phenomenologically informed account of the relationship between human and divine love, the chapter presented a transposition of Lonergan's metaphysically informed account of love to his later phenomenological account. In light of this guiding framework, a selective turn to Marion helped us to penetrate in phenomenological fashion the relationship between the human love of intimacy and the love of God. Marion challenged us to prioritize the question of love as fundamental, to explore what it means to make love in person within the context of an oath and the fecundity of children, and ultimately showed us that we can only love truly because we were already deemed loveable by God. Placed within the natural-supernatural framework, the language of Marion helped us imagine in a more intrinsic way the interconnection of human and divine love, and what it might mean experientially to receive the supernatural gifts of sanctifying grace and the habit of charity.[98] These gifts do not create a new human end, but constitute instead a new relation to this same end. The desire we have for God's essence naturally is transformed into a new way of relating – a way of relating that instils in us a desire for the beatific vision – the very *patria* of Trinitarian life. And our experience of human love in all its vulnerability – with children, with the vulnerable, in sexual intimacy – is not extrinsic to, but inextricably intertwined with, this supernatural inclination.

PART 3

Mimetic Desire, Models of Holiness, and the Love of Deviated Transcendence

6 Incarnate Meaning and Mimetic Desire: Saints and the Desire for God

This part of the book shifts our attention, in a more concentrated way, to other-mediated and socially mediated desire, recognizing the growing emphasis in theological scholarship on the saints as models of desire. How might a consideration of the human desire for God be broadened when the socially mediated, mimetic character of concrete subjectivity is taken seriously? Recall Girard's claim that mimetic desire is also the desire for God.[1]

An exploration of the relationship between theology and models of holiness can be found, for example, in the work of Michael Buckley. Buckley argues for the restoration of religious experience to its legitimate place in theology. Accordingly, he has posed the challenge of developing a more robust account of "religious intellectuality," which is couched in terms of two dynamisms: (1) the permanent orientation of the human mind to truth, goodness, beauty, and justice; and (2) concrete historical disclosures of holiness – persons and encounters that create the conditions for assent to the reality of God.[2]

The former dynamism was treated in chapters 3–5; this chapter and the one to follow respond to Buckley's challenge of discerning the role of the saints in theological discourse.[3] In fact, he finds it "extraordinary that so much Christian formal theology for centuries has bracketed this actual witness," offering it very little intellectual weight.[4] He asks, "Is it not a lacuna in the standard theology, even of our day, that theology neither has nor has striven to forge the intellectual devices to probe in these concrete experiences the disclosure they offer of the reality of God and so render them available for so universal a discipline?" He adds that this "would be a difficult and complex task."[5]

In an attempt, then, to restore concrete disclosures of religious experience to their legitimate place in theology, this chapter first outlines Doran's heuristic framework for integrating the dynamism for self-transcendence and mimetic desire. Building on the ongoing Lonergan-Girard conversation, it then links Lonergan's category of "incarnate meaning" with René Girard's theory of mimetic desire as a means of developing some general-theological terms on which to build a theology of religious disclosure. Finally, it highlights a distinctive feature of a Girardian account of sanctity, humility and resistance to scapegoating, and further suggests a way of integrating Lonergan's account of nature, understood as self-transcendence, into Girard's schema. This will pave the way for a discussion of the metaphysics of holiness and the habit of charity in the next chapter. Both incarnate meaning and mimetic desire recognize the primacy of the interpersonal in human experiences of meaning and truth. The integration of these categories enables us to envision the saints as both sites of incarnate meaning and, more specifically, incarnate models of desire.

Intellectual Desire and Mimetic Desire

I frame this chapter in terms of a more constructive integration of intellectual and mimetic desire. As I mentioned in the introduction to this book, Girardian scholar Kevin Lenehan has suggested that Girard's anthropological emphasis on intersubjectivity, relationality, and the phenomenon of "knowing and willing according to a model" as a ground for "human openness to divine revelation" might complement "the more cognitive approaches of scholasticism and transcendentalism."[6]

In *The Trinity in History*, Doran establishes a framework, based on Lonergan's work, for integrating natural desire and mimetic desire.[7] He grounds this integration in his account of *two ways of being conscious*. The first way of being conscious highlights the passive character of the human spirit. In Thomistic terms, this is a movement from potency to act. This first way involves undergoing passively "what we sense and imagine, our desires and fears, our delights and sorrows, our joys and sadness."[8] Doran refers to this way as the psychic dimension of consciousness. As the kind of data to be understood by depth psychology, it lies in the polyphony or cacophony of our "sensations, memories, images, emotions, conations, associations, bodily movements, and spontaneous intersubjective responses."[9] Doran identifies this first way of being conscious with elicited desire, and contrasts elicited desire with natural or innate desire.[10]

The second way of being conscious involves the unfolding of the transcendental, spiritual, autonomous, and active desire for being and value. It is the pure, unrestricted, detached, disinterested desire for what is, what is true, and what is good. Lonergan's remark about children is especially relevant for the navigation of mimetic and natural desire: "Wearing their parents out with a virtually endless stream of questions is something that children neither are taught nor learn."[11] In Thomistic terms, it is the spiritual dimension of human consciousness that becomes the created analogy for the Trinitarian processions. This is an instance, not of elicited desire, but of natural desire. This is where human consciousness "provides instances of autonomous spiritual processions." The term "autonomous" must be qualified. For Doran, this term does not indicate the "sense of a self-asserting effort at what Ernest Becker called the *causa sui* project."[12] Rather, it recognizes that in the second way of being conscious we are operating under transcendental exigencies for the intelligible, the true, and the real. This is the realm of natural (not elicited) desire, spiritual (not psychic) desire. Lonergan's and Doran's positive references to the "autonomous subject" pose a tension with Girard's and Alison's consistent critique of the romantic lie and metaphysical autonomy. (Recall that the anthropology of grasping perpetuates the romantic lie and the ongoing illusion of autonomy.)[13] It is rooted in what Girard calls "metaphysical desire" – the deviated desire to absorb the mediator of our desire into ourselves, especially the other's imagined autonomy and uniqueness. Doran affirms their critique of autonomy; but he also consciously wants to maintain the language of autonomy, not to defend the enlightenment subject or the romantic subject, but to substantiate the spiritual acts, the intelligible emanations of the human mind that participate in uncreated light and that serve as an analogy for the Trinitarian processions.[14]

For Doran, however, it would be a mistake to separate these two ways of being conscious in hermetically sealed spaces. The first way of being conscious, in fact, "precedes, accompanies, and overarches the intentional operations that constitute the second way of being conscious."[15] In this vein, Doran reorients Heidegger's *Verstehen* (understanding) and *Befindlichkeit* (mood) into his context of vertical finality. "Vertical finality," as we noted in chapter 4, indicates an upward-directed dynamism from the lower to higher levels of being; lower levels set the conditions for the emergence of higher levels. In this context, *Befindlichkeit* is the state of mind, the mood, the dispositions that shape and accompany the human quest for meaningful, intelligent, rational, moral, and loving modes of living.

The following question must be posed to Girard: If one is committed to an account of the second way of being conscious, that is, to the natural desire for meaning, truth, and goodness (to the autonomous spiritual processions), is all desire really mimetic desire? According to Doran, Girard's mimetic desire concerns the first way of being conscious, but also "penetrates our spiritual orientation to the intelligible, the true and the real, and the good, for better and for worse."[16] In other words, distorted mimetic desire can infect the unfolding of the intellectual quest, while positive mimesis may strengthen, enhance, and deepen our commitment to the exigencies of the mind. Positive models have the power to elicit the desire to be faithful to the natural desire for meaning, truth, and goodness. Doran's appropriation of Girard's work emphasizes that Lonergan's first "way of being conscious" is "precisely interdividual in many of its manifestations." For Doran, psychic development entails the negotiation of this interdividual field, which often distorts this second way of being conscious and yet, if authentically negotiated, will allow the second way to flourish in the development of the person.[17] "The intersubjective presence of that other evokes my innate drive for self-transcendence, that is, for fuller or more authentic being-myself."[18]

Doran insists that Girard is correct that "almost all learning is based on imitation" and that even "satisfying the desire to know involves mimetic behavior, however natural the desire to know may be, and however elicited mimetic desire always is."[19] Still, the desire to know, he further insists, is not a matter of acquisitive mimesis, which – recall Alison's "anthropology of grasping" – is a perversion of the pure, detached, disinterested desire to know. It thwarts the eros of the mind. Doran suggests that Girard and Lonergan exhibit both mimetic desire and the natural desire to know. Girard exhibits the latter in integrating his insights over the years into a rational framework and transforming them into real knowledge; his own intellectual performance cannot be reduced to acquisitive mimesis. Similarly, Lonergan was surely influenced by Aquinas in mimetic fashion, but so many of his judgments and decisions – his pioneering intellectual achievements – were also his own.[20]

In light of Doran's integration of these two desires, it is pertinent to note that Girard would probably be more sympathetic than one might at first imagine. As Grant Kaplan has pointed out, Girard does acknowledge other kinds of explanatory tools besides mimetic desire. He is interested in mimetic desire because of its ubiquity and wide application,[21] but his emphasis on mimetic desire ought not to be taken as excluding other types of explanation. For example, Girard says, "I believe in the love that parents have for their children, and I don't see how you could interpret that in mimetic fashion."[22] In a further response to a question about whether all desire is religious, Girard responded, "All desire is a desire for being."[23] Kaplan comments, "Here we have the inchoate basis ... for the possibility of a love that exists apart from the vagaries of mimesis, and desire unrestricted in the sense insisted on by Doran and Lonergan."[24]

In light of this integrating framework, my aim is to widen the scope of desire beyond the intellectual desire associated with the natural desire for God debates discussed in previous chapters. Here I develop an account of the "living texts" of saints as both sites of incarnate meaning and, more specifically, incarnate models of desire. This integration of incarnate meaning and mimetic desire builds primarily on the ongoing Lonergan-Girard conversation. It is not self-evident, however, that Lonergan and Girard should be regarded as pioneers in this task. After all, Lonergan's thick retrievals of St Augustine and St Thomas Aquinas focus overwhelmingly on their scholarly contributions to theology and philosophy. Granted, he refers in many places to St Ignatius Loyola, in whose spirituality Lonergan was formed as a Jesuit. But, in his corpus as a whole, one cannot find the kind of thick and sustained reflection on particular saints as constitutive sites of theological meaning that one can, for example, in Balthasar's use of Thérèse of Lisieux. In addition, Girard's corpus, although his later work is deeply attentive to biblical revelation, offers a more sustained analysis of literary authors – Proust, Dostoevsky, Shakespeare, Cervantes, Flaubert, among others – than it does of the lives and insights of the saints.

Lonergan and Girard, nevertheless, have an important contribution to make to the question of the development of a contemporary theology of the saints as models of desire for God. As much as the saints pervade Balthasar's theology, what is needed is a set of categories to control and illuminate the kind of meaning that a concentration on the saints might provide. Can the integration, then, of Lonergan's category of incarnate meaning with René Girard's theory of mimetic desire contribute to the connection between the saints and the human desire for God? This chapter argues that Lonergan's category of incarnate meaning and its manifestation in art offers a way of articulating the saints as symbolic worlds wherein we may dwell for theological and religious inspiration. Furthermore, Girard's emphasis on mimetic desire enables us to speak of saints not only as sites of incarnate meaning, but more specifically as incarnate models of desire for the Christian community. In this sense Girard's account of mimetic desire illuminates, extends, and complements Lonergan's account of incarnate meaning.

Lonergan on Incarnate Meaning

In *Method in Theology*, Lonergan states that meaning "is embodied or carried in human intersubjectivity, in art, in symbols, in language, and in the lives and deeds of persons."[25] Lonergan labels this latter kind of embodiment or carrier of meaning "incarnate meaning." At the beginning of his very modest section on incarnate meaning, Lonergan quotes one of his most beloved influences, John Henry Newman: *"Cor ad cor Loquitor"* – heart speaks to heart. In *Grammar of Assent*, Newman writes, "The heart is commonly reached, not through reason but through the imagination, by means of direct impressions, by the testimony of facts and events, by history, by description. Persons influence us, voices melt us, looks subdue us, deeds inflame us."[26] In his body of work, Lonergan offers several definitions of the term "incarnate meaning." In *Method*, it is "the meaning of a person, of his way of life, of his words, or of his deeds."[27] With a slight variation to this definition, Lonergan writes elsewhere: "A person, either in his totality or in his characteristic moment, his most significant deed, his outstanding achievement or sacrifice, *is* a meaning. That meaning may be cherished, revered, adored, re-created, lived, or it may be loathed, abominated, contemned."[28] He recognizes that, while the meaning discovered might be limited to one person, more often it may be meaningful for a group or even "for a whole national, or social, or cultural, or religious tradition." This kind of meaning "may attach to group achievement, to a Thermophylae or Marathon, to the Christian martyrs, to a glorious revolution." According to Lonergan, incarnate meaning may also be "transposed to a character or characters in a story or play, to a Hamlet or Tartuffe or Don Juan."[29]

In his essay "Time and Meaning," Lonergan employs the example of John of the Cross to explain his understanding of incarnate meaning.[30] What is noteworthy about Lonergan's account here is his particularly theological interpretation of incarnate meaning. He explains this interpretation by distinguishing the respective ways in which mystics and metaphysicians encounter reality. To put it succinctly, whereas metaphysicians *think* of reality in its totality, mystics more comprehensively and holistically *experience* this reality. "John of the Cross," writes Lonergan, "is a manifestation, a symbolic manifestation, of that experience of reality in its totality."[31]

Lonergan's emphasis on John of the Cross as a paradigmatically theological example of incarnate meaning is quite fitting in the context of Buckley's challenge mentioned above. Not only has Buckley initiated hundreds of students into the mystical world of John of the Cross, but he has also employed the Spanish mystic as a specifically theological response to the respective critiques of Feuerbach and Freud, and their agreement that "what is believed in religion is a projection of the human, that the divine must be 'deconstructed' and disclosed as the human."[32] Buckley's analysis serves as an example of the way incarnate meaning can bear fruit in a theological setting. As Buckley envisions, the task of theology "should be less to refute Feuerbachian and Freudian analysis than to learn from them what they have to teach about the relentless remolding of the image of God by religious consciousness and to suggest alternative stages to the processes they elaborate of anthropological recognition and reduction."[33] The model for an alternative, according to Buckley, is St John of the Cross. Apophatic theology, after all, is not primarily about theological propositions, but is rather a process of religious experience that points beyond language. The dark nights of John of the Cross, in their active and passive dimensions, are "finally dialectical movements in which the human is purified from projection by a 'no' which is most radically a 'yes,' a 'no' that is generated by the initial 'yes.'" In sum, Freud, Feuerbach, and John of the Cross agree that much projection resides in our conceptualization of God. For Freud and Feuerbach, the proper response is to deny the reality of God; for John of the Cross, and other mystics of the apophatic tradition, such an affirmation of projection recognizes that "the evolution or personal development of faith must pass through the contradictions that are the desert and the cross."[34] With Buckley's illumination of Lonergan's category, we can argue that John of the Cross incarnates a theological meaning, namely, the incomprehensibility of God. The example of John of the Cross, in other words, embodies Buckley's own retrieval of a "specifically religious intellectuality" that does not "bracket or excise religious evidence and religious consciousness and the interpersonal that marks authentic religious life and experience."[35]

In light of this connection between incarnate meaning and John of the Cross, I now consider Lonergan's claim that incarnate meaning often combines many of the other carriers of meaning.[36] I confine my exploration to artistic meaning because it offers further resources, in a parallel way to Buckley's theological use of John of the Cross, for envisioning the encounter with the incarnate meaning of a saint as a withdrawal into a symbolic world of dramatic holiness, offering contemplative insight into the holiness of God and the challenge of discipleship. I have examined Lonergan's theory of art in more depth elsewhere.[37] Here I simply highlight three features relevant for this chapter.[38]

First, the artistic experience, for Lonergan, reveals our orientation to transcendent mystery. Lonergan writes, "But the fundamental meaning important to us in art is that, just as the pure desire to know heads on to the beatific vision, so too the break from the ready-made world heads on to God. Man is nature's priest, and nature is God's silent communing with man. The artistic movement simply breaks away from ordinary living and is, as it were, an opening, a moment of new potentiality."[39] Lonergan isolates two fundamental human experiences that naturally orient us to God: the unquenchable desire to know and the artistic break from the ready-made world into a world of transcendent possibility.

Second, for Lonergan, art constitutes a withdrawal into a symbolic world. He isolates art's connection to the complexity of human consciousness and articulates the kind of meaning that it communicates. It is not primarily the kind of meaning we would associate with scientific demonstration. Rather, Lonergan refers to the meaning apprehended in the artistic experience as "elemental" meaning. Elemental meaning is the transformation of one's world. It occurs when one slips out of the ready-made world of one's everyday living – such as one's functions in society, ordinary conversation, and the media. It is the opening up of a new horizon that presents something that is "other, different, novel, strange, remote, intimate – all the adjectives that are employed when one attempts to communicate the artistic experience."[40] Lonergan describes this slip out of the ready-made world as a "withdrawal for return." It is an invitation to participate, to explore a symbolic world. Art is a

> withdrawal from practical living to explore possibilities of fuller living in a richer world. Just as the mathematician explores the possibilities of what physics can be, so the artist explores the possibilities of what life, ordinary living, can be. There is an artistic element in all consciousness, in all living. Our settled modes have become humdrum, and we may think of all our life simply in terms of utilitarian categories. But in fact the life we are

living is a product of artistic creation. We ourselves are products of artistic creation in our concrete living, and art is an exploration of potentiality.[41]

In this artistic experience, we are "transported from the space in which we move to the space within the picture, from the time of sleeping and waking, working and resting, to the time of music, from the pressures and determinisms of home and office, of economics and politics to the powers depicted in dance."[42] Lonergan proceeds to demonstrate this theory by illuminating the function of different types of art: the picture, the statue, architecture, music, poetry, narrative, drama, and the lyric. In doing so, he supports his central claim that art is the exploration of the potentialities of concrete living. Unlike the language of science, whose words have meaning based on logical calculations, deductions, and propositions, literary language has resonance in our consciousness. Literary language, in short, reveals the multidimensional field of subjectivity as experienced, the world of human potential, exhibiting in a concrete manner the many ways in which human beings "apprehend their history, their destiny, and the meaning of their lives."[43]

Finally, art has a kind of sacramental character. Lonergan acknowledges that this withdrawal may be illusory; but he also suggests that it may be regarded as "more true and more real."[44] Just as our mysterious and unquenchable desire to know ultimately reveals our transcendent orientation within the intellectual pattern of experience, the artistic experience can reveal our orientation to the divine within the aesthetic and dramatic patterns. For Lonergan, then, good art has an ulterior significance. It presents "the beauty, the splendor, the glory, the majesty, the 'plus' that is in things and that drops out when you say that the moon is just earth and the clouds are just water."[45] Art has the capacity to direct our attention to the reality "that the world is a cipher, a revelation, an unveiling, the presence of one who is not seen, touched, grasped, put in genus, distinguished by difference, yet is *present*."[46] The sacramental possibility of art points to the tension between the visibility and invisibility operative in the revelation of transcendent mystery. As the patristic scholar Frances Young writes, a "contemplative insight" is required to witness the sacramental depths of reality: that "Scripture along with nature, the incarnation, baptism and eucharist has the quality of witness, revealing yet concealing the hidden reality to which it points, evoking the powerful presence of transcendent mystery."[47]

What then is the connection between artistic meaning and incarnate meaning? Similar to artistic meaning, an experience of the incarnate meaning of the saints – their way of life, their words, and their deeds – constitutes a withdrawal from the ready-made world into the symbolic world of dramatic holiness, and facilitates a return to daily living enriched by contemplative insight into the holiness of God and the challenge of authentic discipleship. This kind of withdrawal mediates elemental meaning and enables us to explore the self-disclosure of God in everyday living. As a way of illuminating this "withdrawal for return," it is relevant to note Cunningham's reflections on the connection between Christian practice and music. The Bible is studied primarily as a text to be embodied, similar to the relationship between a musical score and a musician, namely, "to establish the authenticity of the text" at its deepest level, which is revealed in its performance.[48] "That meaning derives," writes Cunningham, "both from fidelity to the text and as the score is enhanced by the performance of the musician."[49] Recognizing that not all performances are equal, Cunningham adds that "there are those who give a passing nod to the demands of the gospel life, but it is quite something else when someone grasps the same message and performs at a profound level." The saint represents "a classical performer of the word of God."[50]

**An Expansion of Incarnate Meaning:
Girard's Mimetic Desire**

I have explored Lonergan's category of incarnate meaning and enriched it with Buckley's use of John of the Cross. With Lonergan's suggestion in mind, I also integrated incarnate meaning and artistic meaning, envisioning the saints as symbolic worlds wherein we may dwell for theological and religious inspiration. Turning now to the work of René Girard, I show how the French thinker's account of mimetic desire enables us, in a complementary fashion, to speak of saints not only as sites of incarnate meaning but as incarnate models of desire for the Christian community. Girard has written widely about the problematic nature of mimetic desire, especially its tendency towards conflict and violence. In fact, if one were to read selectively from Girard's corpus, one might get the impression that mimetic desire itself is an evil to overcome. In *Things Hidden Since the Foundation of the World*, for example, Girard writes that "following Christ means giving up mimetic desire."[51]

For Girard, mimetic desire leads to envy, rivalry, and violence. A full account of the dark side of mimetic desire would require a longer explanation. For the purposes of this chapter, however, my aim here is only to give the reader a feel for this complex dynamic. For Girard, the fact of mimetic desire in human living is incontestable, evident in the success of the advertising industry. Do we desire products for their intrinsic value or because we imitate the desires of the beautiful person selling the product? And, in terms of human relations, mimetic desire manifests a triangular structure constituted by the "I – object – other" dynamic, whether it is two toddlers fighting over a toy, one family's envy of another family's larger house, or one political leader's imitation of the desire of another political leader for territorial expansion. Girard's claim is that mimetic desire often leads to tension, conflict, and violence. When mimetic desire escalates, cultures experience a crisis. Those involved in a web of rivalry end up transferring their frustrated desires onto a third party, in what Girard calls the single-victim mechanism. This act of scapegoating relieves cultural tension and restores peace to divided communities.[52] Scapegoating takes place in sibling rivalry, in playground disputes, in neighbourhood gossip, in the fields of sports, politics, and religion. It occurred in Hitler's Germany and in the Jim Crowe era in the United States.

I will return to the dark side of mimetic desire below. Here I want first to develop some conceptual foundations on which to build a theology of the saints, to which end a key insight is that "desire itself is essentially mimetic, directed toward the object desired by the model."[53] In other words, mimetic desire is not by its nature violent. The mimetic quality of childhood desire is "universally recognized," according to Girard. In fact, Girard has argued that we should not renounce mimetic desire as such:

> But as to whether I am advocating "renunciation" of mimetic desire, yes and no. Not the renunciation of mimetic desire itself, because what Jesus advocates is mimetic desire. Imitate me, and imitate the Father through me, he says, so it's twice mimetic. Jesus seems to say that the only way to avoid violence is to imitate me, and imitate the Father. So the idea that mimetic desire itself is bad makes no sense. It is true, however, that occasionally I say "mimetic desire" when I really mean only the type of mimetic desire that generates mimetic rivalry and, in turn, is generated by it.[54]

In fact, mimetic desire is not only "the basis of rivalry and murder but of heroism and devotion to others."[55] Girard's emphasis on heroism and devotion in relation to mimetic desire offers a fruitful avenue of investigation in the context of a theology of the saints. He writes, "Nothing is more mimetic than the desire of a child, and yet it is good. Jesus himself says it is good. Mimetic desire is also the desire for God."[56] Girard reinforces this distinction in his more recent work: "Mimetic desire is intrinsically good."[57] He adds that if desire were not mimetic, "we would not be open to what is human or what is divine."[58] Recall that for Lonergan, two experiences reveal the human orientation to transcendent mystery: the pure desire to know and the capacity to break from the ready-made world, the type of experience captured by the artist. For Girard, the fundamental experience of mimetic desire also discloses our human orientation to the divine.

Girard's exploration of mimetic desire is worked out under the formula of "interdividual psychology."[59] For the purposes of this chapter, it is fitting to note Charles Hefling's suggestion of ways in which the work of Girard might complement Lonergan's. Whereas in *Insight*, Lonergan focuses on individual psychology and the patient/therapist relationship, Girard's use of "interdividual" emphasizes dramatic relationships that constitute everyday living. Hefling explores mimesis in a horizon that privileges the language of Lonergan's later *Method in Theology*. He writes, "In 'dramatic,' everyday, commonsense interaction with others, with the *dramatis personae* of my living, I can and do respond to the 'ontic' value of an other, to someone else as be-ing and as a being."[60] "The intersubjective presence of that other," Hefling writes, "evokes my innate drive for self-transcendence, that is, for fuller or more authentic being-myself."[61] The specifically Girardian insight here is that *being-like* another involves wanting what he or she wants. For in this way, in and with admiration for someone, there is evoked a further feeling, or a differentiation of feeling, as a response, not to the 'ontic' value of the other, but more specifically to the value of what the other values."[62] As a complement to Hefling's suggestions, I have argued in this chapter that Lonergan's account of incarnate meaning belongs in this conversation about the drama of interpersonal relations. Incarnate meaning captures the personal and interpersonal concreteness of the human life-world. Depending on how it is construed, it also articulates how the lives and deeds of persons of the past might symbolically shape the dynamic situation of the present, a point that relates to the following key distinction offered by Girard.

In his further specification of mimetic desire and mimetic drama, Girard distinguishes between external and internal mediation. In *Desire, Deceit, and the Novel*, he speaks of external mediation "when the distance is sufficient to eliminate any contact between the two spheres of *possibilities* of which the mediator and the subject occupy the respective centers."[63] Internal mediation, on the other hand, relates to the situation where "this same distance is sufficiently reduced to allow these two spheres to penetrate each other more or less profoundly."[64] Whereas spatial proximity in internal mediation heightens the possibility for mimetic rivalry, in external mediation rivalry with the mediator is impossible.[65] As Girard puts it, "The hero of external mediation proclaims aloud the true nature of his desire. He worships his model openly and declares himself his disciple."[66] The work of Buckley provides some apposite examples.

In his discussion of the categorical dimension of Christian religious experience, Buckley privileges concrete encounters with models of holiness that create the conditions for a desire for and assent to the reality of God.[67] He offers the stories of Edith Stein and Raïssa Maritain as examples of such categorical religious experiences. The noteworthy connection – a connection not explicitly pointed out in Buckley's own commentary – is the mimetic desire operative in both stories. That is, the respective conversions of Edith Stein and Raïssa Maritain were both "socially mediated."

As Buckley recounts, Edith Stein's acceptance of God "emerged from her ability to read personal and intersubjective experience."[68] In the summer of 1921, she by chance picked up the *Autobiography of Teresa of Avila*. After reading through the night she closed the book and reflected: "This is the truth." Buckley comments, "This is not the chance reading of a pious tale by a religious enthusiast. It is the disclosure of the divine within a very complex human history to one who was able to interpret it as such."[69] The relevant point is that mimetic desire was central to Stein's judgment. Stein's desire and recognition for God were mediated through Teresa's desire and recognition. As we stated earlier, for Girard, to say that our desires are imitative or mimetic is to root them neither in objects nor in ourselves, but in a third party, the *model* or *mediator*, whose desire we imitate in the hope of being like the model. Not only did Stein accept the truth of God mimetically, she also became a Carmelite like Teresa and was later canonized under her monastic name as St Teresa Benedicta of the Cross. This corresponds to the phenomenological disclosure of truth discussed in the introduction to this book.

The conversion story of Jacques and Raïssa Maritain, as recounted by Buckley, also has a deeply mimetic quality. In terms of social mediation, the novelist and essayist Léon Bloy was deeply influential on the Maritains. Instead of employing the "apologetic of demonstration,"

Bloy placed before them "the fact of sanctity. Simply, and because he loved [the saints], because their experience was near his own – so much so that he could not read them without weeping – he brought us to know the saints and the mystics."[70] Buckley comments that Bloy "introduced this young couple not to argument and inference, but to narrative, to the lives and writings, i.e., to the experience and holiness, of the saints."[71]

Finally, the conversion of St Ignatius Loyola further illuminates this connection between mimetic desire and the lives of the saints. As recounted in Loyola's *Autobiography*, while he was recovering from injury his usual books of interest – "worldly books of fiction" – were unavailable and so he was given instead a life of Christ and a book of the lives of the saints.[72] Ignatius was prompted to think: "What if I should do what St. Francis did, and what St. Dominic did?" He continues, "St. Dominic did this, therefore, I have to do it; St. Francis did this, therefore I have to do it." During this period of deep reading, Ignatius's desire for the life of God flourished.[73] Similar to the narratives above, Ignatius' desire for God was rooted in the third party, in this case Francis and Dominic; Ignatius desired the object of their desire.

Girardian Sanctity: Pacific Mimesis and the Graced Resistance to Violence

Girard provides the impetus for a further insight into the desire for God, one involving resistance to the dark side of mimetic desire, the lure to envy, scapegoating, and violence, and cultivation of the peaceful desire exhibited by Christ. (My discussion of Thérèse of Lisieux and Etty Hillesum in the next chapter will build on this particular account of sanctity.) Drawing on the work of Grant Kaplan, I suggest that Girard's account of holiness bespeaks of the "humble saint" and not the "Romantic hero."[74] As noted above, Girard was suspicious of the language of autonomy whether in its Kantian or romantic form. Even though I affirmed the use of "autonomy" in a qualified way, I am also sympathetic to the heart of Girard's critique. Romanticism emphasizes the individual's inherent goodness, with sinfulness arising through co-mingling with sinful society: "the Romantic hero … abandons society's norms and lives freely, *naturally*, unencumbered and uninfluenced by culture's fallenness."[75] Qualities such as creativity, imagination, and originality mark the romantic hero. Girard's vision of sanctity, on the other hand, emphasizes humility and receptivity over and against autonomous achievement. Although we are often inspired by the "asceticism, the devotion, and the self-sacrifice" of the saints, the most fundamental disposition of the saints, in Girard's reading, is "the awareness that they have not achieved their holiness on the basis of personal merit."[76] This is Girard's post-romantic account of sanctity.

Girard's mimetic interdividuality – his claim that we are so often given our desires – "does not doom one to non-being or even to sinfulness."[77] Though we are inextricably intertwined with others, Girard finds a solution in Paul ("Be imitators of me, as I imitate Christ"; 1 Cor. 11:1) and Jesus ("Be perfect, as your heavenly Father is perfect"; Mt. 5:48).[78] His solution resides not in refusing to admit we are affected by this reciprocity but in finding "Christ a model for peaceful, non-violent imitation."[79] This entails at its core the exchange of rivalrous imitation for peaceful imitation.

In light of Girard's emphasis on humility and positive mimesis, a specifically theological account requires a more robust mining of religious realities. This is the task of the next chapter. But as a bridge, I will highlight Kaplan's suggestion that "mimetic theory makes available a pneumatology that can inform the role that the Holy Spirit plays in the process of sanctification. Just as mimetic theory lends greater precision to the virtue of humility, so too does it make explicit what is meant by the gift of the Holy Spirit."[80]

In his book *Scapegoat*, Girard argues that the Spirit is working in history "to reveal what Jesus has already revealed, the mechanism of the scapegoat, the genesis of all mythology, the nonexistence of all gods of violence."[81] Thus, a Girardian-coloured account of sanctity involves the overcoming of the dark side of mimetic desire – antagonistic mimesis, envy, scapegoating, and the like. The unity of the Son's and the Spirit's mission becomes clear, as Kaplan suggests, in Jesus's words and actions during John's farewell discourse. In his non-violent acceptance of the cross, "Jesus reveals the mechanism by which the Accuser creates false community at the expense of a hapless victim."[82] Furthermore, in his peaceful return to the disciples, "the risen Jesus uncovers the very structures in our religious psychology that move us from denial, through horrific realization, to true forgiveness."[83] If to be animated by the Holy Spirit "in a real and concrete way means to cultivate the habits and practices made available through the supernatural gift of divine indwelling," then a Girardian pneumatology offers "a fuller picture of what it might mean to be holy in today's postmodern world."[84] "Our imitation of Christ does not mean," suggests Kaplan, "that we grow a beard and speak Aramaic while honing our skills in wood-working.

154 The Givenness of Desire

It means the creative living out of a response to the scapegoating into which we are inculturated."[85]

Sacrificial Violence, Self-Transcendence, and Self-Sacrifice

I end by revisiting the Lonergan-Girard conversation that has framed this chapter in the first place. What is the relationship between Girard's account of mimetic desire and Lonergan's natural desire, which is ultimately, as I argued above, an incipient desire for God?[86] Is it possible to give full weight to Girard's account of conflict and the emergence of the scapegoat mechanism as the way in which we typically resolve the triangular structure of mimesis, while at the same time suggesting that there are other ways of resolving the tensions that arise from mimesis? The other ways require a different account of the origins of culture.[87] Neil Ormerod maps out three possible responses.

The first way is illuminated by Girard's account of "sacrificial violence," described above. To reiterate, this involves the resolution of mimetic conflict "by turning the focus of hostility onto a third party, a scapegoat or innocent victim, whose life is sacrificed, uniting the original combatants in a common purpose and restoring some degree of social harmony."[88] For Girard, this is the emergence of "religion and culture" which, for him, is rooted in "the primal murder of the innocent victim, whose power to bring about reconciliation between the original combatants raises the victim to semi-divine status."[89] This phenomenon was replaced, in large part, by the sacrifice of animals and other goods.

The second possible response is the way of cognitional or moral "self-transcendence," which involves the identification of other means for dealing with the tension. Girard fails to fully account for this response. The way of natural desire, the way of self-transcendence, includes "acts of practical intelligence which identify patterns of sharing in the desired goods, or means of increasing the production of goods" – acts that would diminish the rivalrous conflict.[90] It involves the recognition of the common good, which transcends individual desires, discussed in our account of the human good in previous chapters. This model identifies the origins of culture in terms of the human desire for meaning, truth, and goodness. While this account may not pay enough attention to the distortions of desire and the darkness of the human condition, it does imply that "the way of violent sacrifice is not primordial, but derivative, indeed parasitic upon the more primordial orientation to meaning, truth, and goodness."[91] Recall my account of the importance of "nature" and "natural desire" in chapters 3 and 4 of this book.

The third possible response is that of "self-sacrifice." This mode of resolution is found not in "self-assertion and a sacrifice of the innocent, nor in an appeal to a higher good that may mediate the conflicting desires that arise from mimesis, but in a willing self-sacrifice on the part of one of the participants, who gives up claims on the object of desire, who lays aside the demands of justice and turns the other cheek in the face of threats from the other." It means, Ormerod adds, to hand over "the resolution of the conflict to a divine agency who acts in history to provide both mercy and justice."[92]

According to Ormerod, some forms of political theology neglect the way of self-transcendence and "read human history simply in terms of the clash between sacrificial violence and self-sacrifice."[93] Without an account of "nature," there emerges the temptation to eschew dialogue with the world; there is no common ground between the earthly city and the city of God. With an account of self-transcendence and the natural desire that permeates such acts, the way of violent sacrifice is envisioned as "parasitic on an underlying good" and the "clash between the two ways is no longer ultimate."[94] In sum, there is a tendency to set an "anthropology of grasping" in opposition to an "anthropology of self-giving," recalling my engagement with Alison in chapter 3. I am arguing here for a more integrated, less oppositional account of self-donation and self-transcendence, and submit that that the sacrifice of love does not replace but *restores* human culture to the path of self-transcendence.

Conclusion

This chapter aimed to widen the scope of desire in light of Lonergan's turn to concrete subjectivity, religious experience, and religious love described in previous chapters. With Doran's framework of natural and mimetic desire as background, this chapter attempted to integrate Lonergan's category of incarnate meaning in relation to Girard's account of mimetic desire, in the context of a theology of the saints. Both incarnate meaning and mimetic desire recognize the primacy of the interpersonal in the human experience of meaning and truth. Furthermore, in a complementary fashion, Girard's emphasis on mimetic desire helped us to envision the saints not only as sites of incarnate meaning but as incarnate models of desire – a dynamic that resides at the root of our encounter with the saints. If it is plausible to affirm the deeply mimetic nature of human desire, then it is also fitting to envision saints as models or mediators, whose desire we imitate in the hope of resembling him or her. The chapter ended by highlighting a distinctive feature of a Girardian vision of sanctity – the call to nurture pacific mimesis, on the one hand, and to overcome the dark side of mimetic desire, on the other hand, through a sustained resistance to envy and scapegoating. This distinctive feature paves the way for our more specifically theological analysis of models of holiness in the next chapter.

7 The Metaphysics of Holiness and the Longing for God in History: Thérèse of Lisieux and Etty Hillesum

The last chapter widened the scope of desire beyond the intellectual desire associated with the natural desire for God debates, to encompass the saints as sites of incarnate meaning and specifically as incarnate models of desire. I considered a specifically Girardian account of sanctity, marked by the "humble saint" and not the "Romantic hero." Integral to that explanation was Girard's account of cultivation of the peaceful desire exhibited by Christ, and I noted in passing the Trinitarian roots of this desire. The task of this chapter is to articulate these roots with more explicit attention to the categories being developed throughout this book: what is needed is a "rich and theologically grounded phenomenology of the graced life."[1] This involves, in part, a return to Doran's four-point Trinitarian hypothesis, with particular attention to sanctifying grace and the habit of charity – two supernatural realities that make possible the kind of humble love and nonviolent resistance so integral to Girard's expression of Christian holiness. In light of both the natural-supernatural framework developed throughout the book and the shift of attention to socially mediated, incarnate models of desire, this chapter turns to two specific examples of incarnate meaning in a secular age: Thérèse of Lisieux and Etty Hillesum.

In many ways, the French Carmelite and the Dutch spiritual seeker occupy quite different terrain in the nineteenth- and twentieth-century spiritual landscape. Thérèse was reared in a French pious Catholic household with all of her surviving sisters entering cloistered religious life. Etty was raised in a largely secular Jewish household smattered with an eclectic mix of Christian, Jewish, philosophical, literary, and poetic influences. Thérèse lived as a celibate religious behind the walls of Carmel. Etty lived in the heart of cultured Amsterdam, socialized in circles influenced by Jungian psychology, and engaged in her spiritual seeking in the context of an ongoing, complicated sexual life. In fact, she considered herself "accomplished in bed," just about "seasoned enough" to be "counted among the better lovers."[2]

And yet there are also striking points of contact. Both achieved a level of spiritual maturity at a young age, meeting early deaths in their twenties. Both communicated to us through journals and letters. Both embody not so much a large political program of rooting out systematic injustice, but the "little way" of love alone. This is not to deny a mysterious connection between contemplative life and public-political significance, but only to emphasize that their mutual commitment to simplicity of life and daily contemplative practices fueled their heroic works of charity.

Both women have also been employed for feminist concerns in theology. Despite Thérèse's caricature as saccharine and sentimental, feminist scholars have emphasized that in fact she was "an adult, in a mature stage of faith" who understood "the meaning of her trial of darkness as an experience of profound and mutual relationships."[3] With emphasis on egalitarianism and individuality, Thérèse struggled for autonomy and acquired "an original vision of religious life while living according to the Carmelite Rule which values obedience and conformity to religious customs" handed on from the sixteenth century.[4] In a similar fashion, Etty Hillesum has been hailed for her "free and interreligious holiness, which escaped the restrictive confines separating various religious faiths and denominations."[5] Our postmodern, secular age welcomes, some have argued, "unconventional saints like Etty to carry on proclaiming the freedom of the Spirit and the breath of God's creative love."[6]

While there is much to be explored between these two religious seekers, this chapter considers them within a more explicitly systematic-theological context – that of the Trinitarian basis of the human desire for God both "inside" and "outside" the ecclesial milieu. Accordingly, I revisit Robert Doran's four-point hypothesis and consider Neil Ormerod's extension of this hypothesis as a basis for establishing the "metaphysics of holiness" as "created participation in the divine nature."[7] The approach constitutes a further moment in my response to Feingold's claim – highlighted in chapter 2 and revisited in chapter 5 – that our innate inclination to our connatural end is "capable of transformation into a supernatural inclination to the vision of God through the reception of sanctifying grace, by which we are made mysteriously proportionate to a divine end."[8] After establishing this explanatory ground, the chapter explores Thérèse's desire to be "love in the heart of the Church" and Hillesum's desire to be "the thinking heart of the barracks."

The Four-Point Hypothesis and the Metaphysics of Holiness

In the previous chapter, I noted Robert Doran's integration of the eros of the human spirit and mimetic desire. For Doran, Girard's mimetic desire – whether pacific or destructive – penetrates our spiritual orientation to the intelligible, the true and the real, and the good. In other words, distorted mimetic desire can infect the unfolding of the intellectual quest, while positive mimesis may strengthen, enhance, and deepen our commitment to the exigencies of the mind.[9] Positive models have the power to elicit the desire to be faithful to the natural desire for meaning, truth, and goodness. In other words, there are a variety of imitations. The working of grace in history is a matter of created imitations of and participation in the divine relations. The working of sin in history, on the contrary, involves the imitation of violent and destructive relations, indicated in the aforementioned account of bias, envy, rivalry, scapegoating, and violence. To be an *imago Dei* in history – a theme reflective of de Lubac's retrieval of the Fathers of the Church – lies both in being faithful to the unfolding of the eros of the sprit, that is, to the transcendental precepts to be attentive, intelligent, rational, and responsible, and in the active reception of the divine grace, which is a participation in the active and passive spirations of the Trinitarian relations.

Doran argues that systematics should begin with active and passive spiration as universally accessible realities. Accordingly, the mission of the divine Word is the definitive revelation of God's love that has already been "poured into human hearts everywhere and from the beginning."[10] This constitutes, in short, an emphasis on being on the receiving end of an unqualified love (active spiration) and the invitation to love in an unqualified fashion in return (passive spiration).[11] Genuine evangelization promotes a soteriological differentiation of consciousness – the return of good for evil – which is distinctively articulated in Christianity but is also present "wherever the gift of the Holy Spirit has been gratefully received, however anonymously."[12]

To develop this emphasis on the saints as expressions of the desire for the supernatural in a systematic-theological vein requires a more explanatory account of holiness, rooted in Trinitarian categories.[13] If

160   The Givenness of Desire

Divine Relations	Created, Human Participations	Forms of Sanctity
Active Spiration: Father and Son breathing the Holy Spirit	Sanctifying grace	Sanctity *simpliciter*
Passive Spiration: Holy Spirit as proceeding love to Father and Son	Habit of charity	Apostolic sanctity
Paternity: Father to Son	*Esse Secundarium* of the Incarnation	Saint as sage
Filiation: Son to Father	Beatific vision (Light of Glory)	Saint as mystic

Balthasar is correct in his challenge to theologians to discern the intelligible in the sensible in the concrete lives of the saints, then Ormerod has offered us some explanatory tools for responding to this challenge. Building on Lonergan's and Doran's Trinitarian theology, Ormerod connects the four distinct, created participations in divine nature – sanctifying grace, the habit of charity, in-dwelling divine wisdom, and the beatific vision – with four types of holiness that correspond to these four created participations. The importance of this typology is that it offers a Trinitarian account of holiness that can be applied to other religious traditions. As Ormerod suggests, "Such a possibility could be called a supernatural *vestigia trinitatis*, to supplement the traditional Augustinian understanding of a *vestigia trinitatis* found in the created order."[14]

The basic assumption is that the call to holiness is a historical expression of our participation in and imitation of the divine nature. This biblical command to be holy was given fresh expression in the Second Vatican Council's *Lumen Gentium*.[15] The four types of holiness that correspond to the divine relations and the created participations in these divine relations are: simple sanctity (active spiration, sanctifying grace), apostolic sanctity (passive spiration, habit of charity), saint as sage (secondary *esse* of the Incarnation, in-dwelling divine wisdom), and saint as mystic (beatific vision).

Active spiration/sanctifying grace/sanctity simpliciter. The divine relation of *active spiration* connects to the created reality of *sanctifying grace*. Active spiration refers to the divine relation of the Father and Son "breathing" the Holy Spirit together. This involves the relation between the spirator

Thérèse of Lisieux and Etty Hillesum 161

(Father and Son) and the spirated (Holy Spirit). For Lonergan, sanctifying grace – the reception of the Father's love as including us and becoming our love – participates in and imitates active spiration, that is, the Father and the Son together as they "breathe" the Holy Spirit, and so bears a special relation to the uncreated Holy Spirit. Sanctifying grace corresponds to *sanctity simpliciter*, which emphasizes those who embody a consoling, contemplative rest and transformation by divine love. The "little way" of Thérèse of Lisieux embodies this type of holiness.[16]

Passive spiration/habit of charity/apostolic sanctity. The divine relation of passive spiration connects to the created reality of the habit of charity. The habit of charity proceeds from the reception of sanctifying grace and participates in the proceeding love breathed by the Father and the Son. The habit of charity embraces the return of good for evil in an abiding friendship with God.[17] The habit of charity corresponds to *apostolic sanctity*, and embodies the common work of the Father and Son to build the kingdom of God. This form of sanctity emphasizes the active dimension of the spiritual life and the habitual orientation to enacting God's love in the world – working for the Kingdom, if you will. Ormerod identifies St Ignatius Loyola and Dorothy Day as examples of apostolic sanctity.[18]

Ormerod importantly draws attention to the mutual relationship between simple sanctity/sanctifying grace and apostolic sanctity/habit of charity. This integration of contemplation and action will be emphasized in my discussion of Thérèse of Lisieux and Etty Hillesum below. As ideal types, they are distinct and may in fact be embodied more in one than in another. But there are dangers in severing sanctifying grace and the habit of charity, simple sanctity and apostolic sanctity. A claim to holiness rooted in contemplation divorced from political and personal implications in the ethical sphere, on the one hand, and activist apostolic sanctity divorced from the contemplative nature of simple sanctity, on the other hand, both seem inadequate. This Trinitarian-theological grounding reminds us these two types of sanctity are intrinsically related as "active and passive spiration are related, as two aspects of the single divine procession of the Spirit from the Father and the Son."[19]

Paternity/Incarnation/saint as sage. The in-dwelling of divine wisdom corresponds to the *saint as sage*. This type of holiness relates in a special way to the Logos made flesh who lived in obedience to the Father. Ormerod identifies Thomas Aquinas as a special exemplary of this wisdom. "Those who live this form of holiness," writes Ormerod, "leave a lasting cultural legacy in the life of the Church, providing future generations with an enduring witness to the profundity of the mysteries of faith."[20]

Filiation/beatific vision/saint as mystic. The created participation in the beatific vision (which corresponds to the divine relation of filiation) corresponds to the *saint as mystic*. The beatific vision is the eschatological promise to enjoy the vision of God forever. While mystics have been given glimpses of this vision, the encounter is often expressed "apophatically and ineffably, a stripping away of images and concepts which are inadequate to divine mystery."[21] The Spanish mystics, St Teresa of Ávila and St John of the Cross, exemplify this type of holiness in dramatic ways.

Thérèse of Lisieux: Love in the Heart of the Church

Mindful of these explanatory categories, I turn now to two concrete models of holiness and the human desire for the supernatural. In this chapter I emphasized the first two sets of categories discussed above, participations in active and passive spiration as universally accessible realities. This theological grounding enables me to highlight sanctifying grace and the habit of charity at work both within and without the visible boundaries of the church.

When Thérèse was born in 1873, her father and mother, Louis and Zelie, had already lost four of their children. The five surviving children were all girls – Marie, Pauline, Leonie, Celine, and the youngest, Thérèse. Four years later, Zelie died of breast cancer at the age of forty-six and Louis moved his family to the town of Lisieux. Whereas Etty Hillesum experienced a largely secular upbringing sustained by eclectic classical, philosophical, and religious sources, Thérèse's rearing was thoroughly Catholic and of the French variety. An image that captures this upbringing is of the girls' room on the second floor of their home in Lisieux, which offered a view over Lisieux and its Cathedral of Saint-Pierre, which they regularly attended.[22]

Contemplative Life and Openness to the World

Since my aim is systematic-theological, this section privileges Balthasar's attempt to mediate the theological wisdom of Thérèse as part of his larger project of developing a supernatural phenomenology of the saints.[23] The aim, of course, is not to offer a comprehensive account of her life and thought, but only to consider her as an instance of incarnate meaning in the larger analysis of the human desire for God in the context of concrete subjectivity.

Balthasar presents a multilayered vision of this French Carmelite saint, who died at the age of twenty-four. A full examination of her life and witness would, of course, have to include a historical, biographical, and even psychological analysis. Balthasar's "supernatural phenomenology" aims to penetrate essential dimensions of her mission, without depersonalizing her concrete story or reducing her witness to an abstraction. As Balthasar notes, Thérèse "understood the act of total surrender to the triune God as the highest possible form of engagement on behalf of the world's salvation."[24] While there are many themes to be explored in Balthasar's lengthy account of Thérèse, I focus here on what Balthasar considers to be her distinctive account of the relationship between contemplation and action.

To preface my presentation of her vision, I will say something about Balthasar's concern with the fate of contemplation in the contemporary world. He first published his book on Thérèse of Lisieux in the early 1950s, when the meaning of the contemplative life was not under debate, and reissued a new edition in 1970, when the meaning of the contemplative life had become "so obscure that even the orders living the contemplative life, including the Carmelites, [had] become uncertain."[25] Balthasar was unnerved by the active assault on monasticism, asceticism, and contemplation. Openness to the world, for him, was more than dialogue measured by practical goals and successes. This short-sighted posture ignored the deeper insight of the contemplatives: contemplation is, in fact, "an inward continuation of action" as attested by the incarnation of God. "Far from being a flight from the world," comments Balthasar, "Carmel and all purely contemplative forms of life in the church extrapolate the encounter between the world and the living God of Jesus of Christ to its most radical point."[26]

Little Way as Sanctity Simpliciter

One of the dominant images of Thérèse, technically known as St Thérèse of the Child Jesus and the Holy Face, is the "Little Flower." "It seems to me," writes Thérèse, "that if a little flower could speak, it would tell simply what God has done for it without trying to hide its blessings."[27] This image of the little flower exemplifies "Thérèse's genius for sisterhood" – her way of placing herself as "an equal in the midst of the masses of simple folk who will never be specifically noticed or acclaimed."[28] Thérèse, of course, had intense desires to do great things and was tortured by these great desires. It was only in the discovery of her vocation that the torture subsided. Her story reveals, as does Etty Hillesum's, that "when we come to rest in God, we are simple, singlehearted creatures," but that this same path to simplicity is "complex, often torturous, fraught with painfully conflicting desires and dreams."[29]

The sanctity *simpliciter* of the "little way" is a constitutive dimension of Thérèse's contribution. The little way, in Balthasar's terms, is a way of both "demolition" and "construction." In terms of the first, the little way demolishes an obsession with performing great deeds – a kind of Gospel demolition of religious facades. The living flame of love casts fire upon the earth and sends the saints to spread the flame, not to be dampened by bourgeois Christianity.[30] Thérèse was a fighter by nature – fearless and aggressive – which explains her devotion to Joan of Arc, about whom she wrote poetry and even penned a play. Thérèse's battle was to rid Christianity of Pharisaism and the will to power disguised under the mantle of religion, which in reality functions to assert one's own greatness.[31] She was, therefore, sceptical of ascetical practices that seemed to aim at human perfection. Preferring spiritual childhood more than religious greatness, Thérèse believed sanctity consists not in successfully performing religious acts, but in being ready "to become small and humble in the arms of God, acknowledging our own weaknesses and trusting in his fatherly goodness to the point of audacity."[32]

Even if she downplayed the successful performance of religious acts, she still prioritizes a set of renunciations as a mark of the little way, for they represent "the steps leading directly to the state where each new call of God's love finds its response in faith."[33] She renounced, for example, the desire for the joy and pleasure that accompany love, along with consoling visions that might solidify her faith. With such renunciations, she experiences instead the darkness of naked faith.[34] She also renounced an obsession with progress. She strides endlessly, in Balthasar's words, in "the darkness, below the earth, without bearings" and "puts one foot in front of the other along a road whose direction God alone knows."[35] If Christ fell three times, Thérèse reflects in the intimacy of spousal language, why should she expect a different lot from her spouse? Instead of climbing a mountain, he is waiting for her in the fertile valley of humility. Her standard is neither good feelings nor progress and perfection, but love – the love of God and her total loving response.³⁶

In light of this book's emphasis on developing the interpersonal dimension of religious experience, it is pertinent to note that Thérèse's relationship with God was never controlled by legal language but always bore the marks of the interpersonal. To the average Christian, this love may seem overdone; to the unbeliever, it may seem childish. To those standing outside a relationship of love in general, this "inner, secret realm with a far-ranging geography" seems "incomprehensible."³⁷ But even if misunderstood, lovers delight in roaming in such spaces. In many of her writings, Thérèse expressed desire not so much to be consoled, but to "console Jesus," to "give pleasure to Jesus," to make her heart "a little garden of delight where Jesus may come to find rest."³⁸

Thérèse's model of the little way – of sanctity *simpliciter* – constitutes, in Balthasar's play of words, both *a* way and *the* way. It is *a* way in that there are many other ways to be found in the history of Christian religious experience, including the way of those who emphasize significant penances or receive extraordinary mystical graces. Since these extraordinary dimensions are not absolutely essential in light of the teaching of the Gospel, however, Thérèse's way – which makes love of God and neighbour absolutely central – can also be described as *the* way."³⁹

Thérèse expresses the centrality of love and the unity of her contemplative and missionary vocation in the Church most poignantly in Manuscript B – a document written at the request of her sister Marie of the Sacred Heart. It is in this manuscript that many of the oft-quoted passages from her work reside. Here Thérèse yearns for the "science of Love" and realizes that it is "only love that makes us acceptable to God."⁴⁰

The little way demands not great actions, but simply surrender and gratitude. Thérèse possessed high aspirations to perform heroic deeds by being a warrior, priest, apostle, doctor, and martyr. She hoped that these apostolic missionary ventures would lead her to martyrdom in the manner of other great saints. After meditating on 1 Corinthians 12–13, however, Thérèse realized that even the most heroic deeds are nothing without love. She discovered that her vocation was simply to love. Without love, she understood, martyrs would not sacrifice their lives; love lay at the heart of all vocations.⁴¹

Contemplation and Action: Sanctity Simpliciter as Apostolic Sanctity

As noted above, Ormerod draws attention to the "mutual relationship" between sanctifying grace and the habit of charity, between simply sanctity and apostolic sanctity. This Trinitarian-theological grounding reminds us these two types of sanctity are intrinsically related as "active and passive spiration are related, as two aspects of the single divine procession of the Spirit from the Father and the Son."[42] Thérèse embodied this unity in a distinctive way.

In terms that resonate with being on the receiving end of God's love, her practice involved "complete surrender and openness to the Word of the Lord, reaching beyond all active prayer into a state of being held, of simply receiving and, finally, of necessity, passing on to suffering and to passion."[43] Balthasar attributes to Thérèse a pioneering development of this unity. For him, many of the Fathers had an individualistic conception of contemplation influenced heavily by Stoic and neoplatonic contemplative ideals. Balthasar suggests boldly that the "little Thérèse is the first to rid contemplation of its neoplatonic relics."[44]

> Here we have a doctrine of contemplation, explicitly formulated, such as the medievals never worked out clearly. Contemplation is not superior to action because it allows a person leisure and tranquility, as the ancients thought who despised work as illiberal. Nor even, as St. Thomas argued in stating the traditional doctrine, because contemplation is directly concerned with God, whereas action deals "only" with one's neighbor. It is solely because, of all the church's manifestations of love, contemplation bears the most abundant fruit, so abundant that Thérèse does not hesitate to compare the contemplative vocation to that of the priesthood.[45]

This is an integrating and demanding vision of "fructifying contemplation." The superiority of contemplation, if one wants to speak in these terms, resides not in a zone sealed off from the concrete concerns of everyday life, but "must integrate into itself the whole pathos and strength of action." Thérèse's vision of contemplation is "the very opposite of Quietism: It is the fruit of an endeavor into which one throws all one's energies." It is to be applied to the smallest details of everyday life. Thérèse's vision embodies the motto of Ignatius, *In actione contemplativus*. This integrated vision is shown, for example, when Thérèse was appointed novice mistress. Cognizant that she was taking on a duty beyond her powers, she did not "sit down to work out a scheme for dividing her time between prayer and action." Instead she devoted herself contemplatively to God: "without leaving your arms, without even turning my head, I shall distribute your precious gifts to the souls who come asking for food."[46] Thérèse embodies "an attitude that cannot be described exactly in terms of either contemplation or action."[47] Rather, she is, more accurately stated, "beyond them both in the all-embracing law of love, which governs both receptivity and fruitfulness, both Mary and Martha."[48] In other words, Thérèse transcends the "dualism of passivity and activity, at the point where they meet in Christian love."[49] Too often, in Balthasar's estimation, patristic and scholastic interpretations are strongly influenced by ancient philosophy. Aquinas's interpretation of the Martha-Mary story, for example, relies too heavily on Aristotle's account of the contemplative life in privileging contemplation over action. Thérèse's vision consists not in alternating from one to the other, but in perfecting the two simultaneously.[50] In a letter at the end of her life, she writes:

> I really count on not remaining inactive in heaven. My desire is to work still for the Church and for souls. I am asking God for this and I am certain He will answer me. Are not the angels continually occupied with us without their ever ceasing to see the divine Face and to lose themselves in the Ocean of Love without shores? Why would Jesus not allow me to imitate them?[51]

The beatific vision is often imagined as the cessation of all movement – a resting in God.[52] Unparalleled by any other saint, however, Thérèse regards heaven as the scene for her most intense mission, not unlike Jesus, who retained the vision of the Father in the midst of his earthly mission – a relational vision that shaped every moment of his earthly activity.[53] With this integration of contemplation and action, Thérèse felt closer to Joan of Arc than to any other saint. They are united by their single-hearted commitment to do God's will.

Habit of Charity: Feasting at the Table of Unbelief

Having examined the unity of action and contemplation, the inseparability of active and passive spiration, we focus in this section on Thérèse's embodiment of the habit of charity. Again, the habit of charity is, in Lonergan's terms, the antecedent willingness to respond to evil with love. It is the habitual orientation to enacting God's love in the world. It is the imitation of and participation in passive spiration. I discuss three instances: her conversion during the Christmas of 1886, her response to sisters in the Carmel whom she despised, and her willingness to feast at the table of sorrow of unbelievers.

The story of the Christmas of 1886 seems simple and ordinary, but it had profound implications for her spiritual life.[54] When she was in her early teens, the girls came home from midnight mass and Thérèse immediately ran to her shoes, which she had placed at the chimney, to look for the little gifts she was accustomed to receiving. Her father – fatigued and annoyed – remarked harshly on Thérèse's childishness. Her response would normally involve wounded feelings and crying. It was on this night that she received what she called the grace of her "complete conversion." "Forcing back my tears," Thérèse writes, "I descended the stairs rapidly; controlling the poundings of my heart, I took my slippers and placed them in front of Papa, and withdrew all objects joyfully. I had the happy appearance of the Queen ... I felt *charity* enter my soul, and the need to forget myself and to please others." This ordinary family incident was a profound moment of conversion; Thérèse had discovered "the art of transforming narcissistic hurt into outpoured love."[55]

Second, in Manuscript C, Thérèse addresses the difficulty of the habit of charity, especially to those for whom we have natural antipathy. Yet it is precisely in loving the latter that our love becomes divine.[56] Thérèse despised, for example, a sister in her convent, and yet in her wisdom admits that this sister must be pleasing to God. Exhibiting the habit of charity – the very imitation of and participation in passive spiration – Thérèse reflects:

> Not wishing to give in to the natural antipathy I was experiencing, I told myself that charity must not consist in feelings but in works; then I set myself to doing for this sister what I would do for the person I loved the most. Each time I met her I prayed to God for her, offering Him all her virtues and merits. I felt this was pleasing to Jesus, for there is no artist who doesn't love to receive praise for his works, and Jesus, the Artist of souls, is happy when we don't stop at the exterior, but, penetrating into the inner sanctuary where He chooses to dwell, we admire its beauty. I wasn't content simply with praying very much for this Sister who gave me so many struggles, but I took care to render her all the service possible, and when I was tempted to answer her back in a disagreeable manner,

I was content with giving her my most friendly smile, and with changing the subject of conversation.[57]

Third, Thérèse willingly feasted at the table of sorrow – "the dark banquet of bitter bread."[58] The healing episode of Christmas 1886 described above set forth her missionary vocation to become a fisher of souls. If Thérèse resisted the temptation "to see," she embraced with equal fervour something akin to the dark night of the soul. I will not enter into the debate over whether she experienced the dark night of the soul in the same sense as St John of the Cross and whether she also belongs in the category of saint as mystic, in Ormerod's terms. My point here is that her experience of the "night," which is where "she lives almost the whole time," was integral to her mission of charity to unbelievers.[59] She subjectively absorbed the pain and alienation of unbelief experienced widely in the secular age.

During Easter 1896, after the Good Friday when she first spat up blood, God shows her, as she interprets the experience, that there really are people who have no faith.

> He permitted my soul to be invaded by the thickest darkness, and that the thought of heaven, up until then so sweet to me, be no longer anything but the cause of struggle and torment. This trial was to last not a few days or a few weeks, it was not to be extinguished until the hour set by God himself and this hour has not yet come ... One would have to travel through this dark tunnel to understand its darkness.[60]

These images express a kind of mystical experience of the dark night of the soul. One of the fundamental points about the habit of charity that she learns is that charity is not always a feeling but an act of the will. In the midst of these feelings of darkness, she begs for mercy for her unbelieving brothers and resigns herself to sit with these poor sinners at the table filled with bitterness.[61]

> When I want to rest my heart, weary of the surrounding darkness, by the memory of the luminous country after which I aspire, my anguish only increases. It seems as if the darkness, echoing the voices of sinners, is mocking me, saying, 'You dream of light, of a fragrant homeland, you dream that you will possess the Creator of these wonders for all eternity, you believe that you will one day emerge from this gloom ... Go on! Look forward to death, which will give you – not what you hope – but a still darker night, the night of nothingness.[62]

Though there is still debate over the precise nature of her dark night, most scholars suggest that Thérèse probably experienced significant subjective desolation, without technically losing her faith. Thérèse understood herself "as standing among the sinners, no longer separated in any way from their condition," experiencing "the fullness of alienation from God."[63]

Etty Hillesum: The Thinking Heart of the Barracks

If Thérèse of Lisieux is accessible through her profound yet challenging little way, Etty Hillesum is for some contemporary seekers perhaps even more accessible. Her vivacious demeanour, her erotic pursuits and struggles, her rearing in a house gifted with intellectual and artistic acumen and complicated by mental illness, and her spiritual pluralism make her even more relatable to many sojourners in the secular age.

Born in the Netherlands in 1914, Etty – an assimilated Dutch Jew – was the oldest of four children. The Hillesums were a middle-class, socially well established family. Though they were part of the ethnic Jewish community, they did not participate regularly in Jewish religious practices. According to Etty, her family exuded "a remarkable mixture of barbarism and culture."[64] Louis, her father, was a respected grammar school teacher and a disciplined scholar. "He studied the Jewish and Christian scriptures, read French literature, especially Pascal, explored various German philosophers, and studied Freud."[65] Though Etty had much in common with her father, "she did not share the skepticism which kept him away from social contracts and denominational organizations. His intellectual attitude of situating himself above mundane reality characterized him to the end of his life." Her mother was unbalanced and difficult, extroverted, and domineering. Etty shared "the emotional tonality of her mother's life," though she was well aware of her mother's shortcomings and regarded her mother as "a model of what I must never become."[66] Her brothers, Jaap and Mischa, were both talented and emotionally disturbed. Jaap, who studied medicine, suffered from schizophrenia and Mischa, one of the most promising pianists in Europe, was hospitalized for a time with psychotic episodes. Etty herself fought at times with "periods of inner fragmentation, depression, and immobility, sleeping for long stretches at a time, experimenting with self-medication, and experiencing moments of physical and internal fatigue and extreme mood swings."[67]

During the time of her journals – later published as *An Interrupted Life* – Etty was living in Amsterdam where she worked as a Russian tutor. Her life in Amsterdam revolved around two communities: the household of Han Wegerif, where she lived, and a group of women devoted to the Jungian-influenced psychochiriologist Julius Spier and his practice of a kind of psychotherapy. She had ongoing intimate sexual relationships with both Wegerif and Spier, the latter being the more captivating and transformative relationship in her life. As Eva Hoffman notes, "As part of his therapeutic method, Spier engaged in eroticized tousles with his patients, which were not, apparently, supposed to lead to sexual intercourse."[68] Etty's chronicling of "his tantalizing touches and kisses, of the casual liberties he took with admiring female patients, strike us as highly incorrect, to say the least." Nevertheless, such behavior was not uncommon during the interwar period, which was marked by "eclectic psychoanalytic experiments" and "eccentric adventures in self-exploration." In some ways, Spier's mode of therapy represents an "older tradition of active philosophical teaching": through her "real and metaphorical wrestlings with Spier, Etty "trained herself to check her impulses and restrain the impetuousness of her needs." Indeed, her most difficult battle was with the "problem of sexuality in its modern, feminine variant": she was both "seduced and riven by her desires, torn between romantic yearnings for submergence and the need for independence." As her journals attest, however, she began to learn "the kind of love that is closer to selfless agape than to urgent eros and that combines deep sympathy with calm detachment."

Universal Activity of the Spirit

Richard Galliardetz notes that "while it is true that in her later writing she admits to reading with great interest and sympathy the Gospel of Matthew, the writings of St. Augustine and the medieval mystic, Meister Eckhart," it would be at the same time "misleading to characterize her as a crypto-Christian, as many Christian admirers of her thought have been inclined to do."[69] She drew on a variety of religious, philosophical, and poetic sources: classical literature, Russian literature, art, psychology – with an emphasis on Jung and Adler, Augustine, Thomas à Kempis, and the Bible, and above all Rainer Maria Rilke.[70] In fact, "as she was preparing to go to Westerbork for the last time, she fretted about which books to bring with her and decided upon her bible,

Dostoyevski's *The Idiot*, Rilke's *Book of Hours* and *Letters to a Young Poet*, and her Russian dictionaries."[71]

Mindful of these dangers, it still seems plausible for a theologian to discern vestiges of Trinitarian love at work in a broken, interrupted, unfinished life such as Etty Hillesum's, presuming from the perspective of a Catholic theologian that the Trinitarian God of love continually breaks into history. It is fitting to discern in compelling examples of religious experience the possibility of sanctifying grace – the consoling, complacent love that offers true rest, and the habit of charity – the kind of apostolic sanctity that habitually orients one to enact God's love in the world. This approach avoids "seeking to make sweeping judgments about different religious traditions in themselves, but seeks to identify concretely the way in which God has operated within their traditions, according to a normative Trinitarian template."[72]

I noted in chapter 2 a contemporary theological development on limbo in light of the Christological teaching of the Second Vatican Council. To place this treatment of Hillesum in theological context, it is fitting to note another emerging theological emphasis on the presence of the Spirit outside the visible borders of the church. If indeed the Spirit is manifested in a special way in the Church and in her members, exemplified by Thérèse of Lisieux, still the Spirit's activity is universal and may be discerned in the lived witness of Etty Hillesum. This vision was articulated in Vatican II's *Gaudium et Spes* 22 – a passage that highlights both one ultimate supernatural human end and the penetrating mission of the Spirit:

> All this holds true not only for Christians, but for all men of good will in whose hearts grace works in an unseen way. For, since Christ died for all men, and since the ultimate vocation of man is in fact one, and divine, we ought to believe that the Holy Spirit in a manner known only to God offers to every man the possibility of being associated with this paschal mystery.

I give particular attention here to John Paul II's development of this insight in *Redemptoris Missio* 28.[73] The Church, John Paul II writes, is aware that humanity is continually being stirred by the Spirit of God. This is evident in the ongoing human quest for the meaning of life in the face of the riddle of death. The Spirit, according to John Paul II, resides "at the very source of man's existential and religious questioning, a questioning which is occasioned not only by contingent situations but by the very structure of his being." The Spirit animates not only individual lives, but also "society and history, peoples, cultures and religions." Indeed, the Spirit is "at the origin of the noble ideals and undertakings which benefit humanity on its journey through history." The risen Christ is continually working to both instil "a desire for the world to come" and to animate, purify, and reinforce "the noble aspirations which drive the human family to make its life one that is more human and to direct the whole earth to this end."

Robert Doran's vision both affirms and extends these post–Vatican II developments.[74] In light of the unity of nature and grace in the concrete world order, Doran argues that "we Christians share a religious community with all human beings, including the people of the world's other religions, because of this universal gift of what we call the Holy Spirit."[75] The communities to which we belong are grounded both in "the common orientation of human nature as obediential potency through intentional consciousness to the mystery of love and awe that in fact is the transcendent triune God, and in the universal gift of the transcendent God's triune life through what Christians would confess to be the indwelling of the Holy Spirit"[76]

If the legacy of the Second Vatican Council enables us to discern, in a contemporary mode, the presence of the Spirit at work on a large scale, then Benedict XVI helps us discern this presence more specifically in the life of Etty Hillesum. In his Ash Wednesday audience given shortly after he announced his resignation, Benedict narrated familiar examples of religious conversion, such as St Paul and St Augustine. But, sensitive to the secular age and the prevailing "eclipse of the sense of the sacred," he also challenged his audience to notice "God's grace is at work and works marvels in the life of so many people. The Lord never tires of knocking at man's door in social and cultural milieus that seem engulfed in secularization," he said. Benedict highlights Etty Hillesum as a particular example to be noted in a secular age.[77] "At first far from God," Benedict remarked, "she discovered him looking deep within her and she wrote: 'There is a really deep well inside me. And in it dwells God. Sometimes I am there, too. But more often stones and grit block the well, and God is buried beneath. Then he must be dug out again.'"[78] Benedict adds, "In her disrupted, restless life she found God in the very midst of the great tragedy of the 20th century: the Shoah. This frail and dissatisfied young woman, transfigured by faith, became a woman full of love and inner peace who was able to declare: 'I live in constant intimacy with God.'" Indeed, in a secular age wherein the very plausibility of the question of God is eclipsed, "we may not be surprised to discover modern-day mystics and unconventional instances of contemporary sanctity that fall outside the framework of traditional hagiography."[79]

The Little Way of Etty: Quest for Simplicity and Contemplative Rest in God

It is possible to discern in Hillesum's journals something akin to the sanctity *simpliciter* of Thérèse of Lisieux. This kind of sanctity is a historical expression of sanctifying grace – an embodiment of divine love as "a consoling, complacent love which offers an invitation to rest and be transformed by that love."[80] It is not altogether obvious that she understands the God to whom she refers over four hundred times in her journals as the God of Judaism and Christianity. Still, as time progresses and as the Jewish situation in Amsterdam worsens, Etty develops a more intimate, loving relationship with God. We witness a transition from her speaking of God in the third person to an I-Thou encounter. In a letter from Westerbork, Etty recounts her journal entry from that very afternoon to her friend Tide:

> You have made me so rich, Oh God, please let me share out Your beauty with open hands. My life has become an uninterrupted dialogue with You, oh God, one great dialogue. Sometimes when I stand in some corner of the camp, my feet planted on Your earth, my eyes raised toward Your heaven, tears sometimes run down my face, tears of deep emotion and gratitude. At night too, when I lie in bed and rest in You, oh God, tears of gratitude run down my face, and that is my prayer ... I may never become the great artist I would really like to be, but I am already secure in You, God. Sometimes I try my hand at turning out small profundities and uncertain short stories, but I always end up with just one single world: God. And that says everything, and there is no need for anything more. And all my creative powers are translated into inner dialogues with You. The beat of my heart has grown deeper, more active, and yet more peaceful, and it is as if I were all the time storing up inner riches.[81]

This loving rest in God is captured by a key image in her journals – that of kneeling. Etty described herself as "the girl who could not kneel" but who would later become a "kneeler in training":[82]

> There is a sort of lamentation and loving-kindness as well as a little wisdom somewhere inside me that cries to be let out. Sometimes several

different dialogues run through me at the same time, images and figures, moods, a sudden flash of something that must be my very own truth. Love for human beings that must be hard fought for. Not through politics or a party, but in myself. Still a lot of false shame to get rid of. And there's God. The girl who could not kneel but learned to do so on the rough coconut matting in an untidy bathroom. Such things are often more intimate even than sex. The story of the girl who gradually learned to kneel is something I would love to write in the fullest possible way.[83]

The language that animates these passages – "thou," "kneeling," "love," "intimacy" – expresses the kind of active receptivity and relationality that marked Lonergan's later emphasis on being-in-love as the highest way of being that shapes our quest for self-transcendence.

This same loving-kindness is expressed in her experience of reading and meditating on Paul's profound reflection on love in 1 Cor. 13. Paul's circling meditation, Etty recounts, "worked on me like a divining rod that touched the bottom of my heart, causing hidden sources to spring up suddenly within me." "All at once," she adds, "I was down on my knees beside the little white table and all my released love coursed through me again, purged of desire, envy, spite, etc."[84] Notice a particular kind of Girardian sanctity at work here (see chapter 6)?

Thérèse's contemplative life was marked by a rich relationship between time and eternity, especially as she faced a slow, brutal death by illness. "It seems to me," writes Thérèse, "that love can substitute for a long life. Jesus takes no account of time, since there is none in heaven. He must take account only of love."[85] Hillesum, as her relationship with God progressed, had to similarly focus on being attentive to the present, facing death in the midst of the great atrocities of the twentieth century:

> I must conquer in myself ... Life is difficult ... In the past I would live chaotically in the future, because I refused to live in the here and now. I wanted to be handed everything on a platter, like a badly spoiled child. Sometimes I had the certain if rather undefined feeling that I would "make it" one day, that I had the capacity to do something "extraordinary," and at other times the wild fear that I would "go to the dogs" after all. I now realize why. I simply refused to do what needed to be done, what lay right under my nose. I refused to climb into the future one step at a time ... I no longer think of the future, that is, I no longer care whether or not I shall "make it," because I now have the inner certainty that everything will

be taken care of. Before, I always lived in anticipation, I had the feeling that nothing I did was the "real" thing, that it was all a preparation for something else, something "greater," more "genuine." But that feeling has dropped away from me completely.[86]

In the place of continually anticipating the future, which began to take on for Hillesum a sense of doom, that she would be a part of the mass extermination of Jews under Hitler, she continual reflects on the meaning of the quotidian and the beauty of love.

Every minute of this day seems one great gift and consolation, a memory I shall carry within me as an ever-present reality … We must count neither on being preserved nor on being destroyed. These are extreme possibilities, but neither is a certainty. What matters are the concerns of daily life … the main thing is that even as we die a terrible death we are able to feel right up to the very last moment that life has meaning and beauty, that we have realized our potential and lived a good life.[87]

Similar to Thérèse, the journals of Hillesum reveal an ongoing ascetical process of pruning herself of the desire for greatness, what I called above the "demolition of great deeds," and instead orienting her attention to the little things. Just as Thérèse desired to be a missionary, warrior, and priest, Hillesum desired to be a great writer.

Wash your hands of all attempts to embody those great, sweeping thoughts. The smallest, most fatuous little essay is worth more than the flood of grandiose ideas in which you like to wallow … Your imagination and your emotions are like a vast ocean from which you wrest small pieces of land that may well be flooded again. That ocean is wide and elemental, but what matter are the small pieces of land you reclaim from it. The subject right before you is more important than those prodigious thoughts on Tolstoy and Napoleon that occurred to you in the middle of last night, and the lesson you gave that keen young girl on Friday night is more important than all your vague philosophizings. Never forget that. Don't overestimate your own intensity; it may give you the impression that you are cut out for greater things than the so-called man in the street, whose inner life is a closed book to you. In fact, you are no more than a weakling and a nonentity adrift and tossed by the waves … Keep your eye fixed on the mainland, and don't flounder helplessly in the ocean. And now to the job at hand![88]

As Hillesum's spiritual quest deepened, she became more committed to simplicity of speech and lifestyle, discipline in work, faithfulness in the little things, and finding God in the midst of the concreteness of her life.

> Sometimes I long for a convent cell, with the sublime wisdom of centuries set out on bookshelves all along the wall and a view across the cornfields – there must be cornfields and they must wave in the breeze – and there I would immerse myself in the wisdom of the ages and in myself. Then I might perhaps find peace and clarity. But that would be no great feat. It is right here, in this very place, in the here and now, that I must find them. But it is all so terribly difficult, and I feel so heavyhearted.[89]

When she translated Russian, she felt, for example, that she must write another *Brothers Karamazov* and she was filled "with sudden fears that I might not fulfill the promise of those 'exalted' moments." But she asks reflectively why she feels she has to achieve such noble deeds: "All I need to do is to 'be,' to live and try being a little bit human … and that's probably why I accumulate knowledge, out of a desire to be important." She asks God instead for the "knowledge that leads to wisdom and true happiness and not the kind that leads to power."[90]

A key challenge of the little way is attentiveness to the concreteness of the little things and not to grand, sweeping ideas. This tension is crystallized in Hillesum's experience with and reflection on her father. When she was travelling to visit her father, she was stressed over how to engage him, but reflected: "the main item for this weekend's program: to love my father deeply and sincerely and to forgive him for disturbing my pleasure-seeking life."[91] Thinking about her father prompted a kind of Dostoyevskian insight about the abstract and the particular: whether to approach humanity abstractly through a kind of detached Enlightenment objectivity (Ivan Karamazov) or through an embrace of the world through the concrete particularity of humble love (Fr Zosima)?

> Then something dawned on me. At a fairly advanced age, my father had traded all his uncertainties, doubts, and probably also his physical inferiority complex, his insurmountable marriage problems, for philosophical ideas that though held in perfect sincerity and full of the milk of human kindness are totally vague. Those ideas help him to gloss over everything, to look just at the surface instead of plumbing the depths he knows full well are there, perhaps precisely because he knows it. And so he can never hope to attain clarity. Beneath the surface, his resigned philosophy simply

means: Oh, well, which of us knows anything, all is chaos within and without. And it is that very chaos that also threatens me, that I must make it my life's task to shake off instead of reverting to it time and again. And no doubt my father's expressions of resignation, humor, and doubt appeal to something in me that I share with him, but which I must nevertheless outgrow.[92]

In contrast to her father's abstract approach, Etty grows in her commitment to the little way, to a resting simplicity and a commitment to the concrete details of daily living:

To be very unobtrusive, and very insignificant, always striving for more simplicity. Yes, to become simple and to live simply, not only within yourself but also in your everyday dealings. Don't make ripples all around you, don't try so hard to be interesting, keep your distance, be honest, fight the desire to be thought fascinating by the outside world. Instead, reach for true simplicity in your inner life and in your surroundings, and also work. Yes, work. It doesn't matter at what.[93]

Habit of Charity: "A Balm for All Wounds"

Hillesum's contemplative being-in-love with God – her imitation of and participation in active spiration – is intimately connected to her love and care for others in a dire moment of history. In what way might we envision her in the context of passive spiration – the proceeding love breathed by and proceeding from the Father and the Son – and its historical expression as the habit of charity? In what way did Hillesum embody what Ormerod calls apostolic sanctity – the habitual orientation of enacting God's love in the world? I will focus the analysis here on three dimensions of the habit of charity: her concrete care for the victims of Nazi violence, her return of good for evil, and her embodied transformation of eros into agape.

If Thérèse wanted to be a "balm of consolation" and "love at the heart of the Church," Hillesum desired to serve as a "balm for all wounds" and to be "the thinking heart of the barracks." Her journals reveal a turning point in July 1942, when she realizes more clearly the severity of the Nazi program against the Jews in Amsterdam. Many of the reflections in the section above are set against the backdrop of the increasing ban of Jews from public places, curfews, confiscation of property, and so on. As she grew more independent of Spier and more deeply engaged in the spiritual practices of reading, reflection, and intimate prayer, she was "confronted with the realities of war and her responsibility to become socially active and involved."[94] She accepts a position as typist with the Jewish council, "an organization coopted by the German Nazi regime to help transport Jews out of the country."[95] Aware of the ambiguity that comes with an organization full of intrigue and Nazi accommodation, Hillesum accepted the position with the hope of doing some good in the midst of persecution. A few weeks later she volunteered to be sent to the transit camp at Westerbork, which entailed "living on the campsite and in an environment of cramped and noisy quarters, hospital and prison barracks, deprivation and food shortages, illness and lack of hygiene, and in the constant company of death."[96] The deep prayer life nurtured in solitude in Amsterdam enabled her "to become an embodied presence of compassion, dispensing simple words and gestures of consolation and love" – a "balm for all wounds."[97]

Second, Hillesum embodied the habit of charity in her embrace of the return of good for evil. Her attitude towards the enemy is one of the more remarkable and controversial dimensions of her journals and letters. She embodied a kind of Girardian pacific mimesis. Tzvetan Todorov strongly criticizes Hillesum's approach to evil and the enemy.[98] He finds her fascinating and even admits that when we read her "we feel in the presence of someone whom we would want to spend time with, to count among our friends, to love."[99] Nevertheless, Todorov is convinced that her approach ends up contributing to the kind of "fatalism and passivity" that lent itself to "the murderous project of the Nazis."[100] He identifies in Hillesum's writings an indifference to things outside the self, an acceptance of evil, and even at times a preference for suffering. In fact, he thinks her navigating of evil and suffering often resembles stoicism, quietism, and even Taoism – a religious tradition to which she does refer. Though she prefers "ordinary virtues (caring) to heroic virtues (war)," she goes further in a way that proves to be disturbing to Todorov: "Instead of doing something about the causes of evil, she is content to be 'the balm for all wounds.' She lives not in resignation but rather in joyful acceptance of the world and thus of evil as well."[101] "And this is why," Todorov adds, "despite her uncontestable nobility, I cannot commend her position to the downtrodden of the earth."[102]

Todorov's criticisms should be considered carefully. An eclectic spirituality that sloppily combines Christian and Taoist imagery is destined for ambiguity. That said, from the theological framework established in this book, it is possible to discern a key dimension of the habit of charity as it is expressed in the Christian tradition in the Sermon on the Mount and the Law of the Cross – the command to return evil with love. While there are many legitimate moral responses to a mass atrocity like the Shoah – Dietrich Bonhoeffer discerned after all that it was legitimate for a Christian to assassinate Hitler – Hillesum's little way of fighting against hatred embodies traces of the Trinitarian relation of passive spiration as it is embodied in the habit of charity in history. Furthermore, in light of our discussion of mimetic desire in the previous chapter, I want to suggest that her journals reveal a progressive movement from antagonistic mimesis to peaceful mimesis. One finds in Hillesum a mature transformation of mimetic desire from envy to peacefulness. Even if there are other ways of dealing with the horror of the Nazis, as Todorov indicates, this does not nullify her mimetic spirituality of committing to the sustained work of overcoming hatred, scapegoating, and other types of mimetic snowballing. For example, she writes:

> It is the problem of our age: hatred of Germans poisons everyone's mind … I had a liberating thought that surfaced in me like a hesitant, tender young blade of grass thrusting its way through a wilderness of weeds: if there were only one decent German, then he should be cherished despite that whole barbaric gang, and because of that one decent German it is wrong to pour hatred over an entire people.[103]

Akin to the unity of contemplation and action envisioned by Thérèse above and to Girardian sanctity, Hillesum sees "no other solution" than "to turn inward and to root out all the rottenness there." "I no longer believe that we can change anything in the world until we have first changed ourselves," she writes.[104] Her developing spirituality of returning evil with good is captured in her encounter with a young Gestapo officer, who verbally abused her. The real import of the story, according to her, was not that she was wronged but that she "felt no indignation," but instead a "real compassion." She wanted to ask him: "Did you have a very unhappy childhood, has your girlfriend let you down?" Recognizing that the officer looked harassed, sullen, and weak, she reflected: "the blame must be put on the system that uses such people. What needs eradication is the evil in man, not man himself."[105]

This dimension of the habit of charity, this nurturing of peaceful mimesis, was given pointed expression as she lay upon her bed in

Amsterdam listening to Bach. Cognizant that "any minute now a piece of shrapnel could come through that window," she still felt "so peaceful and grateful":[106]

> All disasters stem from us. Why is there a war? Perhaps because now and then I might be inclined to snap at my neighbor. Because I and my neighbor and everyone else do not have enough love. Yet we could fight war and all its excrescences by releasing, each day, the love that is shackled inside us, and giving it a chance to live. And I believe that I will never be able to hate any human being for his so-called wickedness, that I shall only hate the evil that is within me ... In any case, we cannot be lax enough in what we demand of others and strict enough in what we demand of ourselves.[107]

Hillesum advises us to open up to "cosmic sadness." She repeatedly contemplates the beauty of life even in the midst of horror. This involves an incipient embrace of the Law of the Cross as the humble way to freedom – a resistance to the perpetual temptation to nurture hatred.

> Yes, life is beautiful and I value it anew at the end of every day, even though I know that the sons of mothers, and you are one such mother, are being murdered in concentration camps. And you must be able to bear your sorrow; even if it seems to crush you, you will be able to stand up again, for human beings are so strong, and your sorrow must become an integral part of yourself, part of your body and your soul, you mustn't run away from it, but bear it like an adult. Do not relieve your feelings through hatred, do not seek to be avenged on all German mothers, for they, too, sorrow at this very moment for their slain and murderous sons. Give your sorrow all the space and shelter in yourself that is its due, for if everyone bears his grief honestly and courageously, the sorrow that now fills the world will abate. But if you do not clear a decent shelter for your sorrow, and instead reserve most of the space inside you for hatred and thoughts of revenge – from which new sorrows will be born for others – then sorrow will never cease in this world and will multiply. And if you have given sorrow that space its gentle origins demand, then you may truly say: life is beautiful and so rich. So beautiful and so rich that it makes you want to believe in God.[108]

Third, as her journals attest, Hillesum also began to learn "the kind of love that is closer to selfless agape than to urgent eros and that combines deep sympathy with calm detachment."[109] As mentioned above, Hillesum experienced a dominant erotic spirit, which was at times expressed in envious mimetic desire. This kind of antagonistic mimesis occurred, for example, amidst the women who were involved in the social circle associated with Spier. Hillesum expresses her jealousy that other women, the "Aryan girls," find him attractive.[110] Their desire for physical and spiritual intimacy with Spier escalated mimetically; they desired according to the desires of one another. Still, one witnesses in her journals an elevation and transformation of her erotic desires into agapic commitments. As Richard Gaillardetz suggests:

> Her journal presents the reader with a flawed woman who nevertheless embodied "passionate living" in both of its senses: erotic passion, and the willingness to suffer. Moreover, her writing suggests that these two capacities may flow from the same wellspring, a willing to risk powerlessness and vulnerability. Surrounded by a climate of fear, suspicion and hatred, Hillesum opted for a vulnerable presence to and with others. Her remarkable capacity to face suffering and death for the sake of others should not be separated from her willingness to explore the erotic and sensual dimensions of her being. For both authentic sexual intimacy and suffering demand the embrace of powerlessness and vulnerability that lie at the heart of passionate living.[111]

Galliardetz is suggesting that her sometimes "reckless exploration of human sexuality, while fraught with danger, may indeed activate that mysterious capacity latent within all of us to be vulnerable not just to our intimates but before the world." Her passionate life was certainly not always lived within the boundaries of religious moral teaching. Yet, while living with passion may complicate life, "such *passion*, whether realized through human sexual intimacy, or the arts or in any number of other directions, can give rise to *compassion*, a capacity to suffer in solidarity with others." Such compassionate living is "trafficking in the divine."[112]

Conclusion

This chapter tied together several themes that emerged throughout the book. First, mindful of Lonergan's shift to concrete religious experience, it examined particular examples of being-in-love with God that marked his attention to concrete subjectivity. Second, in a related manner, it responded to the contemporary challenge of integrating concrete models of holiness as theological sources and did so by establishing – by way of Doran and Ormerod – the Trinitarian roots of the human desire for God. This constitutes a further moment in my response to Feingold's claim – highlighted in chapters 2 and 5 – that our innate inclination to our connatural end is "capable of transformation into a supernatural inclination to the vision of God through the reception of sanctifying grace, by which we are made mysteriously proportionate to a divine end."[113] Accordingly, I revisited Robert Doran's four-point hypothesis and considered Neil Ormerod's extension of this hypothesis as a basis for establishing the metaphysics of holiness as created participation in the divine nature. I then explored Thérèse's of Lisieux's desire to be "love in the heart of the Church" and Etty Hillesum's desire to be "the thinking heart of the barracks." This chapter suggested, albeit in a speculative manner, that sanctifying grace and the habit of charity – two supernatural realities that make possible the kind of humble love and non-violent resistance so integral to Girard's expression of Christian holiness – were especially operative in the lives of these two very different models of holiness, who both embodied a Trinitarian basis of the human desire for God both "inside" and "outside" the ecclesial milieu.

8 Distorted Desire and the Love of Deviated Transcendence

In thinking about a way beyond the neo-Thomist-Lubacian impasse, Edward Oakes suggested that the term "desire" is "still spoken of too abstractly, without a due allowance being made to the phenomenology of desire in the light of original sin – with its legacy of the *fomes peccati*, that is, of temptation and concupiscence."[1] This chapter argues that attention to concrete subjectivity protects against the temptation of too easily equating the natural desire for being with the natural desire for God without simultaneously acknowledging the widespread distortion of desire in human life – the very misdirection of human loves to false and deviated transcendence. I examine distorted desire in the form of contemporary consumerism and do so through the prism of Lonergan and Girard – the very line of conversation that has animated part 3 of this book.[2]

Though our living is artistic and dramatic, though we participate in our own self-making, we are also limited as concrete subjects in the degree to which we fully shape our lives. We are "already constituted biologically in a particular way," and in large part human identity and self-understanding is a product of "a multifaceted process of socialization."[3] The facticity of our lives – the already given, the already constituted – is the material out of which we "shape our drama"; it is within the "already constituted horizon of meanings and value that the drama of human living unfolds."[4] With a sense of historical consciousness, this chapter takes seriously "hermeneutic interiority" and the communal and cultural formation of our concrete subjectivity in the world. Human receptivity involves the meanings and values handed on to us in our communities.[5] Attentive to concrete subjectivity, this chapter notes our vulnerability to the all-pervasive cultural moods that shape the very meaning and meaningfulness (or lack thereof) of the question of God.

It is important to note that I do not address the very difficult questions related to political economy. I am more concerned with the formation of human subjectivity in an age of global consumerism. A socially dominant vision of the human being in our culture is, in Nicolas Boyle's terms, the self as consumer – an anonymous, identity-less generator of a "never-ending series of new wishes demanding instantaneous satisfaction."[6] In Alasdair MacIntyre's characterization, persons are educated "to regard themselves primarily as consumers whose practical activities are no more than a means to consumption." "Unsurprisingly," MacIntyre comments, "*pleonexia*, the drive to have more and more, becomes treated as a central virtue."[7]

A Civilization of Consumption: The Challenge of Catholic Social Teaching

Pope Francis in *Evangelii Gaudium* emerges not so much as an enemy of capitalism as a prophetic critique of some of the deleterious effects of global consumerism: "The great danger in today's world, pervaded as it is by consumerism," he writes, "is the desolation and anguish born of a complacent yet covetous heart, the feverish pursuit of frivolous pleasures, and a blunted conscience."[8] When our interior lives are marked by egoism, "there is no longer room for others, no place for the poor. God's voice is no longer heard, the quiet joy of his love is no longer felt, and the desire to do good fades" (*EG* 2). Francis explicitly uses the language of idolatry in his diagnosis of some of the challenges of today's world. "The worship of the ancient golden calf (cf. Ex. 32:1–35) has returned in a new and ruthless guise in the idolatry of money and the dictatorship of an impersonal economy lacking a truly human purpose" (*EG* 55). In light of Francis's indictment of the idols of consumerism, I turn briefly to selected themes from Catholic social teaching, with special attention to the writings of John Paul II.

The first theme I highlight is the problem of superdevelopment. A phenomenon not unrelated to the massive challenge of underdevelopment, superdevelopment, John Paul II has noted, is the "excessive availability of every kind of material good for the benefit of certain social groups."[9] Superdevelopment enslaves us to immediate gratification of desire, and confines us to a narrow horizon marked by the multiplication or continual replacement of things. This civilization of consumption exhibits both a "crass materialism" and a "radical dissatisfaction." The deeper aspirations of the human heart remain unsatisfied (*SRS* 28.2).

Second, Catholic social teaching highlights the distinction between "having" and "being" (*SRS* 8.3). Employing the language of human subjectivity, John Paul writes, "To 'have' objects and goods does not in itself perfect the human subject, unless it contributes to the maturing and enrichment of that subject's 'being,' that is to say unless it contributes to the realization of the human vocation as such" (*SRS* 28.3). This is, in part, a question of individual authenticity and the dialectic of the subject, but is situated within the dialectic of the social and cultural life. The unjust distribution of goods and services creates the following scenario: the few who possess much do not grow in *being* because they are stifled by by the cult of *having*. And those who have little cannot realize their basic human vocation because they are deprived of basic goods (*SRS* 28.5). If our deepest desire is to engage in the "dramatic artistry of living," then the neglect of vital needs by oppressive social structures "remove[s] the conditions of the possibility of satisfying the deeper desire and the pattern of experience in such a way that the prosecution of this desire becomes impossible."[10] In *SRS*, John Paul II introduces his notion of "structures of sin" and encourages us to analyse consumerism as a form of modern "imperialism."

Third, in light of the priority of being over having, Catholic social teaching challenges us "to create life-styles" that prioritize "the quest for truth, beauty, goodness and communion with others" for the sake of the common good.[11] As we identify new needs and the new means to meet them, we must be guided by a comprehensive understanding of the human person. An economic system as such "does not possess criteria for correctly distinguishing new and higher forms of satisfying human needs from artificial new needs which hinder the formation of a mature personality" (*CA* 36.1). This requires significant cultural and educational work.[12]

Finally, the historical experience of the West has shown that the so-called good life, with its emphasis on unsustainable superdevelopment, on having over being, on an unrestrained use of the earth's resources, has created the conditions for widespread alienation and the loss of meaning. This loss of authentic meaning is precipitated by consumerism, which confines human beings to a web of superficial gratifications instead of an experiencing personhood in authentic and concrete ways, that is, in solidarity and communion with others (*CA* 41). A society is alienated, a culture distorted, if "its forms of social organization, production and consumption make it more difficult to offer this gift of self and to establish this solidarity between people" (*CA* 41.2). Benedict XVI, in his important contribution to Catholic social teaching *Caritas in Veritate*, identifies the continual emergence of a consumerist and utilitarian view of the world, which distracts us from the anthropological centrality of gift and gratuity (*CV* 34). The good life, in reality, involves the contemplative space for nurturing a "disinterested, unselfish and aesthetic attitude that is born of wonder in the presence of being and of the beauty which enables one to see in visible things the message of the invisible God who created them" (*CV* 37.1).

Idolatry and Deviated Transcendence: Consumerist Practice in the Realm of the "Sacred"

Contemporary Catholic social teaching has diagnosed some of the deleterious effects of consumerism and has exposed its anthropological, ecological, and ontological deficiencies. If human beings are oriented by nature to truth, goodness, and beauty – if indeed human beings are made for gift – then a consumerist culture at its worst offers only simulacra of the realities that truly satisfy the deepest desires of the human heart. Though we intuitively frame consumerism as a secularism to be resisted, I want to suggest that consumerism is in fact a more like a sacralization to be resisted – a deleterious form of idolatry. Of course, the terms "secularization" and "sacralization" are fluid, and it is therefore useful to examine two terms central to this chapter – "idolatry" and "false" or "deviated transcendence" – and highlight some sacral, liturgical dimensions of consumer culture.

One of the central questions guiding Aquinas's treatment of idolatry – a treatment that is deeply Augustinian – is whether it should be considered as a species of superstition or unbelief.[13] This question is pertinent here because it reorients the question of idolatry, shifting it from what we believe to what we love, that is, what we worship, the object of what we desire as ultimate. For Aquinas, idolatry is a species of superstition. Superstition involves the distortion of worship, and this is done chiefly when "divine worship is given to whom it should not be given." Aquinas contrasts the act of superstition with the virtue of "religion," which is marked by worshipping "the most high uncreated God alone."[14] Hence, Aquinas writes, "superstition is a vice contrary to religion by excess, not that it offers more to the divine worship than true religion, but because it offers divine worship either to whom it ought not, or in a manner it ought not."[15] Aquinas also distinguishes superstition and heresy; heresy is a species of unbelief, belonging to those who profess the Christian faith, but corrupt its dogmas,[16] whereas superstition is a confession of unbelief, not by false opinion, but by false external worship.[17]

False or deviated transcendence, then, can be the object of idolatrous worship. According to Girard, the "true guide of human beings is not abstract reason but ritual."[18] For Girard, human society is "the work of the mimetic process that is disciplined by ritual."[19] In fact, religion gave birth to culture. And primitive religion, in Girard's writings, often restored peace through controlled, ritualized violence. As scandal, chaos, and disorder are part of living cultures, the religious response that emerged was the practice of killing or expelling a victim – a response that restores order and solidarity among the community. This religious act of sacrifice reveals a double transference: a shift of blame to the victim and yet a paradoxical divinization of the victim, who gets credit for peace and prosperity. Girard argues that this religion is illusory, protecting humans from violence and chaos by means of sacrificial rituals. That said, although this system is grounded in an illusion, "its action in the world is real to the extent that idolatry, or false transcendence, commands obedience."[20]

Connected to this false transcendence, for Girard, are the powers and principalities, the thrones and dominions that perpetuate forms of false worship.[21] As we look ahead, this connection is relevant insofar as consumerism can be considered a kind of imperialism operative in the world – a global phenomenon marked, in the words of Doran, by an "objectless disposition" and "unlimited forcible expansion" not of capitalism as such, but of the kind of unbridled capitalism scrutinized by Catholic social teaching.[22] Furthermore, this kind of consumerist imperialism is perpetuated through an array of cultural liturgies, as we suggest below. Girard writes, "On the one hand, these powers are "worldly" and "dwell concretely in the world." On the other hand, they are "celestial," meaning that there is a "religious dimension," the "prestige that thrones and sovereigns enjoy among humankind and that is always perceived as a little supernatural." Girard notes a paradox at work in "organizations or institutions that are very real but rooted in a transcendence that is unreal and yet effective." Human language "does not command the necessary resources to express the power of bringing people together that false transcendence possesses in the real, material world, in spite of its false and imaginary nature."[23]

Having situated idolatry within a sacralized sphere[24] – within the context of worshiping a false sacred – I end this section by highlighting a related dimension of the work of James K. A. Smith. Smith offers an account of the human person as a liturgical, desiring animal and illuminates the variety of ways we participate in the liturgies of consumption, aiding us in identifying some often ignored, "sacral" dimensions of consumer culture. He argues that we are first liturgical, desiring animals. Human identity is shaped by what we love – and what we love as ultimate, what orients our being-in-the-world and gives us a sense of meaning and purpose.[25] Smith expresses then in a different way Lonergan's and Marion's emphasis on the priority of love, highlighted in chapter 5. The desiring person intends the world in the mode of love, embodied in the structure of desire or longing.[26]

To say that to be human is to love, for Smith, is to suggest that this vision of the good life becomes "inscribed or infused in our habits and dispositions and thus woven into our precognitive (second) nature."[27] (Recall Lonergan's account of habits and grace in chapter 4.) These habits are formed by the texts – the compelling visions in stories, songs, films, and the like – that shape our desires. They are inscribed in us through bodily practices and rituals that train us to desire certain ends.[28] Smith identifies the desire-forming practices of what he calls our "cultural liturgies." His aim is not to be simply anti-cultural, but "to raise the stakes of what it means for us to be immersed in such cultural rituals."[29] Hence, he frames the "consuming transcendence" of "mall religion" not merely in terms of opposing worldviews, but as a set of liturgical practices with a holistic, affective, embodied anthropology.[30] The mall, he argues, is an intensification of consumerism with marketing as its evangelism, with advertising in all its emerging varieties as its outreach. The rituals and practices of the mall capture our imaginations through the senses. The embodiments of a sexy ideal are offered in the icon-like mannequins in the windows, offering a variety of hagiographies about what constitutes the good life. The mall communicates its "transcendent" story "not through tracts and didactic lectures but through visual embodiments of the happy life" – functioning as an effective liturgy and pedagogy of desire, forming us into "a certain kind of people without ever realizing it."[31] Mindful of the injustice at the heart of consumer culture noted above, however, this kind of liturgical training for the good life also requires massive consumption of natural resources, along with the use of cheap and exploitive labour. The liturgy of consumption creates "a desire for a way of life that is destructive of creation itself" and a way of life "that we can't feasibly extend to others, creating a system of privilege and exploitation."[32]

Consumerism as a "Sacralization to Be Dropped"

To this point I have highlighted Catholic social teaching's diagnosis of the problems associated with superdevelopment and the challenge of reorienting our desires to truth, beauty, communion, and justice. Smith's analysis helped us to situate the challenge of consumerism within a sacralized context by pointing out the often unnoticed, quasi-liturgical practices at work in our civilization of consumption. Even if Smith's case is at times exaggerated, he is still correct in illuminating the primacy of desire in human experience and directing our attention to what's at stake in our participation in the quasi-liturgies of our culture. In sum, he helped us frame consumerism as a false sacralization to be resisted.

I turn once again to Lonergan, Doran, and Girard, all of whom give due attention to the primacy of desire in human experience in complementary ways, as I have noted in previous chapters. Earlier in the book, I offered a more comprehensive account of the relationship between Lonergan's natural desire for meaning, truth, and goodness and Girard's positive account of mimetic desire – both of which can contribute in a more explanatory way to John Paul II's challenge to create lifestyles that prioritize the quest for truth, beauty, goodness, and communion with others for the sake of the common good. I limit my analysis here to Lonergan's account of sacralization and secularization, and am especially mindful of Doran's development of this account in light of the work of Girard.

In "Sacralization and Secularization," Lonergan challenges us to distinguish between (1) a sacralization to be dropped and (2) a sacralization to be fostered; (3) a secularization to be welcomed and (4) a secularization to be resisted.[33]

Mindful of my treatment of the *ressourcement* challenge in chapters 1 and 2, it is relevant to note that Lonergan centres his reflection on the positions of M.D. Chenu and J. Daniélou.[34] Though I have treated *ressourcement* thinkers as a unity in this book so far, this Chenu-Daniélou conversation illuminates the fact that the movement was not a monolith. In fact, one can detect different theological emphases between the Jesuits at Lyon-Fourvière and the Dominicans at Le Saulchoir. As Boersma notes, "The difference between the Jesuit and the Dominican theologians may point, on the one hand, to a predilection among the Fourvière Jesuits for the Greek Fathers with their neoplatonic inclinations; and, on the other hand, to a more pronounced interest among the

Dominicans from Le Saulchoir in St. Thomas with his Aristotelian background."[35] Hence de Lubac's emphasis on the upward natural desire for a supernatural end had a sacramental focus; Chenu's downward focus on the Incarnation prioritized this-worldly historical realities. Chenu and the Saulchoir theologians tended to emphasize the relative autonomy of the created order and the need to adapt to modern culture. Their subtle differences, however, were "emphatically theological in nature," and cannot be reduced to a conservative-progressive divide.[36]

In Lonergan's reading, Chenu is a "disciple of Aquinas," who "broke with the symbolic thought of his medieval predecessors and contemporaries" – one who "acknowledged the reality of human nature and the legitimacy of its proper sphere of activity."[37] In terms of the sacralization to be dropped and a secularization to be welcomed, Chenu welcomes "the contemporary movement of secularization and laicization insofar as it compels us through the force of circumstance to get out of the mental and institutional complex of Christendom."[38] Chenu suggests the abandonment of outdated institutions and some of the heavy-handed procedures of the past. Christians are called more to be missionaries of the gospel and less to concern themselves with the Church as protector of a civilization.

In terms of a new sacralization to be fostered, Lonergan (via Chenu) refers to the Council's call for Christians to discern the signs of the times. Such signs include the humanization and socialization of the human person, peace among nations, and the emerging signs of conscience that can be discerned globally. These signs reveal "the autonomous process proper to the world," but they are also "toothing stones," a new kind of *"praeparatio evangelica"* pointing to ultimate human destiny.[39] The aim is not to "bring about a sociological Christianization of the masses, or to set up a Christian world alongside the world, but to be in the world without being of it, to respect and promote its genuine values without being confined to them and without identifying Christian values with them."[40]

To find a secularization to be dropped, Lonergan turns to Jean Daniélou. While Daniélou abandoned the dream of a Christendom, he still advocated for some kind of "sociological preparation for the faith, certain zones where sacred and religious elements are preserved so that the faith of the poor is not left without social and cultural foundations."[41] Although it is clear that Lonergan is not fully satisfied with Daniélou's analysis, he still assigns significant value to his contribution. All human beings need symbols and, in reality, most do not transcend the limitations of symbolic thinking. Hence, in a developed culture, Lonergan notes, "religion has to be pluralist: it needs some measure of symbolization for all; it needs only a limited measure for the few that get beyond symbolic thinking; and it needs a bounteous dose for the many that do not."[42]

If one is sympathetic with Lonergan's account of the relationship between the natural and supernatural, as I am, then one is inclined to sympathize with the broad lines of Chenu's vision. Still, it is plausible to question whether such a seamless vision of the supernatural elevation of the autonomous secular process allows due attention to the false sacralizations at work in human cultures, including the processes of global consumerism. Lonergan reveals a great deal of wisdom, I believe, by including Daniélou's voice. In fact, the analysis of cultural, consumerist quasi-liturgies that form and deform our desires on such a ubiquitous scale heightens our attention to the wisdom of Daniélou. In many ways, the liturgies of consumption do what Daniélou suggested: they create through the predominance of images and symbols, narratives and practices a kind of "sociological preparation" for allegiance to the priority of having over being, to unfulfilling kinds of false transcendence. In the contemporary era, human identity and the human desire for meaning, truth, goodness, beauty, and love are massively shaped by the forces of global consumerism. As Kelton Cobb observes, we now live in an era in which "whole generations in the West have had their basic conceptions of the world formed by popular culture":

> Television, movies, a multitude of genres of music, amusement parks, fast food franchises, action heroes, Dr. Seuss, Disney, Dream Works, comic books, advertising, soundtracks, mail order catalogs, video games, contemporary fiction, sports, celebrities, journalism, wall art and science fictions have been the primary sources of the myths, parables, iconographies, hagiographies, devils and heroes that orient them in life. From this plethora of material whole generations are now attempting through *bricolage* to invest life with meaning and find a justification for their lives."[43]

As the sociologist Juliet Schor has argued in her book *Born to Buy: The Commercialized Child and the New Consumer Culture*, "Children have become conduits from the consumer marketplace into the household, the link between advertisers and the family purse."[44] As eager and often naive "repositories of consumer knowledge and awareness," young people are "the first adopters and avid users of many of the new technologies" and are often "the household members with the most passionate consumer desires," sometimes almost mystically united to brands and consumer products. Marketing is, she argues, "fundamentally altering the experience of childhood. Corporations have infiltrated the core activities and institutions of childhood, with virtually no resistance from government or parents." "We have become," she adds, "a nation that places a lower priority on teaching its children how to thrive socially, intellectually, even spiritually, than it does on training them to consume. The long-term consequences of this development are ominous."[45] With the diminishing relevance of the gatekeeper model of parenting, advertisers have secured parent-free access to children through a variety of media.[46] If this diagnosis is correct, then Daniélou's call for a "sociological preparation for the faith," for "certain zones where sacred and religious elements are preserved so that the faith of the poor is not left without social and cultural foundations," seems indispensable for nurturing the desire for God. How are we to open up more enriching, challenging, and holy ways of living in the modern world – ways rooted not in the images and practices of global consumerism but in the symbols, images, and practices of a Christian form of life?

In this same essay, Lonergan contrasts the "religion of the infrastructure" with the "religion of the superstructure." In terms of "religious infrastructure," he has in mind primitive religion and primitive societies. Citing Toynbee, he writes that the "pith of primitive religion is not belief but action, and the test of conformity is not assent to a creed but participation in ritual performances."[47] There is a certain immediacy associated with the religion of the infrastructure: "it will fixate on sacred objects; it will acknowledge sacred places, it will hallow sacred times, it will celebrate sacred rites; it will conform to the dictum that the metaphysics of primitive man are expressed in the sedate and rhythmic movements we associate with dance."[48] According to Lonergan, the religions of the infrastructure, more than any other, are "open to palpable idolatry and superstition, to orgiastic and cruel cults, even to the ritual murder of human sacrifice," a problem explored painstakingly by Girard.[49] As Doran notes, "the probability is far greater that religions of the infrastructure will misplace, misidentify, misconstrue precisely what constitutes 'the substance of the sacred.'"[50] What if the substance of the sacred is dictated by the sacralization of consumerism – with its lived emphasis on surface image and the vacuity of signs, the trumpeting of exchange value over use value, the detachment of the signifier and the signified, and the compulsion to desire "desire itself"? Not to

194   The Givenness of Desire

mention its corresponding rituals and practices, along the lines indicated by Smith above? What if our experience of mystery, our images of human flourishing, and the orientation of our fundamental desires are shaped primarily by the quasi-liturgies of consumerism? Can we not, in some analogous way, call this a religion of the infrastructure, prone to a kind of idolatry similar to that which we find in pagan religious traditions? Does not consumerism as a kind of religion of the infrastructure offer several sacrifices inimical to the human good: the flourishing of the targeted children, the flourishing of the underdeveloped who produce the products for our conspicuous consumption, even the flourishing of the "superdeveloped," the flourishing of our natural ecology?

Girard on Consumerism and Mimetic Desire

Robert Doran interprets Lonergan's account of a sacralization to be dropped and a secularization to be dropped by creatively integrating the thought of Girard, especially the French literary scholar's illumination of deviated transcendence, as we defined above. For Doran, Girard is most helpful in identifying a sacralization to be resisted: "any and all attempts to employ the name or word of God or any other sacral trappings to justify persecution, exclusion, and scapegoating."[51] In light of Doran's interpretation of and elaboration on Lonergan's essay, I will integrate several Girardian themes to bolster the case that consumerism can be interpreted under certain conditions as a sacralization to be resisted.

First, Girard's expansive account of mimetic desire offers an explanatory term with which to illuminate Smith's account of the lure of the liturgies of consumerism. "The goods and aspects of human flourishing painted by these alluring pictures of the good life," Smith writes, "begin to seep into the fiber of our being and thus govern and shape our decisions, actions, and habits. Thus we become certain kinds of people; we begin to emulate, mimic, mirror the particular vision that we desire."[52] Smith's account of emulation and mimicry can be explained in a more painstaking way by Girard's account of mimetic desire. Recall from chapters 6 and 7 that mimetic desire names the all-pervasive other-mediated and socially mediated nature of our desire.

In an audio interview with Robert Harrison of Stanford University, Girard captures the kind of mimetic desire at the heart of consumer culture: "Why have all girls been baring their navels for the last five years? Obviously, they didn't all think by themselves that it would be nice to show one's navel or maybe one is too hot in the navel and one must do something about this. We see the mimetic nature of their desire the day that fashion collapses. Suddenly it becomes very old-fashioned to show one's navel and no one will show it anymore. And it will be because of other people, just as now it is because of other people that they show it."[53]

Second, this fundamental reality of mimetic desire creates the conditions, especially in a consumer society, for the proliferation of rivalry and envy among neighbours. Girard's interpretation of the romantic lie brings this to light in a crystallized way. We noted in a previous chapter Girard's critique of the romantic or autonomous lie. Influenced as we are by expressive, indeed excessive, individualism, we presume that we are autonomous individuals, that we are individual agents who create our own desires and do not desire the goods of our neighbours. Does the tenth commandment of the Decalogue forbid an uncommon and perverse human desire – the coveting of our neighbour's possessions, his wife, and his goods? For Girard, the Decalogue prohibits a widespread common desire – a desire in fact constitutive of all human beings – acquisitive mimetic desire. To understand the inadequacy of the expressive individualist account of desire, all one has to do is "to watch two children or two adults who quarrel over some trifle."[54] In other words, "we tend to desire what our neighbor has or what our neighbor desires."[55] If this is true, then "rivalry exists at the very heart of human social relations. The rivalry, if not thwarted, would permanently endanger the harmony and even the survival of all human communities."[56] In sum, we are not, for Girard, "autonomous individuals," but rather "interdividuals" whose desires are socially mediated through a complex web of internal and external mediations. The following passage captures the essence of Girard's (not uncontroversial) claim:

> We do not each have our own desire, one really our own. The essence of desire is to have no essential goal. Truly to desire, we must have recourse to people about us; we have to borrow their desires. This borrowing occurs quite often without either the loaner or the borrower being aware of it. It is not only desire that one borrows from those whom one takes for models; it is a mass of behaviors, attitudes, things learned, prejudices, preferences, etc. And at the heart of these things the loan that places us most deeply into debt – the other's desire – occurs often unawares. The only culture really ours is not that into which we are born; it is the culture whose models we imitate at the age when our power of mimetic assimilation is the greatest.[57]

And Girard explicitly acknowledges a sacramental-liturgical element of the workings of mimetic desire in consumer culture. "If you really look at advertising," Girard says, "they are never trying to demonstrate to you that the object they are selling is the best possible from an objective point of view, from the point of view of scientific objectivity."[58] Rather, they are "always trying to prove to you that this object is desired and possessed by the people we would like to be." Coca-Cola, for example, offers the setting of "a very beautiful beach, marvelous sun, a bunch of people sun tanning in an ideal way, while always between the ages of 16 and 22." He adds, "And therefore there is something sacramental; religion is always mixed up these things. If you consume Coca-Cola, maybe if you consume a lot of it, you will become a little bit like these people you would like to be. It's like a kind of Eucharist that will turn you into the person you really admire."

Third, Girard recognizes that the "consumption society has simply become a system of *exchange of signs*, rather than an exchange of actual objects."[59] As a by-product of superdevelopment, there are also cultural currents Girard identifies in which consumption as "a sign of wealth is no longer appealing," precipitating a mimetically inspired "minimalist" or "anorexic" trend.[60] Drawing on the work of Thomas Frank, Girard notes a phenomenon known as the commodification of discontent. Practitioners of this trend of non-consumption perceive themselves as representing the height of cultural refinement. Hence, this conspicuous non-consumption is only "superficially discontinuous with the attitude it supersedes" and "at a deeper level, it is a mimetic escalation of the same process."[61]

Fourth, if Girard is correct in his reading of the Decalogue, then in his view the heart of neo-paganism is a subversion of the wisdom of the commandments in terms of desire, part of a widespread neo-Nietzschean heritage. Girard interprets contemporary secularization in sacralized terms, noting the centrality of sacrifice in contemporary paganism. Neo-paganism treats Judeo-Christian morality as an expression of intolerable violence, and longs for its complete abolition. Girard identifies neo-paganism with ubiquitous consumerism and the multiplication of desires. "Neopaganism locates happiness," he writes, "in the unlimited satisfaction of desires, which means the suppression of all prohibitions."[62] Yet in one respect the multiplication of available products weakens certain mimetic rivalries: "By making the same objects, the same commodities available to everybody, modern society has reduced the opportunity for conflict and rivalry."[63] Wide availability leads to undesirability. Still, Girard warns that this weakening of mimetic desire does not end the sacrificial solution so widespread in human culture. "Like all sacrificial solutions," he writes, "the consumer society needs to reinvent itself periodically. It needs to dispose of more and more commodities in order to survive."[64] An inflation of objects leads to the kind of "throw-away," superdeveloped cultures critiqued by John Paul II, where objects "go directly from the shop to the bin, with hardly a stop in between."[65] "One buys objects with one hand," Girard says, "and throws them away with the other – in a world where half of the human population goes hungry."[66] Also attentive to the ecological consequences discussed above, Girard points out a new kind of sacrificial performance: "the market society is devouring the earth's resources, just as primitive society devoured its victims."[67]

Finally, for Girard, the dissatisfaction generated in a consumer society can also turn us into mystics "in the sense that it shows us that objects will never satisfy our desires."[68] While it can certainly "lead us to all sorts of useless activities," it can also "bring us back to an awareness of our need for something entirely different. Something that the consumer society cannot provide."[69] As the searching Augustine reflected in Book 4 of the *Confessions*: "There is no rest where you seek for it. Seek for what you seek, but it is not where you are looking for it. You seek the happy life in the region of death; it is not there. How can there be a happy life where there is not even life?"[70]

Consumerist Idolatry and the Distortion of the Scale of Values

I have situated the phenomenon of consumerism in the realm of "religion" and the "sacred" and have explored consumerism as a kind of idolatry – as a sacralization to be dropped. Although Lonergan did not often use the term "idolatry," when he did he captured its heart, namely, the orientation of our desires, our ultimate loves, to something other than God: "for only idolatry would bestow" this state of being in love on anyone or anything of this world."[71] To raise the question of idolatry, then, is not to deny that we love and we worship, but that our ultimate concerns, our deepest desires, our highest loves are attached to the wrong things. If Lonergan and Marion are correct (see chapter 5) – that in religious matters "love precedes knowledge" – in what ways do our distorted loves shape the way we desire, understand, judge, and deliberate? What if we fall in love with the wrong object: how does this affect the "new organization" of our world?[72] If the proper human response to "transcendent mystery is adoration," what happens when we adore pseudo-mysteries, false gods, alluring idols with the same kind of adoration?[73] And what implications might this have for social and cultural life?

Though I suggested in passing that consumerism operates as a kind of global imperialism, I also recognize that the term "imperialism," as Doran notes, is a largely descriptive term.[74] A more adequate explanatory framework consists in the "integral scale of values" and a "set of distinct but related and currently distorted dialectics of the subject, culture, and community," noted earlier in the book.[75] Accordingly, I reiterate Robert Doran's interpretation of this scale:

> From above, then, religious values condition the possibility of personal integrity; personal integrity conditions the possibility of authentic cultural values; at the reflexive level of culture, such integrity will promote an authentic superstructural collaboration that assumes responsibility for the integrity not only of scientific and scholarly disciplines, but even of everyday culture; cultural integrity at both levels conditions the possibility of a just social order; and the just social order conditions the possibility of the equitable distribution of vital goods. Conversely, problems in the effective and recurrent distribution of vital goods can be met only by a reversal of distortions in the social order; the proportions of the needed reversal are set by the scope and range of the real or potential maldistribution; the social change demands a transformation at the everyday level of culture proportionate to the dimensions of the social problem; this transformation frequently depends on reflexive theoretical and scientific developments at the superstructural level; new cultural values at both levels call for proportionate changes at the level of personal integrity; and these depend for their emergence, sustenance, and consistency on the religious development of the person.[76]

While Doran explains the mutual conditioning among the different dimensions of the scale, the point I want to emphasize here is Doran's claim that "personal integrity and authentic religion" lie in a sense "beyond both the infrastructure and the superstructure," but that they are "essential to the integral functioning" of a just society.[77] In light of the argument of this chapter, I suggest that consumerism as a form of idolatry – as quasi-liturgical worship of false transcendence – is not simply part of everyday cultural meanings and values that distort the social infrastructure, but is first and foremost an inauthentic ordering of religious love, leading to a distortion of the scale, as it were, from the beginning. This communicates perhaps a more explanatory way of integrating the theme of the "ordering of loves" so prominent in the tradition. The ordering of loves, after all, is what distinguishes Augustine's two cities in the *City of God*. The heavenly city and the earthly city in Augustine's rendition are not two geographical regions, but are divided by contradictory, ultimate loves: the heavenly city is directed to love of God and neighbour, the earthly city to a disordered love of self. The heavenly city is identified with the common good, humility, and rest, the earthly city with arrogant love of domination, pride, and restlessness. The heavenly city is imbued with truth, goodness, and justice, the earthly city with greed, envy, and corruption.[78]

If this kind of "secularized sacred" distorts the scale of values, then the "sacralization to be fostered will be found precisely in the dynamics of the redemptive process that is a constitutive feature of the structure of history, that is, in the Law of the Cross." The Law of the Cross – the response of self-giving religious love – "characterizes all genuine and sustained fidelity to the integral scale of values."[79] Instead of the distorted anthropology and soteriology of consumer liturgies, a genuine anthropological differentiation of consciousness prioritizes "being over having," while a genuine soteriological differentiation of consciousness brings to light the "mysterious intelligibility" of "the pattern of suffering servanthood assumed by the world-transcendent measure of integrity become human flesh."[80]

I return in this light to Lonergan's appropriation of Daniélou and the importance of creating particular communal spaces for the communication of and formation in the "really sacred." If indeed we are moved by the "transcendent" stories, the visual embodiments, the liturgies and pedagogies of desire of consumer culture without even realizing it, then it seems fitting to suggest that a bounteous dose of symbols is needed as an antidote, illuminating a massive cultural need for a self-appropriation of one's empirical consciousness. This kind of affective or psychic conversion effects an ongoing habitual conversion to phantasms, restoring the "natural" orientation of the human spirit, which is, as I argued in chapter 4, intimately connected to the desire for God. It involves understanding the manner in which symbols express and influence our affective state and challenges us to the nurturing of redemptive symbols to elevate and heal the culture.[81] This kind of conversion is a "transformation of desire."[82] We are, of course, moving beyond the scope of this chapter into the realm of ecclesiology and liturgical theology. That is, we are raising questions about the need for the church and the church's liturgy to be "sacred zones" for the ongoing ritualized encounter with authentic mystery, stories of transcendence, visions of the good life, marked by the priority of the gift and the self-giving communion of persons.

Conclusion

Walker Percy treated this theme of disordered loves masterfully in his novel *Love in the Ruins*. The lukewarm Catholic protagonist, Dr Tom More, a distant descendent of St Thomas More, exclaims: "I believe in God and the whole business, but I love women best, music and science next, whiskey next, God fourth, and my fellow man hardly at all."[83] In other words, it is not a matter of whether we love, but what or whom we love, and how we order our loves. Tom More in Percy's narrative did not doubt God's existence, so it was not first a matter of belief or unbelief. It was a question of what he loved ultimately. This disordering created the conditions for the malaise and anxiety that marked his life in the novel and, I suggest, marks our lives within the contemporary horizon of consumerist superdevelopment. Could it be that our fundamental choice – at least in the affluent West – is not between theism and atheism, but between the God of Life and the idolatry of deviated transcendence? Akin to Girard's suggestion that a consumer society can turn us into mystics, perhaps it is fitting to end with Lonergan's reflection on the importance of the right ordering our religious loves: "Unless religion is totally directed to what is good, to genuine love of one's neighbor and to a self-denial that is subordinated to a fuller goodness in oneself, then the cult of God that is terrifying can slip over into the demonic, into an exultant destructiveness of oneself and of others."[84]

Conclusion

This book constructed a multifaceted language for the human desire for God in the context of concrete subjectivity. The problematic situation to which the inquiry responded was the work of Henri de Lubac and the widespread reconsideration of his writings on the supernatural that continues to emerge in contemporary theological discourse.

Lonergan's voice proved to be especially fruitful because, over the course of his career, he engaged in a highly serious way the writings of Thomas on nature and grace expressed in metaphysical categories and then later integrated the insights of phenomenology and existentialism – concrete subjectivity, meaning, religious experience, the gift-character of love. This tension between metaphysics and phenomenology, broadly conceived, has shaped the theological debates between the neo-scholastics and the *ressourcement* Lubacians from the Danielou-Garrigou-Lagrange exchange in the late 1940s down through the Schindler-Long debate at the dawn of the third millennium.

What particular value, then, did the hermeneutical lens of concrete subjectivity offer to ongoing conversations about the human desire to see God? What is the significance of this inquiry?

1. *Concrete subjectivity bears the resources for responding to the Lubacian emphasis on concrete and historical nature, on the one hand, and the neo-Thomist call to develop a substantive and ontologically dense understanding of nature, on the other hand.* In contrast to many neo-Thomists, Lonergan marginalized the theorem of pure nature, but he consistently affirmed a rich and dynamic account of nature, expressed in both his retrieval of Aquinas and in his transposition of Thomistic wisdom in his account of emergent probability. Lonergan affirmed what might be called the

"relative autonomy" of the created order.[1] His treatment of vertical finality and obediential potency over and against a static-essentialist vision of the relationship between the natural and supernatural orders offered a reconciling voice to the debate. He also possesses the resources, more than any other interlocutor in this book, for constructive integration of the natural sciences. His substantive account of "nature" both preserves the gratuity of the supernatural order and creates the conditions for multidisciplinary and interreligious deliberation about social life. It emphasizes that what binds us together is the transcultural call to be attentive, intelligent, rational, responsible, and loving. What unites us is the common vocation to be faithful to the eros of self-transcendence and to root out bias wherever it surfaces. The normative scale of values constitutes, as I suggested in these pages, a contemporary reformulation of the nature-grace synthesis with greater attention to the social and historical dimensions of human subjectivity.

Furthermore, this shift from intellectual desire to a more holistic account of the concrete subject paved the way for integrating Lonergan's emphasis on the centrality of love into this conversation on the human desire for God. Establishing a phenomenological transposition of a metaphysical framework enabled me to articulate the Trinitarian roots (sanctifying grace and the habit of charity) of the human desire for the supernatural and to enrich this vision with the interpenetration of agapic and erotic subjectivity.

One particular defence of "pure nature," for example, suggests that the value of this theological term lies in its nurturing of epistemological humility. Bernard Mulcahey argues that Christian believers cannot fully grasp any given domain of created reality, and that includes theologians, bishops, and even popes who transgress their competence on particular secular topics.[2] Pure nature reminds theologians that the world and human beings are intelligible to natural reason, and hence to recognize both the "limits of their competence" in other disciplines and "the rightful autonomy of secular learning." Lonergan's dynamic account of the eros of self-transcendence and its relation to building the human good affirms the general thrust of this claim. His vision of nature as emergent probability requires, for example, a multidisciplinary exploration. That said, in light of Lonergan's account of concrete subjectivity, the claim about "the rightful autonomy of secular learning" also requires attention to the way individual, dramatic, group, and general bias may affect the eros of the mind at work in these other authorities on knowledge. Holding too dearly to "pure nature" may in fact falsely convey a kind of purity in secular learning and diminish the challenge of rooting out bias that is required of every kind of disciplinary inquiry. In the words of the Lubacian thinker David Schindler, the fundamental question is whether in one's abstraction – the seeking of common ground, the appeal to reason, the methodological differentiation of academic disciplines – one remains "dynamically open" in one's interior disposition and in the content of one's inquiry "to the realities of grace and sin that are always already operative in the one historical order."[3]

2. *Concrete subjectivity provides the space for theological reflection on the human desire for God with heightened attention to the contemporary cultural milieu.* In recent years, Benedict XVI has identified a particular narrowing of reason in the West, and has urged us to rethink an account of reason that is open to God.[4] He has challenged the modern cultural superstructure in the west (philosophy, science, scholarship, art, literature, etc.) to nurture meaningful spaces for the question of God to emerge as a constitutive question of the human condition.[5] Benedict referred to the question of God as the crucial question: "faith and culture are permanently connected heights, a manifestation of that *desiderium naturale vivendi Deum* that is present in every person."[6] Benedict resituates the natural desire to see God within the horizon of the question of God: "The question of the Truth and the Absolute – the question of God – is not an abstract investigation divorced from daily life, but is the *crucial question* on which the discovery of the meaning of the world and life depends."[7] Understanding the human quest as a search for truth and goodness enlarges the scope of reason and diminishes the temptation of making scientific discoveries a means of power and enslavement. This narrowing of reason identifies real scientific knowing with the interplay of mathematical and empirical elements. This methodological approach, then, by its very nature "excludes the question of God, making it appear an unscientific or pre-scientific question."[8]

In this light, Lonergan's shifts of emphasis from an intellectual proof of God's existence in the tradition of natural theology to the variety of ways *the question of God* arises in the intellectual, moral, and religious dimensions of our concrete lives is highly relevant. That is, he emphasized the human call to self-transcendence and the way acts of self-transcendence enable the *question of God* to emerge in one's conscious horizon. The plausibility of even asking "the question of God" cannot be taken for granted in the secular age.

With his emphasis on concreteness, Lonergan was concerned with the difference the natural human desire for God and natural human knowledge of God made to human living and human society. For Lonergan, this natural desire means that the reality of God resides within the horizon of human knowing and doing – that "religion represents a fundamental dimension in human living."[9] He, of course, understood that many contemporary wayfarers regard religion as little more than a comforting illusion. This dimension of the modern social imaginary communicated, for him, a "profound ignorance" of the "real nature" of the human person, and may have "a gravely distorting effect on the conduct of human affairs."[10] Thus, the question of the human desire for God is intrinsically connected to the human quest for self-transcendence. Although the intellectual, the moral, and the religious are quite distinct, they are not disparate. They are, in fact, three distinct phases in the unfolding of the human spirit. Lonergan was avoiding an extrinsicist account of nature and grace – expressed here, of course, in a new idiom. The acceptance or rejection of the call to self-transcendence, which includes openness to the question of God, has real consequences for concrete living.

In addition to the cultural issue of the narrowing of reason, the challenge of consumerism also distorts the natural desire for God. *Concrete subjectivity resists the tendency of equating too easily the natural desire for being with the natural desire for God without at the same time acknowledging the widespread distortion of desire.* As I argued in the previous chapter, consumerism is a distorted form of worship, a misdirected love of false and deviated transcendence. The quest for the "good life" in Western culture, and its predilection for having over being, have created the conditions for widespread experience of alienation and the loss of meaning. Concrete subjectivity recognizes the dominance of "hermeneutic interiority," that is, of the communal and cultural formation of our concrete being-in-the-world. Human receptivity has to do with the meanings and values that are handed on to us in our communities.[11] Concrete subjectivity challenges us to account for our vulnerability to the all-pervasive cultural moods that shape the very meaning and meaningfulness (or lack thereof) of the question of God as shaped by our communal history.

3. *Concrete subjectivity attends to the impact of other-mediated, mimetic desire in the human life-world, and provides fertile soil for thinking theologically about the role of the religious experience of the saints and concrete models of holiness in eliciting the human desire for God.* The rise of academic theology in the Middles Ages tended to separate the study of the saints from theological discourse.[12] The work of Hans Urs von Balthasar resists

this division, representing the most pioneering contemporary attempt to employ the saints as a theological resource in Catholic systematic theology.[13] Lawrence Cunningham has suggested that the "theological foundations of sainthood have received short shrift in the theological tradition partially, one suspects, because of the perceived notion that the saints are part of the 'popular' tradition of Catholicism rather than central to the Catholic doctrinal tradition."[14] With particular attention to the ongoing Girard-Lonergan conversation, this book integrated the categories of natural desire, incarnate meaning, and mimetic desire, and further developed an explanatory account of holiness, with particular attention to sanctifying grace and the habit of charity. These two supernatural realities help explain in a systematic-theological way the kind of humble love and non-violent resistance so integral to Girard's account of Christian sanctity. With the development of these theological categories, the book explored in a theologically fruitful way two examples of the human desire for God in a secular age – Thérèse of Lisieux and Etty Hillesum.

I began this book with the example of the ancient seeker Augustine and his grasp of the true longing and all-too-common distortion of human desire; it is perhaps fitting to end with a contemporary wayfarer, Dorothy Day, who mused as she found herself stopping by St. Joseph's Church in New York at six a.m. after a long night out: "Sooner or later I would have to pause in the mad rush of living and remember my first beginning and last end."[15] Such is the human desire for God in all its concreteness.

Notes

Introduction

1 St Augustine, *Confessions*, trans. Henry Chadwick (Oxford: Oxford University Press, 1998), 3.
2 St Augustine, *Confessions*, 64.
3 Noteworthy examples include Hans Urs von Balthasar, *The Theology of Karl Barth*, trans. Edward T. Oakes (San Francisco: Ignatius, 1992); John Milbank, *The Suspended Middle: Henri de Lubac and the Debate Concerning the Supernatural* (Grand Rapids: Eerdmans, 2005); David L. Schindler, *Heart of the World, Center of the Church: Communio Ecclesiology, Liberalism, and Liberation* (Grand Rapids: Eerdmans, 1996); Edward T. Oakes, "The *Surnaturel* Controversy: A Survey and a Response," *Nova et Vetera*, English ed., 9.3 (2011): 625–56; Nicholas J. Healy, "Henri de Lubac on Nature and Grace: A Note on Some Recent Contributions to the Debate," *Communio: International Catholic Review* 35 (Winter 2008): 535–64; and David Grumett, "De Lubac, Grace, and the Pure Nature Debate," *Modern Theology* 31.1 (2015): 123–46.
4 See Lawrence Feingold, *The Natural Desire to See God According to St. Thomas Aquinas and His Interpreters* (Ave Maria: Sapientia, 2010); Steven A. Long, *Natura Pura: On the Recovery of Nature in the Doctrine of Grace* (New York: Fordham University Press, 2010); Reinhard Hütter, *Dust Bound for Heaven: Explorations in the Theology of Thomas Aquinas* (Grand Rapids: Eerdmans, 2012); Bernard Mulcahy, *Aquinas's Notion of Pure Nature and the Christian Integralism of Henri de Lubac: Not Everything Is Grace* (New York: Peter Lang, 2011); Guy Mansini, "Henri de Lubac, the Natural Desire to See God, and Pure Nature," *Gregorianum* 83.1 (2002): 89–109; Mansini, "The Abiding Significance of Henri de Lubac's *Surnaturel*," *The Thomist* 73.4 (2009): 593–619; Thomas Joseph White, "Imperfect Happiness and the

Final End of Man: Thomas Aquinas and the Paradigm of Nature-Grace Orthodoxy," *The Thomist* 78.2 (2014): 247–89; Christopher J. Malloy, "De Lubac on Natural Desire: Difficulties and Antitheses," *Nova et Vetera*, English ed., 9.3 (2011): 567–624; David Braine, "The Debate between Henri de Lubac and His Critics," *Nova et Vetera*, English ed., 6 (2008): 543–90; Thomas J. Bushlack, *Politics for a Pilgrim Church: A Thomistic Theory of Civic Virtue* (Grand Rapids: Eerdmans, 2015), esp. chap. 4; Adam G. Cooper, *Naturally Human, Supernaturally God: Deification in Pre-conciliar Catholicism* (Minneapolis: Fortress, 2014); Andrew Dean Swafford, *Nature and Grace: A New Approach to Thomistic Ressourcement* (Eugene: Pickwick, 2014). See also the many pertinent essays in Serge-Thomas Bonino, ed., *Surnaturel: A Controversy at the Heart of Twentieth-Century Thomistic Thought*, trans. Robert Williams and Matthew Levering (Ave Maria: Sapientia, 2009).

5 Feingold, *The Natural Desire to See God*, xxxvi.

6 Narcisse, "The Supernatural in Contemporary Theology," in Bonino, *Surnaturel*, 308.

7 I draw on many Lonergan scholars throughout the book, but especially note the fundamental influence of Robert M. Doran's *The Trinity in History: A Theology of the Divine Missions*, vol. 1: *Missions and Processions* (Toronto: University of Toronto Press, 2012); *What Is Systematic Theology?* (Toronto: University of Toronto Press, 2005); and *Theology and the Dialectics of History* (Toronto: University of Toronto Press, 1990). I also note the work of Neil Ormerod. See notes 8 and 26 below.

8 That said, notable contributions include J. Michael Stebbins, *The Divine Initiative: Grace, World-Order, and Human Freedom in the Early Writings of Bernard Lonergan* (Toronto: University of Toronto Press, 1995); Neil Ormerod, "The Grace-Nature Distinction and the Construction of a Systematic Theology," *Theological Studies* 75.3 (2014): 515–36; Ormerod, "Addendum on the Grace-Nature Distinction," *Theological Studies* 75.4 (2014): 890–8; Brian Himes, "Lonergan's Position on the Natural Desire to See God and Aquinas' Metaphysical Theology of Creation and Participation," *Heythrop Journal* 54 (2013): 767–83; Raymond Maloney, "De Lubac and Lonergan on the Supernatural," *Theological Studies* 69 (2008): 509–27; Joshua R. Brotherton, "The Integrity of Nature in the Grace-Freedom Dialectic: Lonergan's Critique of Banezian Thomism," *Theological Studies* 75.3 (2014): 537–63; Guy Mansini, "Lonergan on the Natural Desire in the Light of Feingold," *Nova et Vetera*, English ed., 5.1 (2007): 185–98.

9 Bernard Lonergan, "Natural Right and Historical Mindedness," in *A Third Collection: Papers by Bernard J.F. Lonergan, S.J.*, ed. Frederick E. Crowe (New York: Paulist, 1985), 169–83.

10 Lonergan, "Natural Right and Historical Mindedness," 172.
11 Lonergan, "Natural Right and Historical Mindedness," 172.
12 Bernard Lonergan, "*Existenz* and *Aggiornamento*," in *Collection, Collected Works of Bernard Lonergan* (henceforth *CWL*) 4, ed. Frederick E. Crowe and Robert M. Doran (Toronto: University of Toronto Press, 1993), 223.
13 Lonergan, "*Existenz* and *Aggiornamento*," 223.
14 In his essay "Eighteen Days in 1968: An Essay on the Maturation of Lonergan's Intentionality Analysis," *Method: Journal of Lonergan Studies*, n.s., 3.2 (2012), Jeremy W. Blackwood identifies a key moment of development in an eighteen-day time span from Lonergan's lecture "The Subject" to his lecture "Horizons": "Succinctly put, 'The Subject' expressed the summit of conscious subjectivity as the place at which the *individual* subject's personal character and essence are at stake, while 'Horizons' expressed the summit of conscious subjectivity as a *social* genuine personhood" (2). In sum, the social, interpersonal element "became a constitutive element of the immanent intelligibility of human subjectivity" (26).
15 Robert M. Doran, *Theology and the Dialectics of History*, 20.
16 Brian J. Braman, *Meaning and Authenticity: Bernard Lonergan and Charles Taylor on the Drama of Authentic Human Existence* (Toronto: University of Toronto Press, 2008), 49.
17 Braman, *Meaning and Authenticity*, 49.
18 Lonergan, *Phenomenology and Logic: Lectures on Mathematical Logic and Existentialism, CWL* 6, ed. Philip J. McShane (Toronto: University of Toronto Press, 2001), 315–16.
19 See Robert Sokolowski, *Introduction to Phenomenology* (Cambridge: Cambridge University Press, 1999), 159.
20 Sokolowski, *Introduction to Phenomenology*, 186.
21 Bernard Lonergan, "Dimensions of Meaning," in *Collection, CWL* 4, ed. Frederick E. Crowe and Robert M. Doran (Toronto: University of Toronto Press, 1988), 242.
22 See, for example, Daniel A. Rober, *Recognizing the Gift: Toward a Renewed Theology of Nature and Grace* (Minneapolis: Fortress, 2016). Rober helpfully integrates the work of Marion and Ricouer into nature-grace conversations.
23 Lonergan, "Dimensions of Meaning," 242.
24 Lonergan, "Dimensions of Meaning," 243.
25 Girard, "The Goodness of Mimetic Desire," in *The Girard Reader*, ed. James G. Williams (New York: Crossroad, 1996), 64.
26 See, for example, John D. Dadosky, "'Naming the Demon': The 'Structure' of Evil in Lonergan and Girard," *Irish Theological Quarterly* 75.4 (2010):

355–72; Dadosky, "Woman without Envy: Toward Reconceiving the Immaculate Conception," *Theological Studies* 72.1 (2011): 16–40; Robert M. Doran, *The Trinity in History*; Charles Hefling, "About What Might a 'Girard-Lonergan Conversation' Be?," in *Lonergan Workshop Journal* 17, ed. Frederick Lawrence (Chestnut Hill: Boston College, 2002), 95–123; Neil Ormerod, "Questioning Desire: Lonergan, Girard and Buddhism," *Louvain Studies* 36.4 (2014): 356–71; Ormerod, "Desire and the Origins of Culture: Lonergan and Girard in Conversation," *Heythrop Journal* 54.5 (September 2013): 784–95; Ormerod, "Doran's *The Trinity in History*: The Girardian Connection," *Method: Journal of Lonergan Studies,* n.s., 4.1 (2013): 47–59.

27 Kevin Lenehan, "Girard and the Tasks of Theology," in *Violence, Desire, and the Sacred*, vol. 1: *Girard's Mimetic Theory across the Disciplines*, ed. Scott Cowdell, Chris Fleming, and Joel Hodge (New York: Bloomsbury, 2012), 114.
28 See chap. 9, "The Dialectic of Desire," in Doran's *The Trinity in History*. In his essay "New Paths for a Girard/Lonergan Conversation: An Essay in Light of Robert Doran's *Missions and Processions*," *Method: Journal of Lonergan Studies*, n.s., 4.1 (2013), Grant Kaplan says that Doran's book "continues the most serious engagement with mimetic theory carried out over the last two decades by Lonergan scholars" (24).
29 Doran, *The Trinity in History*, 204.
30 Hefling, "About What Might a 'Girard-Lonergan Conversation' Be?," 104.
31 Lonergan, *Method in Theology* (New York: Herder and Herder, 1972), xi.

1. De Lubac's Lament: Loss of the Supernatural

1 Milbank, *The Suspended Middle*, 3–4.
2 Christopher M. Cullen, "The Natural Desire for God and Pure Nature: A Debate Renewed," *American Catholic Philosophical Quarterly* 86.4 (2012): 705.
3 Henri de Lubac, *Surnaturel: Études historiques* (Paris: Aubier, 1946); "The Mystery of the Supernatural," in *Theology in History*, trans. Anne Englund Nash (San Francisco: Ignatius, 1996), 281–316; *The Mystery of the Supernatural*, trans. Rosemary Sheed (New York: Crossroad, 1998); *Augustinianism and Modern Theology*, trans. Lancelot Sheppard (New York: Crossroad, 2000).
4 Feingold, *The Natural Desire to See God*, xxxiv.
5 Milbank, *The Suspended Middle*, 4.
6 De Lubac, "Disappearance of the Sense of the Sacred," in *Theology in History*, trans. Anne Englund Nash (San Francisco: Ignatius, 1996), 236.
7 Joseph A. Komonchak, "Theology and Culture at Mid-Century: The Example of Henri de Lubac," *Theological Studies* 51 (1990): 602.
8 De Lubac, "Disappearance of the Sense of the Sacred," 225.

9 De Lubac, "Disappearance of the Sense of the Sacred," 227.
10 I am following here Fergus Kerr's analysis in "French Theology: Yves Congar and Henri de Lubac," in *The Modern Theologians: An Introduction to Christian Theology in the Twentieth Century*, 2nd ed., ed. David F. Ford (Malden: Blackwell, 1997), 105–6.
11 Kerr, "French Theology," 106.
12 Komonchak, "Theology and Culture at Mid-Century," 597.
13 Henri de Lubac, *A Theologian Speaks* (interview by Angelo Scola) (Los Angeles: Twin Circle, 1985), 1.
14 Hans Boersma, *Nouvelle Théologie and Sacramental Ontology: A Return to Mystery* (New York: Oxford University Press, 2009), 89.
15 Henri de Lubac, *The Drama of Atheist Humanism* (San Francisco: Ignatius, 1995), 266.
16 De Lubac, "Disappearance of the Sense of the Sacred," 237–9.
17 For his own memories of this period, see Henri de Lubac, *Christian Resistance to Anti-Semitism: Memories from 1940–1944*, trans. Elizabeth Englund (San Francisco: Ignatius, 1990).
18 Gabriel Flynn, "Introduction: The Twentieth-Century Renaissance in Catholic Theology," in *Ressourcement: A Movement for Renewal*, ed. Gabriel Flynn and Paul D. Murray (New York: Oxford University Press, 2012), 13.
19 Komonchak, "Theology and Culture at Mid-Century," 598.
20 De Lubac, "Letter to My Superiors," in *Theology in History*, trans. Anne Englund Nash (San Francisco: Ignatius, 1996), 429–31. This letter is dated "Lyons, April 25, 1941."
21 De Lubac, "Letter to My Superiors," 430–2.
22 De Lubac, "Letter to My Superiors," 438.
23 Boersma, *Nouvelle Théologie and Sacramental Ontology*, 89.
24 De Lubac, "Disappearance of the Sense of the Sacred," 230.
25 De Lubac, "Disappearance of the Sense of the Sacred," 230–1.
26 Bernard Mulcahy, *Aquinas's Notion of Pure Nature*, 8.
27 I am drawing heavily here from Feingold's substantive summary of Suárez (*The Natural Desire to See God*, 221–59).
28 Feingold, *The Natural Desire to See God*, 230.
29 Even though uncomfortable with the doctrine, John Milbank recognizes the "admirably compassionate humanism" of Aquinas – a humanism that might be said "to leave the souls of unbaptized babies eternally as *baby-souls* playing idly and creatively throughout all ages" (*The Suspended Middle*, 81).
30 See II Sent., d. 33, q. 2, a. 2 and De Malo, q. 5. a.3. See also Feingold, *The Natural Desire to See God*, 247–50, and Malloy, "De Lubac on Natural Desire," 585–7.
31 Feingold, *The Natural Desire to See God*, 276.

32 Feingold, *The Natural Desire to See God*, 277–8. See also de Lubac, *Augustinianism and Modern Theology*, 1–30.
33 De Lubac, *Augustinianism and Modern Theology*, 2.
34 Feingold, *The Natural Desire to See God*, 278.
35 De Lubac, *Augustinianism and Modern Theology*, 3. "Doctrinally, Baius's naturalism is the equivalent of Pelagius'. The only difference is the point of application or the way in which naturalism occurs in both, and this difference is possibly more a question of temperament or mentality that of deep thought. Pelagius, in St. Jerome's phrase, thought that God has wound man up, once and for all, like a clock, and then gone to sleep; Baius's clock needs continually to be rewound. The perfect Pelagian would be the proud man who wishes never to owe anything to anyone. The perfect Baianist, on the other hand, would be the haggling litigant, always pleading poverty and claiming his due. Baius is a Pelagius turned beggar. Pelagianism means pure asceticism, Baianism pure juridicism. Both, each in his own order and his own way, hold a pure naturalism" (De Lubac, *Augustinianism and Modern Theology*, 5).
36 De Lubac, *Augustinianism and Modern Theology*, 2.
37 Feingold, *The Natural Desire to See God*, 280.
38 Feingold, *The Natural Desire to See God*, 281.
39 This is the title of chapter 5 of *Augustinianism and Modern Theology*. See also *Surnaturel*, part 2, esp. chaps. 4 and 5.
40 See *Surnaturel*, part 1, chaps. 1–7, and *Augustinianism and Modern Theology*, chaps. 1–3. Against Feingold's claim that de Lubac falls unintentionally into a kind of Jansenism, see David Grumett's critique in "De Lubac, Grace, and the Pure Nature Debate," 137ff. See also Mulcahy, *Aquinas's Notion of Pure Nature*, chap. 5 for a more historically conscious account of de Lubac's relationship to Jansenism and its implications for the limits of blaming pure nature and scholasticism for French disaffection for the Catholic faith.
41 I suggest that de Lubac would not disagree with Feingold's designation of this as a "consensus," though he also acknowledges certain tensions. De Lubac writes: "The turning-point in the history of Thomistic thought is marked chiefly by the work of Cajetan (1468–1534), though this was of course laid on ground already prepared, and was accompanied, and then continued and to some extent transformed, by the work of others. The sixteenth-century theologians took note of it. Suárez, for instance, while following Cajetan on essentials, recognized the innovations in the latter's position, though he looked for some solid traditional support for Cajetan's eclecticism" (*Mystery of the Supernatural*, 7).

42 Malloy, "De Lubac on Natural Desire," 567.
43 See Louis Dupré, introduction to de Lubac, *Augustinianism and Modern Theology*, xv.
44 De Lubac, *The Mystery of the Supernatural*, 38.
45 De Lubac, *The Mystery of the Supernatural*, 39.
46 De Lubac, *The Mystery of the Supernatural*, 52.
47 De Lubac, *The Mystery of the Supernatural*, 54–5.
48 De Lubac, *The Mystery of the Supernatural*, 55.
49 Narcisse, "The Supernatural in Contemporary Theology," 296.
50 See de Lubac, *Surnaturel*, 483, and *The Mystery of the Supernatural*, 114–15.
51 De Lubac, *At the Service of the Church*, 184.
52 De Lubac, *Surnaturel*, 484.
53 For both a summary and a critique of this position, see Feingold, *The Natural Desire to See God*, 312, 386–7.
54 De Lubac, *Surnaturel*, 484.
55 De Lubac, *Surnaturel*, 486.
56 De Lubac, *The Mystery of the Supernatural*, 81–2.
57 "For the actual desire, though it certainly exists in every man, being inherent in his nature, is not in him *personaliter*, as the early writers say: it is only in him *simpliciter* or *naturaliter*" (De Lubac, *The Mystery of the Supernatural*, 216).
58 For an indication see chaps. 6–9 of *The Mystery of the Supernatural*. See also de Lubac's 1948 book *Paradoxes of Faith* (San Francisco: Ignatius, 1987).
59 De Lubac, *The Mystery of the Supernatural*, 140–66. The title of chapter 8 of *The Mystery of the Supernatural* is "A Paradox Rejected by Common Sense." See also Boersma, *Nouvelle Théologie and Sacramental Ontology*, 92.
60 Boersma, *Nouvelle Théologie and Sacramental Ontology*, 92–3.
61 De Lubac, *The Mystery of the Supernatural*, 108.
62 See de Lubac, *The Mystery of the Supernatural*, 7, 146–7.
63 Cited in de Lubac, *Augustinianism and Modern Theology*, 130. Feingold identifies Soto's position with the more general line of thinking associated with Scotus and his argument for the innate inclination to the beatific vision. Soto's position was diametrically opposed to the positions of both Cajetan and Sylvester of Ferrara: "De Soto's interpretation is important in that he seems to be the first major Thomist who interprets St. Thomas's natural desire to see God in Scotist terms, following the logic of Scotus's system rather than that of St. Thomas (Feingold, *The Natural Desire to See God*, 206).
64 De Lubac, *The Mystery of the Supernatural*, 140.
65 De Lubac, *Surnaturel*, 428.
66 De Lubac, *The Mystery of the Supernatural*, 178.

67 See Fergus Kerr, *Twentieth Century Catholic Theologians: From Neoscholasticism to Nuptial Mysticism* (Malden: Blackwell, 2007), 74; and Malloy, "De Lubac on Natural Desire," 572.
68 Kerr, *Twentieth Century Catholic Theologians*, 75.
69 De Lubac, *The Mystery of the Supernatural*, 47.
70 Malloy, "De Lubac on Natural Desire," 573
71 Malloy, "De Lubac on Natural Desire," 574. Though I am drawing on Malloy's helpful piece here, the choir metaphor is my own.
72 De Lubac, "Disappearance of the Sense of the Sacred," 231.
73 De Lubac, "Disappearance of the Sense of the Sacred," 231.
74 De Lubac, "Disappearance of the Sense of the Sacred," 232.
75 Mulcahy, *Aquinas's Notion of Pure Nature*, 141.
76 Mulcahy, *Aquinas's Notion of Pure Nature*, 141.
77 Cited in Peter Henrici, "A Sketch of Von Balthasar's Life," in *Hans Urs von Balthasar: His Life and Work*, ed. David L. Schindler (San Francisco: Ignatius, 1991), 13.
78 Henrici, "A Sketch of Von Balthasar's Life," 13.
79 Leo XIII, *Aeterni Patris*, http://w2.vatican.va/content/leo-xiii/en/encyclicals/documents/hf_l-xiii_enc_04081879_aeterni-patris.html, 31.
80 Leo XIII, *Aeterni Patris*, 31.
81 *Gravissime Nos*, cited in Jose Pereira, "Thomism and the Magisterium: From *Aeterni Patris* to *Vertitas Splendor*," *Logos: A Journal of Catholic Thought and Culture* 5.3 (2002): 156. Pereira points out that Pope Leo was commenting on the Fifth Congregation of the Jesuits (1593–94). The Fifth Congregation "had decreed that all members of the Society accept Aquinas as their Doctor and support his major propositions; otherwise, they were at liberty to believe what they thought right. In the words of the 56th decree of that Congregation: 'For those who are genuinely devoted to St. Thomas will not, it is certain, deviate from him except quite reluctantly and very rarely (*nisi gravate admodum et rarissime*)'" (156).
82 Jared Wicks, "A Note on 'Neo-Scholastic' Manuals of Theological Instruction, 1900–1960," *Josephinum Journal of Theology* 18.1 (2011): 242.
83 Jared Wicks, *Doing Theology* (New York: Paulist Press, 2009), 20.
84 Wicks, "A Note on 'Neo-Scholastic' Manuals," 242.
85 See Pereira, "Thomism and the Magisterium," 159–61, for a connection between Pius X's continuation of the themes of *Aterni Patris* and his condemnation of modernism.
86 Kerr, *Twentieth-Century Catholic Theologians*, 5.
87 De Lubac, "Disappearance of the Sense of the Sacred," 233–4.

88 De Lubac, "Disappearance of the Sense of the Sacred," 234.
89 Boersma, *Nouvelle Théologie and Sacramental Ontology*, 17.
90 Boersma, *Nouvelle Théologie and Sacramental Ontology*, 5.
91 John Paul II writes in *Fides et Ratio*: "While, on the one hand, philosophical thinking has succeeded in coming closer to the reality of human life and its forms of expression, it has also tended to pursue issues – existential, hermeneutical or linguistic – which ignore the radical question of the truth about personal existence, about being and about God. Hence we see among the men and women of our time, and not just in some philosophers, attitudes of widespread distrust of the human being's great capacity for knowledge. With a false modesty, people rest content with partial and provisional truths, no longer seeking to ask radical questions about the meaning and ultimate foundation of human, personal and social existence. In short, the hope that philosophy might be able to provide definitive answers to these questions has dwindled" (http://w2.vatican.va/content/john-paul-ii/en/encyclicals/documents/hf_jp-ii_enc_14091998_fides-et-ratio.html, 5).
92 "Les Orientations presents de la pensée religieuse," *Études* 249 (1946): 1–21. The English appears as "Present Orientations of Religious Thought," *Josephinum Journal of Theology* 18.1 (2011): 51–62.
93 Komonchak, "Humani Generis and Nouvelle Théologie," in *Ressourcement: A Movement for Renewal*, 143.
94 Komonchak, "Humani Generis and Nouvelle Théologie," 144.
95 See Erick H. Hedrick-Moser, "The Formation of Jean Daniélou's Vision for Catholicism in Secular France, 1925–1950," doctoral diss., Saint Louis University, 2015, 229–30. Hedrick-Moser insightfully interprets "Les Orientations" in the context of other papers, articles, and private correspondence that Daniélou wrote at this time.
96 Daniélou, "Present Orientations," 51–2.
97 Daniélou, "Present Orientations," 52.
98 Daniélou, "Present Orientations," 52.
99 Daniélou, "Present Orientations," 52.
100 Daniélou, "Present Orientations," 56–7.
101 Daniélou, "Present Orientations," 57.
102 Daniélou, "Present Orientations," 59.
103 Daniélou, "Present Orientations," 59.
104 Daniélou, "Present Orientations," 60–1.
105 Daniélou, "Present Orientations," 61.
106 Daniélou, "Present Orientations," 61.

107 Daniélou, "Present Orientations," 61.
108 "La nouvelle théologie, va-t-elle?" *Angelicum* 23 (1946): 126–145. The English translation appears as "Where Is the New Theology Leading Us?" *Josephinum Journal of Theology* 18.1 (2011): 63–78.
109 Garrigou-Lagrange, "Where Is the New Theology Leading Us?" 67.
110 Garrigou-Lagrange, "Where Is the New Theology Leading Us?" 66.
111 Garrigou-Lagrange reminds his readers that "on December 1, 1924, the Holy Office condemned 12 propositions taken from the philosophy of action, among which was number 5, on the new definition of truth" (67).
112 Garrigou-Lagrange, "Where Is the New Theology Leading Us?" 68.
113 Garrigou-Lagrange, "Where Is the New Theology Leading Us?" 69.
114 Garrigou-Lagrange, "Where Is the New Theology Leading Us?" 69.
115 Garrigou-Lagrange, "Where Is the New Theology Leading Us?" 73.
116 Garrigou-Lagrange, "Where Is the New Theology Leading Us?" 77.
117 Komonchak, "Humani Generis and Nouvelle Théologie," 147.
118 De Lubac, *A Theologian Speaks*, 3.
119 Komonchak, "Humani Generis and Nouvelle Théologie," 146.
120 De Lubac, *A Theologian Speaks*, 3.
121 Given the centrality of Lonergan's thought in this book, it is worth noting that Charles Boyer, SJ, directed Lonergan's doctoral thesis at the Pontifical Gregorian University in Rome; Lonergan defended his thesis in 1940.
122 Komonchak, "Theology and Culture at Mid-Century," 602.
123 Francesca Aran Murphy, "Gilson and the *Ressourcement*," in *Ressourcement: A Movement for Renewal*, 52–3.
124 Gabriel Flynn, "Introduction: The Twentieth-Century Renaissance in Catholic Theology," in *Ressourcement: A Movement for Renewal*, 12.
125 De Lubac, *At the Service of the Church*, 144.
126 De Lubac, *At the Service of the Church*, 144.
127 http://w2.vatican.va/content/pius-xii/en/encyclicals/documents/hf_p-xii_enc_12081950_humani-generis.html.
128 Pope Pius XII, *Humani Generis*, 6.
129 Pope Pius XII, *Humani Generis*, 17. Komonchak speculates: "Clearly referring to the views of Bouillard and de Lubac, these paragraphs remind one of Garrigou-Lagrange's articles. If he had any part in writing *Humani Generis*, I would place it here" ("Humani Generis and Novelle Théologie," 150).
130 Pope Pius XII, *Humani Generis*, 18.
131 Pope Pius XII, *Humani Generis*, 26.
132 De Lubac, *A Theologian Speaks*, 4.

133 Boersma, *Nouvelle Théologie and Sacramental Ontology*, 29. Boersma also mentions de Lubac's teaching on the Mystical Body of Christ as a possible target: "And de Lubac's *Corpus mysticum* seemed referenced when the encyclical argued that some theologians regarded the consecrated species merely as 'efficacious signs of the spiritual presence of Christ and of His intimate union with the faithful members of His Mystical Body'" (29, citing Pope Pius XII, *Humani Generis*, 26).

134 De Lubac's very measured account is that no "legitimate authority of the Church ever took action against me. Having failed to avert the storm, my superior general asked me (not through a formal written order, however) to interrupt my teaching and to inform the cardinal myself that I was doing so. I was, for several years, officially 'on leave' and was myself supposed to choose my personal 'replacement'" (De Lubac, *A Theologian Speaks*, 4).

135 Mulcahy, *Aquinas's Notion of Pure Nature*, 171.
136 De Lubac, *At the Service of the Church*, 143.
137 De Lubac, *At the Service of the Church*, 143–4.
138 Milbank, *The Suspended Middle*, 4–5.
139 De Lubac, "The Church in Crisis," *Theology Digest* 17.4 (1969): 312–25.
140 De Lubac, "The Church in Crisis," 315.
141 De Lubac, "The Church in Crisis," 317.
142 See de Lubac, "The Church in Crisis," 317, 319.
143 De Lubac, "The Church in Crisis," 322.
144 De Lubac, "The Church in Crisis," 320–1.
145 De Lubac, "The Church in Crisis," 323.
146 See de Lubac, "The Church in Crisis," 322–4.
147 De Lubac, "The Church in Crisis," 324–5.

2. *Ressourcement* and Neo-Thomism: A Narrative under Scrutiny, A Dialogue Renewed

1 Edward T. Oakes, "The *Surnaturel* Controversy," 625.
2 For a substantive snapshot of Rahner's theology of nature and grace, see Gerald A. McCool, ed., *A Rahner Reader*, (New York: Seabury, 1975), 173–244.
3 Walter Kasper, *Theology and Church*, trans. Margaret Kohl (New York: Crossroad, 1989), 1. See Oakes, "The *Surnaturel* Controversy," 625–6.
4 Kasper, *Theology and Church*, 1. See also Robert Barron's embrace of the Lubacian reading in *Exploring Catholic Theology: Essays on God, Liturgy, and Evangelization* (Grand Rapids: BakerAcademic, 2015), 100–1.

5 Oakes, "The *Surnaturel* Controversy," 626.
6 Long, *Natura Pura*, 4.
7 See Swafford, *Nature and Grace*. Swafford helpfully argues that the nineteenth-century thinker Matthias Scheeben serves as a model of integration.
8 See Matthew Levering and Reinhard Hütter, eds., *Ressourcement Thomism: Sacred Doctrine, the Sacraments, and the Moral Life* (Washington, DC: Catholic University of America Press, 2010); Jean-Pierre Torell, *Christ and Spirituality in St. Thomas Aquinas*, trans. Bernhard Blankenhorn (Washington, DC: Catholic University of America Press, 2011); Thomas Joseph White, *Incarnate Lord: A Thomistic Study in Christology* (Washington, DC: Catholic University of America Press, 2015); Matthew Levering, *Scripture and Metaphysics: Aquinas and the Renewal of Trinitarian Theology* (Malden: Blackwell, 2004); Thomas G. Guarino, "Nature and Grace: Seeking the Delicate Balance," *Josephinum Journal of Theology* 18.1 (2011): 151–62; Swafford, *Nature and Grace*; and Anthony Sciglitano, "Leaving Neo-Scholasticism Behind: Aspirations and Anxieties," *Josephinum Journal of Theology* 18.1 (2011): 216–39. This is a small sample of a much larger body of literature.
9 William F. Murphy, Jr, "Thomism and the *Noevelle Theologie*: A Dialogue Renewed?" *Josephinum Journal of Theology* 18.1 (2011): 6. See also Robert M. Doran, *What Is Systematic Theology?* (Toronto: University of Toronto Press, 2005), for a different but not unrelated proposal for an integration of neo-Thomism, the *Ressourcement* project, and the praxis component expressed in certain expressions of liberation theology: Catholic theology "will be able to go forward confidently into the future, with some hope of generating a sequence of interrelated systematic positions, to the extent that some principle or set of principles can be expressed that will relate these three emphases to one another and integrate them" (87).
10 Sciglitano, "Leaving Neo-Scholasticism Behind," 217.
11 Hütter, *Dust Bound for Heaven*, 138.
12 Hütter, *Dust Bound for Heaven*, 138.
13 Hütter, *Dust Bound for Heaven*, 139.
14 Hütter, *Dust Bound for Heaven*, 141.
15 David Grumett, "Henri de Lubac: Looking for Books to Read the World," in *Ressourcement: A Movement for Renewal*, ed. Gabriel Flynn and Paul D. Murray (New York: Oxford University Press, 2012), 237.
16 Feingold, *The Natural Desire to See God*, xxxv.
17 Feingold, *The Natural Desire to See God*, 11.
18 Feingold, *The Natural Desire to See God*, xxxvi.

19 Feingold, *The Natural Desire to See God*, 443.
20 Feingold, *The Natural Desire to See God*, 442.
21 Feingold, *The Natural Desire to See God*, 11.
22 "For example, when St. Thomas speaks of an *inclination* coming from the very nature of the will, it is clear that he is referring to an innate appetite. On the contrary, when he speaks of a natural desire that is a *movement* or *act* of the will, aroused by prior knowledge, then it is clear that he is speaking of an elicited desire" (16). Feingold recognizes, however, that for Aquinas "the term 'innate' is roughly synonymous with 'natural,' and thus it is not used to distinguish two types of natural desire" (15n20).
23 Feingold, *The Natural Desire to See God*, 15.
24 Drawing on the work of Torrell, Feingold places the texts in the following order: (1) 1260–64: *Summa contra Gentiles* III, chaps. 25, 50–1, 57; (2) 1265–67: *Compendium theologiae* I, chap. 104; (3) 1266–68: *Summa theologiae* I, q. 12, a. 1; (4) 1265–68: *Super I epistolam ad Corinthios lectura* 13:12; (5) 1269–70: *Super Evangelium S. Matthaei lectura* 5:8; (6) 1270–72: *Super Evangelium S. Ioannis lectura* 1:18; (7) 1270–71: *Summa theologiae* I–II, q. 3, a. 8; (8) 1271–72: *Quaestio disputata de virtutibus in communi* q. un., a. 10. This is simply a list of the key passages. See Feingold, *The Natural Desire to See God*, 30–4.
25 Feingold, *The Natural Desire to See God*, 34.
26 Feingold, *The Natural Desire to See God*, 34.
27 Feingold, *The Natural Desire to See God*, 44.
28 Feingold, *The Natural Desire to See God*, 44.
29 Feingold, *The Natural Desire to See God*, 45.
30 Feingold, *The Natural Desire to See God*, 45. This is largely de Lubac's interpretation. In appendix D of *Surnaturel*, for example, de Lubac considers whether Thomas wishes to affirm the natural desire to see God. He concludes that our beatitude lies in one supernatural end. See de Lubac, *Surnaturel*, 471.
31 Feingold, *The Natural Desire to See God*, 433.
32 These four states are outlined in Feingold, *The Natural Desire to See God*, 433, on which my summary relies.
33 Feingold, *The Natural Desire to See God*, 434.
34 Feingold, *The Natural Desire to See God*, 434.
35 Feingold, *The Natural Desire to See God*, 433.
36 Feingold, *The Natural Desire to See God*, 434.
37 Feingold, *The Natural Desire to See God*, 435.
38 Nicholas J. Healy, "Henri de Lubac on Nature and Grace: A Note on Some Recent Contributions to the Debate," *Communio* 35 (Winter 2008): 535–64.
39 De Lubac, *The Mystery of the Supernatural*, 76.

40 Hütter, *Dust Bound for Heaven*, 151. Feingold remains unsatisfied with de Lubac's move from a distinction of twofold gift as a "phantom of the imagination" to a legitimate distinction. See Feingold, *The Natural Desire to See God*, 317ff.
41 Healy, "Henri de Lubac on Nature and Grace," 551.
42 Healy, "Henri de Lubac on Nature and Grace," 551.
43 Healy, "Henri de Lubac on Nature and Grace," 551.
44 Feingold, *The Natural Desire to See God*, 385.
45 Healy, "Henri de Lubac on Nature and Grace," 563.
46 Healy, "Henri de Lubac on Nature and Grace," 562.
47 Healy, "Henri de Lubac on Nature and Grace," 564.
48 De Lubac, *The Mystery of the Supernatural*, 54.
49 De Lubac, *Surnaturel*, 456.
50 De Lubac, *The Mystery of the Supernatural*, 200–1.
51 De Lubac, *The Mystery of the Supernatural*, 201.
52 *The Divine Comedy: Inferno*, canto 4, vv. 27–30, 41–2.
53 De Lubac, *The Mystery of the Supernatural*, 54.
54 See also Serge-Thomas Bonino's important essay "The Theory of Limbo and the Mystery of the Supernatural in St. Thomas Aquinas," in *Surnaturel*, 117–54: "Even if today we must give up the doctrine of limbo and consider it merely as a thought experiment, the study of this thematic element in St. Thomas remains a useful path to understanding his conception of man and his destiny" (118).
55 Malloy, "De Lubac on Natural Desire," 586.
56 Feingold, *The Natural Desire to See God*, 352.
57 Malloy, "De Lubac on Natural Desire," 586.
58 Feingold, *The Natural Desire to See God*, 352.
59 Oakes, "The *Surnaturel* Controversy," 640–1.
60 Pelagius was acknowledging the passage from John 3:5: "No one can enter the kingdom of God unless he is born of water and the Spirit."
61 Oakes, "Catholic Eschatology," 422.
62 Oakes, "Catholic Eschatology," 421–3.
63 *Gaudium et Spes*, http://www.vatican.va/archive/hist_councils/ii_vatican_council/documents/vat-ii_const_19651207_gaudium-et-spes_en.html, 22.
64 Oakes, "The *Surnaturel* Controversy," 642ff. The theme of solidarity also plays a part in the International Theological Commission's document "The Hope of Salvation for Infants Who Die Without Being Baptized," http://www.vatican.va/roman_curia/congregations/cfaith/cti_documents/rc_con_cfaith_doc_20070419_un-baptised-infants_en.html, 88.

65 Oakes, "Catholic Eschatology," 429.
66 International Theological Commission, "The Hope of Salvation for Infants," 93; Oakes, "Catholic Eschatology," 429. See also Basil Cole, "Is Limbo Ready to Be Abolished? Limbo Revisited," *Nova et Vetera*, English ed., 6.2 (208): 403–18.
67 Benedict XVI, *Spe Salvi*, http://w2.vatican.va/content/benedict-xvi/en/encyclicals/documents/hf_ben-xvi_enc_20071130_spe-salvi.html, 14.
68 This citation and the rest of the citations in this paragraph are from *Spe Salvi*, 48.
69 Long, *Natura Pura*, 85.
70 De Lubac, *The Mystery of the Supernatural*, 54.
71 De Lubac, *The Mystery of the Supernatural*, 55.
72 De Lubac, *The Mystery of the Supernatural*, 59.
73 De Lubac, *The Mystery of the Supernatural*, 63, 64.
74 Mansini, "The Abiding Theological Significance of Henri de Lubac's *Surnaturel*," *The Thomist* 73 (2009): 618. Though Mansini argues for the ongoing significance of de Lubac's work, he is also highly critical of his systematic positions.
75 De Lubac, *The Mystery of the Supernatural*, 69.
76 De Lubac, *The Mystery of the Supernatural*, 71.
77 De Lubac, *The Mystery of the Supernatural*, 73.
78 De Lubac, *The Mystery of the Supernatural*, 231.
79 De Lubac, *The Mystery of the Supernatural*, 230.
80 That I identify here a common line of reasoning in de Lubac and Balthasar is not meant to indicate an easy collapse of one into the other. Balthasar, of course, wrote a book in homage to de Lubac, whom he called his friend and master, published as *Theology of Henri de Lubac: An Overview* (San Francisco: Ignatius, 1991). But others have written on what they understand to be significant differences between the two thinkers. John Milbank, for example, in *The Suspended Middle* argues that a "careful reading of von Balthasar's account of the supernatural in his Barth book suggests a certain divergence from de Lubac and a kind of Germanic Protestant residue in the Francophile Swiss theologian" (66). Balthasar seems "to edge de Lubac's position slightly towards a Barthian 'grace over-against nature'" (67). For Milbank's full critique, which includes Balthasar's trilogy, see chap. 6 of *The Suspended Middle*.
81 Balthasar, *The Theology of Karl Barth*, 283.
82 Balthasar, *The Theology of Karl Barth*, 284. A similar claim is expressed in *Theo-Logic I: Truth of the World*, trans. Adrian J. Walker (San Francisco: Ignatius, 2000): "the supernatural takes root in the deepest structures of

being, leavens them through and through, and permeates them like a breath or an omnipresent fragrance. It is not only impossible, it would be sheer folly to attempt at all costs to banish and uproot this fragrance of supernatural truth from all philosophical inquiry; the supernatural has impregnated nature so deeply that there is simply no way to reconstruct it in its pure state (*natura pura*)" (12).

83 Balthasar, *The Theology of Karl Barth*, 284.
84 Balthasar, *The Theology of Karl Barth*, 284.
85 Balthasar, *The Theology of Karl Barth*, 285.
86 Balthasar, *The Theology of Karl Barth*, 286.
87 Balthasar, *The Theology of Karl Barth*, 290.
88 Balthasar, *The Theology of Karl Barth*, 287.
89 Balthasar, *The Theology of Karl Barth*, 288.
90 Balthasar, *The Theology of Karl Barth*, 285–6, 291. Balthasar referred to this cross-fertilization of philosophy and theology as movement within the "suspended middle." In *The Theology of Henri de Lubac*, he writes: "De Lubac soon realized that his position moved into a suspended middle in which he could not practice any philosophy without its transcendence into theology, but also no theology without its essential inner substructure of philosophy. This center has been the vital environment of his thought from the beginning to the present, at the beginning in opposition to the modern dichotomy that Cajetan has projected into Thomas, today in opposition to a new form of Christian schizophrenia that yields so much to post-Kantian scientific rationalism and secularism ... that the only thing left for the sphere of faith is a groundless fideism" (15).
91 Feingold, *The Natural Desire to See God*, 335.
92 Feingold, *The Natural Desire to See God*, 336.
93 Feingold, *The Natural Desire to See God*, 337.
94 Long, *Natura Pura*, 2.
95 Long, *Natura Pura*, 1.
96 Long, *Natura Pura*, 84–5.
97 Long, *Natura Pura*, 201.
98 Long, *Natura Pura*, 200–1.
99 Long, *Natura Pura*, 98.
100 Long, *Natura Pura*, 100 (emphasis in the original).
101 David Braine, "The Debate between Henri de Lubac and His Critics," *Nova et Vetera*, English ed., 6.3 (2008): 570.
102 Braine, "The Debate between Henri de Lubac and His Critics," 571.
103 Jean-Pierre Torrell, "Nature and Grace in Thomas Aquinas," *Surnaturel*, 155–88.

104 Torrell, "Nature and Grace in Thomas Aquinas," 169.
105 Torrell, "Nature and Grace in Thomas Aquinas," 169.
106 Torrell, "Nature and Grace in Thomas Aquinas," 171.
107 Torrell, "Nature and Grace in Thomas Aquinas," 179.
108 John Milbank, *The Suspended Middle*, 89.
109 *Letters of Étienne Gilson to Henri de Lubac*, annotated by Henri de Lubac (San Francisco: Ignatius, 1988), 82–3.
110 *Letters of Étienne Gilson to Henri de Lubac*, 81.
111 *Letters of Étienne Gilson to Henri de Lubac*, 82.
112 De Lubac, *The Mystery of the Supernatural*, 141.
113 De Lubac, *The Mystery of the Supernatural*, 141–2.
114 De Lubac, *Surnaturel*, 428: "Le surnaturel n'est certes pas anormal a la facon de l' 'effet surnaturel' qu'est le miracle."
115 De Lubac, *The Mystery of the Supernatural*, 143. In chapter 7 of *The Natural Desire to See God*, Feingold attempts to vindicate Cajetan from de Lubac's caricature.
116 Feingold, *The Natural Desire to See God*, 105.
117 Feingold, *The Natural Desire to See God*, 107.
118 Feingold, *The Natural Desire to See God*, 112.
119 Feingold, *The Natural Desire to See God*, 113.
120 See also Christopher J. Malloy, "De Lubac on Natural Desire: Difficulties and Antitheses," *Nova et Vetera*, English ed., 9.3 (2011): 618.
121 Healy, "Henri de Lubac on Nature and Grace," 562. Steven A. Long argues in a more critical manner that de Lubac's failure to fully appreciate "specific obediential potency" has severe consequences for the life of the church in the world (cf. 28–36). De Lubac drained the natural order of its own distinctive finality and intelligibility. "It is not the first time," Long writes, "that a physician unintentionally has communicated the plague he nobly sought to resist" (44). In the same essay cited above, Healy critically evaluates Long's work (see 558ff.).
122 Feingold, *The Natural Desire to See God*, 276.
123 Milbank, *The Suspended Middle*, 84.
124 Feingold, *The Natural Desire to See God*, 276.
125 Milbank, *The Suspended Middle*, 86.
126 Duffy, *The Graced Horizon*, 76. For a defense of "pure nature" and a critique of de Lubac, see Feingold, *The Natural Desire to See God*, chaps. 14–16.
127 Milbank, *The Suspended Middle*, 21.
128 Milbank, *The Suspended Middle*, 23.
129 Feingold, *The Natural Desire to See God*, 394.

224 Notes to pages 60–67

130 Feingold, *The Natural Desire to See God*, 394.
131 Feingold, *The Natural Desire to See God*, 395.
132 See Buckley, *Denying and Disclosing God*, chaps. 1 and 2.
133 Buckley, *Denying and Disclosing God*, 37.
134 Long, *Natura Pura*, 196.
135 Long, *Natura Pura*, 196–7.
136 Long, *Natura Pura*, 186.
137 Bushlack, *Politics for a Pilgrim Church*, 144ff.
138 Long, *Natura Pura*, 178.
139 Long, *Natura Pura*, 178.
140 Bushlack, *Politics for a Pilgrim Church*, 148.
141 Bushlack, *Politics for a Pilgrim Church*, 151, 152.
142 Bushlack, *Politics for a Pilgrim Church*, 129.

3. The Erotic Roots of Intellectual Desire

1 See Frederick G. Lawrence, "The Fragility of Consciousness: Lonergan and the Postmodern Concern for the Other," in *The Fragility of Consciousness: Faith, Reason, and the Human Good*, ed. Randall S. Rosenberg and Kevin M. Vander Schel (Toronto: University of Toronto Press, 2017), 229–277.
2 See Benedict XVI, "The Regensburg Lecture," published an as appendix to James V. Schall, *The Regensburg Lecture* (South Bend: St. Augustine's Press, 2007).
3 I draw here mainly on David Tracy's *The Analogical Imagination: Christian Theology and the Culture of Pluralism* (New York: Crossroad, 1981). A fuller discussion would require an engagement with the many nuances of both strands of thinking. See, for example, D. Stephen Long, *Speaking of God: Theology, Language, and Truth* (Grand Rapids: Eerdmans, 2009). See also the many helpful essays in *The Analogy of Being: Invention of the Antichrist or the Wisdom of God*, ed. Thomas Joseph White (Grand Rapids: Eerdmans, 2011). Also noteworthy is the new translation of and introduction to Erich Przywara, *Analogia Entis: Metaphysics: Original Structure and Universal Rhythm*, trans. John R. Betz and David Bentley Hart (Grand Rapids: Eerdmans, 2014).
4 Tracy, *The Analogical Imagination*, 408.
5 Tracy, *The Analogical Imagination*, 409.
6 Tracy, *The Analogical Imagination*, 413.
7 Tracy, *The Analogical Imagination*, 413.
8 Tracy, *The Analogical Imagination*, 415.
9 Tracy, *The Analogical Imagination*, 417.

10 Thomas Joseph White, "Imperfect Happiness and the Final End of Man: Thomas Aquinas and the Paradigm of Nature-Grace Orthodoxy," *The Thomist* 78 (2014): 247–89.
11 White, "Imperfect Happiness," 247. In any discussion of Barth and analogy, one must be attentive to dispute over the development of his thinking on this issue. See Bruce L. McCormack, "Karl Barth's Version of an 'Analogy of Being': A Dialectical No and Yes to Roman Catholicism," in *The Analogy of Being: Invention of the Antichrist or the Wisdom of God?*, 88–144.
12 White, "Imperfect Happiness," 249.
13 White, "Imperfect Happiness," 247.
14 White, "Imperfect Happiness," 247–8.
15 White, "Imperfect Happiness," 250.
16 White, "Imperfect Happiness," 250.
17 In this section, I limit the analysis to James Alison, *The Joy of Being Wrong: Original Sin through Easter Eyes* (New York: Crossroad, 1998).
18 Alison, *The Joy of Being Wrong*, 27.
19 Alison, *The Joy of Being Wrong*, 45.
20 Alison, *The Joy of Being Wrong*, 45–6.
21 Alison, *The Joy of Being Wrong*, 46.
22 Alison, *The Joy of Being Wrong*, 47.
23 Alison, *The Joy of Being Wrong*, 47.
24 Marion, *The Erotic Phenomenon*, trans. Stephen E. Lewis (Chicago: University of Chicago Press, 2007). A fuller integration of Marion's voice in the Lubacian-Thomist conversation would require attention to his essay dedicated to Henri de Lubac. See Marion, "What is the *Ego* Capable of? Divinization and Domination: *Capable / Capax*," in *Cartesian Questions: Method and Metaphysics*, trans. Jeffrey L. Kosky, 67–95 (Chicago: University of Chicago Press, 1999). See also Rober, *Recognizing the Gift*, chap. 3.
25 This section focuses on Marion's critique of contemporary philosophy and its loss of the primacy of desire. The more intersubjective and sexual dimensions of the erotic reduction are discussed in chapter 6, and can be read as largely in sympathy with Alison's emphasis on receptivity and gratuity.
26 Marion, *The Erotic Phenomenon*, 3.
27 Marion, *The Erotic Phenomenon*, 2.
28 Marion, *The Erotic Phenomenon*, 2.
29 Descartes is perhaps Marion's most prized interlocutor. See, for example, his *Cartesian Questions* and *On Descartes' Metaphysical Prism: The Constitution and Limits of Onto-theo-logy in Cartesian Thought*, trans. Jeffrey L. Kosky (Chicago: University of Chicago Press, 1999).

30 Marion, *The Erotic Phenomenon*, 6.
31 Marion, *The Erotic Phenomenon*, 7.
32 Marion, *The Erotic Phenomenon*, 8.
33 Marion, *The Erotic Phenomenon*, 11.
34 Narcisse, "The Supernatural in Contemporary Theology," 308.
35 Narcisse, "The Supernatural in Contemporary Theology," 308.
36 Lonergan, *Verbum: Word and Idea in Aquinas*, 105.
37 Lonergan, *Insight*, 372.
38 See Lonergan, *Insight*, 275–9.
39 See chap. 11, "Self-Affirmation of the Knower," in *Insight*, 343–71.
40 Lonergan, *Ontological and Psychological Constitution of Christ*, in *CWL* 7, trans. Michael G. Shields (Toronto: University of Toronto, 2002), 255.
41 Lonergan, *Ontological and Psychological Constitution of Christ*, 255.
42 Walker Percy, "Symbol as Need," in *The Message in the Bottle: How Queer Man Is, How Queer Language Is, and What One Has to Do with the Other* (New York: Farrar, Straus, and Giroux, 1985), 297.
43 Augustine, *The Confessions*, ed. David Vincent Meconi, trans. Maria Boulding (San Francisco: Ignatius, 2012), 162.
44 Augustine, *Confessions*, 163.
45 Augustine, *Confessions*, 186.
46 Anders Nygren, "Eros and Agape," in *Eros, Agape, and Philia: Readings in the Philosophy of Love*, ed. Alan Stroble (St. Paul: Paragon House, 1998), 93.
47 Lonergan, *Insight*, 247.
48 Lonergan, *Insight*, 28.
49 Lonergan, *Insight*, 28–9.
50 In this paragraph, I am drawing on *Method in Theology*, 11.
51 Lonergan, *Method in Theology*, 53, 55.
52 Lonergan, *Method in Theology*, 55.
53 Lonergan, *Insight*, 706.
54 Thomas Joseph White, *Wisdom in the Face of Modernity: A Study in Thomistic Natural Theology* (Ave Maria: Sapientia, 2009), xxvi.
55 White, *Wisdom in the Face of Modernity*, xxiv.
56 White, *Wisdom in the Face of Modernity*, xxiv. It is still wise to acknowledge the real limitations of such knowledge. As John R. Betz notes with reference to the position of Erich Przywara: "But if the *analogia entis* is essentially a code word for our natural knowledge of God, this knowledge, as merely natural knowledge, is severely limited. Indeed, this is why natural theology, without the light of revelation, is always on the verge of idolatrously collapsing the distinction between Creator and creature that the *analogia entis* hold open. In other words, positively stated, it is only

in the light of revelation that the full scope of the *analogia entis*, both the radical immanence *and* radical transcendence of God, appears" ("After Barth: A New Introduction to Erich Przywara's *Analogia Entis*," in *The Analogy of Being: Invention of the Antichrist or the Wisdom of God?*, 52).

57 David Bentley Hart, *The Experience of God: Being, Consciousness, Bliss* (New Haven: Yale University Press, 2013).
58 Hart, *The Experience of God*, 2.
59 Hart, *The Experience of God*, 152.
60 Hart, *The Experience of God*, 152.
61 Lonergan, *Insight*, 695.
62 Hefling, "Revelation and/as Insight," in *The Importance of Insight: Essays in Honour of Michael Vertin*, ed. John J. Liptay Jr. and David S. Liptay (Toronto: University of Toronto Press, 2007), 103.
63 Lonergan, *Insight*, 669–671.
64 Hart, *The Experience of God*, 234.
65 Hart, *The Experience of God*, 234.
66 Lonergan, "Theology in Its New Context," in *A Second Collection*, ed. W.F.J. Ryan and Bernard J. Tyrrell (Toronto: University of Toronto Press, 1996), 55.
67 Lonergan, "Theology in Its New Context," 63–4.
68 Lonergan, "Theology in Its New Context," 67.
69 Lonergan, *Method in Theology*, 101–3.
70 Lonergan, "Lecture 3: The Relationship between Philosophy of God and the Functional Specialty 'Systematics,'" in *Philosophical and Theological Papers 1965–1980*, CWL 17 (Toronto: University of Toronto Press, 2004), 207.
71 Lonergan, "Lecture 3," 207.
72 Lonergan, "Lecture 3," 207.
73 Lonergan, "Lecture 3," 207.
74 Lonergan, "Lecture 3," 208.
75 Lonergan, "Lecture 3," 209.
76 As Bernard Tyrrell writes, Lonergan regularly noted that if it took such "an acute genius as St. Augustine to realise that he had identified his notion of the 'really real' with body, how much greater confusion must exist in those of lesser talent who have never clearly and distinctly faced the problem, let alone resolved it, and how very important it is for these individuals in some way at least to grasp a certain need for conversion. One might extend the remark to the spheres of the ethical and the religious" (*Bernard Lonergan's Philosophy of God* [Notre Dame: University of Notre Dame Press, 1974], 32).
77 See *Philosophical and Theological Papers 1965–1980*, CWL 17, 157–218.

78 Lonergan, "Horizons," *CWL* 17, 11.
79 Lonergan, "Lecture 1: Philosophy of God," *CWL* 17, 172.
80 Chapter 19 contains Lonergan's philosophical argument for the existence of God, which we briefly considered above. He later reformed his understanding of the proper context for such an argument, as the paragraph suggests.
81 Lonergan, *Philosophical and Theological Papers 1965–1980*, CWL 17, 172.
82 Lonergan, "Lecture 3," 208.
83 Lonergan, "Lecture 3," 202.
84 Lonergan, "The Subject," in *A Second Collection*, 71.
85 Lonergan, "The Subject," 72.
86 Lonergan, "Lecture 3," 203.
87 Lonergan, "Lecture 3," 203.
88 Note the first sentence of *Method in Theology*: "Theology mediates between a cultural matrix and the significance and role of religion in that matrix" (xi).
89 Joseph C. Mudd, *Eucharist as Meaning: Critical Metaphysics and Contemporary Sacramental Theology* (Collegeville: Liturgical Press, 2014), 39.
90 Mudd, *Eucharist as Meaning*, 61.
91 Lonergan, *Insight*, 214.
92 For a more detailed discussion of dramatic bias, see chap. 6 of *Insight*, 196–230; for discussion of individual, group, and general bias, see chap. 7, 232–69.
93 Miller, *The Quest for God and the Good Life* (Washington, DC: Catholic University of America Press, 2013), 125.
94 Lonergan, *Insight*, 249.
95 Lonergan, *Insight*, 249.
96 Lonergan, *Insight*, 250.
97 Lonergan, *Insight*, 251.
98 Miller, *The Quest for God and the Good Life*, 133.
99 Lonergan, *Method in Theology*, 55.
100 Lonergan, *Method in Theology*, 55.
101 Lonergan, *Insight*, 257.
102 Lonergan, *Insight*, 257.

4. Concretely Operating Nature: Lonergan on the Natural Desire to See God

1 Narcisse, "The Supernatural in Contemporary Theology," 308.
2 Lonergan, *Phenomenology and Logic*, 350.
3 Lonergan, *Insight*, 769.

4 Stebbins, *The Divine Initiative*, xvii–xviii.
5 Frederick E. Crowe, "Introduction to 'De ente supernaturali,'" *Early Latin Theology*, CWL 19, 53–60.
6 Bernard Lonergan, *Grace and Freedom: Operative Grace in the Thought of St. Thomas Aquinas*, CWL 1, ed. Frederick E. Crowe and Robert M. Doran (Toronto: University of Toronto Press, 2000).
7 Lonergan, *Grace and Freedom*, 6.
8 Lonergan, *Grace and Freedom*, 7.
9 Lonergan, *Grace and Freedom*, 15–20.
10 Neil Ormerod, *Creation, Grace, and Redemption* (Maryknoll: Orbis, 2007), 13–16.
11 Lonergan, *Phenomenology and Logic*, 354–5.
12 This distinction between imperfect and perfect happiness in Aquinas is germane to the argument of Thomas Joseph White in his essay "Imperfect Happiness and the Final End of Man." White focuses on "Aquinas's interpretation of Aristotelian contemplation of God via natural causes as a form of 'imperfect natural happiness'" (250). He argues that the "natural desire for the vision of God is a rational, philosophical desire and is distinct from the hope for the beatific vision inspired by infused theological virtues" (250–1). Our natural desire is indicative of a teleological openness to God and should not be regarded as a "natural inclination toward the formally supernatural as such" (251). As White notes: "Against Barth and with de Lubac, there exists a natural point of contact in us such that grace is not alien to human nature and can lead human nature without violence through the ascent upward into the supernatural life of God. It does so in profound accord with nature's own highest inclinations and through an accomplishment of those aspirations that nature cannot realize for itself. Aristotelian philosophy thus vindicates Augustinian theology. An Aristotelian sense of the imperfection of the natural happiness disposes us to see the ways that the restless heart of man in the economy of God's grace can be elevated to find its most perfect rest only in the supernatural life of God" (288–9).
13 Lonergan, *Phenomenology and Logic*, 354.
14 Lonergan, *Phenomenology and Logic*, 354–5.
15 Lonergan, *Insight*, 428.
16 Ormerod, *Creation, Grace, and Redemption*, 119.
17 Lonergan, "The Natural Desire to See God," *Collection*, CWL 4, 90. Feingold questions Lonergan's marginalization of "pure nature": "The mature de Lubac, in harmony with *Humani Generis*, has argued that the possibility of a state of pure nature should be affirmed. Nevertheless, he holds it to be

basically irrelevant to defending or understanding the gratuitousness of grace. Bernard Lonergan concurs with de Lubac on both points, and holds it to be a 'marginal theorem'" (*The Natural Desire to See God*, 437). "Yet if this were really a marginal theorem," Feingold poses, "it would be hard to understand the degree of controversy generated by it for over half a millennium. Great historical debates reveal critical underlying problems. In defense of Lonergan, it is true that this problem, like many others, has at times been formulated in ways that were less helpful, obscuring what is at stake" (437).

18 Lonergan, "The Natural Desire to See God," 81–91.
19 Lonergan, "The Natural Desire to See God," 84.
20 Joshua Brotherton highlights this tension with reference to both Feingold and Mansini. See his "The Integrity of Nature in the Grace-Freedom Dynamic: Lonergan's Critique of Báñezian Thomism," *Theological Studies* 75.3 (2014): 537–63.
21 Feingold, *The Natural Desire to See God*, 211.
22 Feingold, *The Natural Desire to See God*, 217.
23 Feingold, *The Natural Desire to See God*, 217.
24 Feingold, *The Natural Desire to See God*, 276.
25 Feingold, *The Natural Desire to See God*, 432–3.
26 Lonergan, "The Supernatural Order," 141.
27 Lonergan, "The Natural Desire to See God," 84.
28 Guy Mansini, "Lonergan on the Natural Desire in the Light of Feingold," *Nova et Vetera*, English ed., 5.1 (2007): 191.
29 Mansini, "Lonergan on the Natural Desire," 191.
30 Lonergan, "The Natural Desire to See God," 87. Mansini mistakenly indicates that this passage is on p. 90.
31 Mansini, "Lonergan on the Natural Desire," 192.
32 Lonergan, "Excursus: The Natural Desire of the Intellect," in *The Triune God: Systematics*, CWL 12, ed. Robert M. Doran and H. Daniel Monsour, trans. Michael G. Shields (Toronto: University of Toronto Press, 2007), 645–59.
33 Lonergan, "Excursus," 647; emphasis added.
34 Lonergan, "Excursus," 653.
35 Brian Himes, "Lonergan's Position on the Natural Desire to See God and Aquinas' Metaphysical Theology of Creation and Participation," *Heythrop Journal* 54.5 (September 2013): 777.
36 Lonergan, "Excursus," 649.
37 Himes, "Lonergan's Position," 777.
38 Lonergan, "Excursus," 657.

39 Mansini, "The Abiding Theological Significance of Henri de Lubac's *Surnaturel*," 605–6.
40 I develop a more fully worked out relationship between this natural desire and sanctifying grace later in the book in response to this important challenge from Feingold's third and fourth states of the human desire for God. See chapter 5.
41 Lonergan, "The Supernatural Order," 147.
42 Lonergan, "The Natural Desire to See God," 84.
43 Lonergan, "The Natural Desire to See God," 84; emphasis added.
44 Stebbins, *The Divine Initiative*, 172.
45 Lonergan, "The Natural Desire to See God," 84–85.
46 Stebbins, *The Divine Initiative*, 172. It is helpful to note Brotherton's slight tension with Stebbins's exposition, though he certainly acknowledges his debt to Stebbins's work. Brotherton suggests that Stebbins wants to align Lonergan a little closer to de Lubac's position than is merited. See Brotherton, "Lonergan's Critique," 541n13.
47 Lonergan, "The Natural Desire to See God," 85.
48 Malloy, "De Lubac on Natural Desire," 594–5n115.
49 Malloy, "De Lubac on Natural Desire," 595n115.
50 Lonergan, "The Natural Desire to See God," 85.
51 Stebbins, *The Divine Initiative*, 176.
52 Matthew L. Lamb, *Solidarity with Victims: Toward a Theology of Social Transformation* (New York: Crossroad, 1982), 126–7.
53 Miller, *The Quest for God*, 14.
54 Miller, *The Quest for God*, 14.
55 See Lonergan, *Insight*, 57ff.
56 For a thorough discussion of the complementarity of classical and statistical investigations, see chapter 4 of *Insight*, 126–62.
57 Cynthia Crysdale, "Revisioning Natural Law: From the Classicist Paradigm to Emergent Probability," *Theological Studies* 56.3 (September 1995): 471.
58 Lonergan, *Insight*, 141.
59 Lonergan, *Insight*, 149–50.
60 Stoeger, "Physics and Astronomy in a Catholic Framework," in *Teaching the Tradition: Catholic Themes in Academic Disciplines*, ed. John J. Piderit and Melanie M. Morey (Oxford: Oxford University Press, 2012), 367. I integrate several insights from Stoeger in this section. In my estimation, he articulates several realities that express in an accessible way what Lonergan is arguing in his account of emergent probability.
61 Stoeger, "Physics and Astronomy," 367.

62 Stoeger, "Physics and Astronomy," 367.
63 Stoeger, "Physics and Astronomy," 365.
64 See, for example, Cynthia Crysdale and Neil Ormerod, *Creator God, Evolving World* (Minneapolis: Fortress, 2013); Nancy Murphy and William R. Stoeger, eds., *Evolution and Emergence: Systems, Organisms, Persons* (Oxford: Oxford University Press, 2007); and Stoeger, "Contemporary Physics and the Ontological Status of the Laws of Nature," in *Quantum Cosmology and the Laws of Nature: Scientific Connections on Divine Action*, ed. Robert John Russell, Nancy Murphy, and C.J. Isham (Vatican City State: Vatican Observatory, 1993), 209–34.
65 William R. Stoeger, "Physics and Astronomy," 368.
66 Peter F. Ryan, "How Can the Beatific Vision Both Fulfill Human Nature and Be Utterly Gratuitous?" *Gregorianum* 83.4 (2002): 748.
67 Ryan, "How Can the Beatific Vision, 747.
68 Ryan, "How Can the Beatific Vision," 749–50.
69 Ryan, "How Can the Beatific Vision, 750.
70 Ryan, "How Can the Beatific Vision, 753.
71 *Gaudium et Spes*, 39.
72 Lonergan, *Insight*, 622.
73 Lonergan, "*Insight* Revisited," in *A Second Collection*, 272.
74 See Lonergan, *Method in Theology*, 47.
75 Lawrence, *The Fragility of Consciousness*, 332.
76 Lonergan, *Method in Theology*, xi.
77 Lonergan, "The Absence of God in Modern Culture," in *A Second Collection*, 101.
78 Lonergan, *Method in Theology*, xi.
79 For an elaboration, see Lawrence, *The Fragility of Consciousness*, 333–41.
80 Doran, *Theology and the Dialectics of History*, 118.
81 Doran, *Theology and the Dialectics of History*, 96–7.
82 Ormerod, "The Grace-Nature Distinction and the Construction of a Systematic Theology," *Theological Studies* 75.3 (2014): 530.
83 Ormerod, "The Grace-Nature Distinction," 531–2.
84 Ormerod, "The Grace-Nature Distinction," 532.
85 Ormerod, "The Grace-Nature Distinction," 530.
86 Malloy, "De Lubac on Natural Desire," 618–19.
87 It is also relevant to note Lonergan's critique of Hegelian sublation: "Hegel's sublation is through a reconciling third concept, but our development is both the accumulation of insights moving to higher viewpoints and the reversal of the aberrations that were brought about by the interference of alien desire" (*Insight*, 447).
88 Stoeger, "Physics and Astronomy," 365.

89 Stoeger, "Physics and Astronomy," 366.
90 The following analysis is based largely on Lonergan's "Mission and Spirit," in *A Third Collection*, ed. Frederick E. Crowe, SJ (New York: Paulist, 1985), 23–34. See also his "Finality, Love, Marriage," in *Collection*, CWL 4, 19–23.
91 Arthur Peacocke, "Biological Evolution – A Positive Theological Appraisal," in *Evolutionary and Molecular Biology: Scientific Perspectives on Divine Action*, ed. Robert John Russell, William R. Stoeger, and Francisco J. Ayala (Vatican City State: Vatican Observatory Publications/Berkeley: Center for Theology and the Natural Sciences, 1998), 359.
92 "The Supernatural Order," 149.
93 "The Supernatural Order," 149.
94 "The Supernatural Order," 149.
95 Brotherton, "The Integrity of Nature in the Grace-Freedom Dynamic," 551.
96 "The Supernatural Order," 159.
97 Lonergan, *Method in Theology*, 241.
98 I am citing for the rest of the paragraph from Stebbins, *The Divine Initiative*, 163.
99 Raymond Maloney, "De Lubac and Lonergan on the Supernatural," *Theological Studies* 69 (2008): 509–27.
100 Maloney, "De Lubac and Lonergan on the Supernatural," 525.
101 Mansini, "Lonergan on the Natural Desire in the Light of Feingold," *Nova et Vetera*, English ed., 5.1 (2007): 193.
102 Mansini, "Lonergan on the Natural Desire," 194.
103 Maloney, "De Lubac and Lonergan on the Supernatural," 525.
104 Stebbins, *The Divine Initiative*, 157–8.
105 Lonergan, "The Supernatural Order," 153. To remain consistent with my interlocutors, I depart from the published English translation in my use of "fittingness" rather than "appropriateness." The Latin text reads: "Proinde, cognita possibilitate visionis in genere, ad eius possibilitatem in homine exhibendam argumenta convenientiae inveniri possunt" (152).
106 Lonergan, "The Supernatural Order," 153.
107 Stebbins, *The Divine Initiative*, 158.
108 See Mansini, "Lonergan on the Natural Desire," 194.
109 Bernard Lonergan, "The Notion of Fittingness: The Application of Theological Method to the Question of the Purpose of the Incarnation," in *Early Latin Theology*, CWL 19, 483.
110 Lonergan, "The Notion of Fittingness," 489.
111 Lonergan, "The Notion of Fittingness," 491, 495.

5. Being-in-Love and the Desire for the Supernatural: Erotic-Agapic Subjectivity

1 Henri de Lubac, "The Total Meaning of Man and the World," *Communio: International Catholic Review* 35 (Winter 2008): 618.
2 De Lubac, "The Total Meaning," 619.
3 De Lubac, "The Total Meaning," 619–20.
4 De Lubac, *The Mystery of the Supernatural*, 227.
5 De Lubac, *The Mystery of the Supernatural*, 236.
6 De Lubac, *The Mystery of the Supernatural*, 228.
7 Feingold, *The Natural Desire to See God*, xxxvi.
8 Feingold, *The Natural Desire to See God*, xxxv, xxxvi.
9 Cited in Feingold, *The Natural Desire to See God*, 417n75.
10 Pope Francis remarked in an interview that "grace is not part of consciousness, it is the amount of light in our souls, not knowledge nor reason. Even you, without knowing it, could be touched by grace" (http://www.repubblica.it/cultura/2013/10/01/news/pope_s_conversation_with_scalfari_english-67643118/?refresh_ce).
11 Feingold, *The Natural Desire to See God*, 435.
12 Feingold, *The Natural Desire to See God*, 435.
13 Feingold, *The Natural Desire to See God*, 435.
14 Lonergan, *Grace and Freedom*, 53.
15 Lonergan, *Grace and Freedom*, 55.
16 Lonergan, *Grace and Freedom*, 58.
17 Lonergan, "The Supernatural Order," 73.
18 Lonergan, "The Supernatural Order," 163.
19 Lonergan, *Method in Theology*, 105, 107, 289.
20 Lonergan, *Method in Theology*, 105. See L. Matthew Petillo, "The Theological Problem of Grace and Experience: A Lonerganian Perspective," *Theological Studies* 71 (2010): 586–608.
21 Lonergan, *Method in Theology*, 105–6.
22 Jeremy Wilkins, "Grace and Growth: Aquinas, Lonergan, and the Problematic of Habitual Grace," *Theological Studies* 72.4 (December 2011): 729.
23 Wilkins, "Grace and Growth," 729.
24 Doran, *The Trinity in History*, 22.
25 Doran, *The Trinity in History*, 23.
26 Doran, *The Trinity in History*, 127.
27 Neil Ormerod, "The Grace-Nature Distinction and the Construction of a Systematic Theology," *Theological Studies* 75.3 (2014): 535. Although in

my judgment the four-point hypothesis is a plausible theory with fruitful implications, it is important to note that it is not without its thoughtful critics. See David M. Coffey, "*Quaestio Disputata*: Response to Neil Ormerod, and Beyond," *Theological Studies* 68.4 (2007): 900–15.
28 Doran, *The Trinity in History*, 17.
29 Doran, *The Trinity in History*, 137.
30 Doran, *The Trinity in History*, 138.
31 Doran, *The Trinity in History*, 127.
32 There has been a long conversation in Lonergan circles about whether a "fifth level" exists. This level is identified as the level of being in love – the level of interpersonal relations. See Robert M. Doran, "Consciousness and Grace," *Method: Journal of Lonergan Studies* 11 (1993): 51–75; Michael Vertin, "Lonergan on Consciousness: Is There a Fifth Level?" *Method: Journal of Lonergan Studies* 12 (1994): 1–36; Tad Dunne, "Being in Love," *Method: Journal of Lonergan Studies* 13 (1995): 161–75; Patrick Byrne, "Consciousness: Levels, Sublations, and the Subject as Subject," *Method: Journal of Lonergan Studies* 13 (1995): 131–50; Christian Jacobs-Vandegeer, "Sanctifying Grace in a Methodical Theology," *Theological Studies* 68.1 (2007): 52–76; Jeremy W. Blackwood, "Sanctifying Grace, Elevation, and the Fifth Level of Consciousness," *Method: Journal of Lonergan Studies*, n.s., 2.2. (2011): 143–61; and Jeremy W. Blackwood, "Trinitarian Love in the Dialectics of History," *Method: Journal of Lonergan Studies*, n.s., 4.1 (2013): 1–16.
33 Doran, *The Trinity in History*, 125.
34 Doran, *The Trinity in History*, 129–30.
35 Doran, *The Trinity in History*, 130.
36 Blackwood, "Sanctifying Grace," 158; Blackwood, "Trinitarian Love," 9.
37 John D. Dadosky, "Is There a Fourth Stage of Meaning?" *Heythrop Journal* 51.5 (2010): 768–80; John D. Dadosky, "Midwiving the Fourth Stage of Meaning: Lonergan and Doran," *Meaning and History in Systematic Theology: Essays in Honor of Robert M. Doran, S.J.*, ed. John D. Dadosky (Milwaukee: Marquette University Press, 2009), 71–92. As I mentioned in the introduction to this book, Jeremy Blackwood has identified a period of eighteen days in which Lonergan develops his position to include the interpersonal element as a constitutive element of the immanent intelligibility of human subjectivity. Blackwood suggests that if his argument is correct, then it supports Dadosky's claim. See Blackwood, "Eighteen Days," 26.
38 I am building here on Neil Ormerod's argument in "Addendum on the Grace-Nature Distinction," *Theological Studies* 75.4 (2014): 890–8.

39 Ormerod, "Addendum," 895.
40 Ormerod, "Addendum," 896.
41 Lonergan, "Finality, Love, Marriage," in *Collection*, CWL 4, 29.
42 Lonergan, "Finality, Love, Marriage," 30–2.
43 Lonergan, "Finality, Love, Marriage," 44, 45.
44 Lonergan, "Finality, Love, Marriage," 45, 51.
45 Lonergan *Insight*, 709.
46 Lonergan, *Insight*, 740.
47 Lonergan, *Insight*, 719.
48 Lonergan, *Insight*, 721.
49 This responds to Feingold's call for an account of two different loves for God – natural and supernatural. See Feingold, *The Natural Desire for God*, 416–21.
50 Lonergan, *Insight*, 721.
51 Lonergan, *Insight*, 718.
52 Lonergan, *Insight*, 722.
53 See Jeremy Wilkins' suggestion for a transposition of these virtues in light of intentionality analysis: "Rather than linking the virtues to particular faculties of the soul, one might go on to explore the particular components that together form an effective circle of schemes for responding to adversity (fortitude), regulating desires (temperance), relating to others (justice), and practical moral reasoning (prudence). Again, one might explore how these schemes are sublated into the still higher circles of efficacious befriending of God and all things in God (charity), persevering in the law of the cross in the face of the objective absurdity that is the cumulative effect of sin (hope), and discerning the finger of God at work in the world (faith)" ("Grace and Growth," 740).
54 See, for example, John van den Hengel, "God With/Out Being," *Method: Journal of Lonergan Studies* 12 (1994): 251–79. For a fuller treatment of Marion's contribution to conversations about nature and grace, see Rober, *Recognizing the Gift*, chap. 3.
55 Balthasar, *Glory of the Lord: A Theological Aesthetics*, vol. 5: *The Realm of Metaphysics in the Modern Age*, trans. Oliver Davies et al. (San Francisco: Ignatius, 1991), 615. Hereafter cited as *GL 5*.
56 Balthasar, *GL 5*, 616.
57 Balthasar, *GL 5*, 616.
58 Lonergan, *Method in Theology*, 115.
59 Lonergan, *Method in Theology*, 106.
60 Lonergan, *Method in Theology*, 115.
61 Lonergan, *Method in Theology*, 340.

62 Lonergan, *Method in Theology*, 341.
63 Marion, *On Descartes' Metaphysical Prism: The Constitution and Limits of Onto-Theo-Logy in Cartesian Thought*, trans. Jeffrey L. Kosky (Chicago: University of Chicago Press, 1999). For a discussion of Pascal, see especially chap. 5.
64 Robyn Horner, *Jean-Luc Marion: A Theo-logical Introduction* (Burlington: Ashgate, 2005), 67.
65 Marion, *On Descartes' Metaphysical Prism*, 316.
66 Lonergan, *Method in Theology*, 122–3.
67 Dadosky, "Desire, Bias, and Love," 257.
68 Dadosky, "Desire, Bias, and Love," 259.
69 Marion, *The Erotic Phenomenon*, 40. Marion contrasts this vision of love with what he calls the "empire of vanity": "for under the rule of vanity, I can very certainly recognize 'I think, therefore I am' – only immediately to annul this certainty by asking myself, 'What's the use?' The certainty of my existence is never enough to make it just, or good, or beautiful, or desirable – in short, it is never enough to assure it. The certainty of my existence simply demonstrates my solitary effort to establish myself in being by my own account; of course a certainty produced by my own act of thinking remains my initiative, my work, and my business – the autistic certainty and narcissistic assurance of a mirror always mirroring another mirror, a repeated void" (22).
70 I am building on Robyn Horner's helpful schematic offered in *Jean-Luc Marion*, chap. 11.
71 Jean Vanier, *From Brokenness to Community* (Mahwah: Paulist Press, 1992), 14.
72 Vanier, *From Brokenness to Community*, 14.
73 Vanier, *From Brokenness to Community*, 17–18.
74 See Emmanuel Levinas, *Totality and Infinity*, trans. Alphonso Lingis (Pittsburgh: Duquesne University Press, 1969), 194–297. The face of the other "summons me to my obligations and judges me. The being that presents himself in the face comes from a dimension of height, a dimension of transcendence whereby he can present himself as a stranger without opposing me as an obstacle or enemy … The Other who dominates me in his transcendence is thus the stranger, the widow, and the orphan, to whom I am obligated" (215).
75 See Levinas, *Totality and Infinity*, 199: "This infinity, stronger than murder, already resists us in his face, is his face, is the primordial *expression*, is the first word: 'you shall not commit murder.' The infinite paralyses power by its infinite resistance to murder, which, firm and insurmountable, gleams

in the face of the Other, in the total nudity of his defenceless eyes, in the nudity of the absolute openness of the Transcendent" (199).
76 Marion, *The Erotic Phenomenon*, 126.
77 Marion, *The Erotic Phenomenon*, 126. Marion's more subtle critique here finds resonance in David Bentley Hart's trenchant critique of Levinas in *The Beauty of the Infinite: The Aesthetics of Christian Truth* (Grand Rapids: Eerdmans, 2003). Though explicitly drawing on Levinas's terminology of "totality" and "infinity," Hart employs these themes differently in a self-conscious contrast to Levinas. According to Hart, "'infinity,' as Levinas uses the word, indicates a kind of purely ethical sublime, recognizably Kantian in its joyless rigor" (14). "Infinity" within a Christian frame, however, is "'ethical' only because it is first 'aesthetic'; it opens up being and beings – to knowledge or love – only within free orderings of its beauty, inviting a desire that is moral only because it is *not* disinterested" (15). This aesthetic and rhetorical vision of the concreteness and particularity of being and truth finds little sympathy with Levinas. Hart writes, "the distance of the other, crossed by the rhetorical *excess* of the other, may awaken one to the truth of the other as along as one can receive that excess as glory. One could not stand here at a farther remove from the Levinasian understanding of the exteriority of the face, which for him must of necessity be seen as a trace, an effaced face, absent from itself and every context, from all being and light. The face of the other, for Christian eyes, must of necessity be visible *only* in the peculiarities of its features, and only within an unforeclosable sequence of perspectives and supplementations; it is always an aesthetic event" (144).
78 Marion, *The Erotic Phenomenon*, 9.
79 Marion, *The Erotic Phenomenon*, 115–16.
80 Marion, *The Erotic Phenomenon*, 116.
81 Marion, *The Erotic Phenomenon*, 116–17.
82 Marion, *The Erotic Phenomenon*, 118.
83 Marion, *The Erotic Phenomenon*, 118.
84 Wendell Berry, *The Art of the Commonplace: The Agrarian Essays of Wendell Berry*, ed. Norman Wirzba (Berkeley: Counterpoint, 2002), 174. The essay is selected from his book *Sex, Economy, Freedom & Community* (New York: Pantheon, 1993).
85 Berry, *The Art of the Commonplace*, 175.
86 Berry, *The Art of the Commonplace*, 175.
87 Berry, *The Art of the Commonplace*, 176.
88 Berry, *The Art of the Commonplace*, 176.
89 Marion, *The Erotic Phenomenon*, 185.

90 Marion, *The Erotic Phenomenon*, 195.
91 Marion, *The Erotic Phenomenon*, 202.
92 Marion is offering a kind of wordplay: "adieu" (farewell) and "à Dieu" (to God).
93 Marion, *The Erotic Phenomenon*, 215.
94 Horner, *Jean-Luc Marion*, 141.
95 Marion, *The Erotic Phenomenon*, 215.
96 Marion, *The Erotic Phenomenon*, 222.
97 Marion, *The Erotic Phenomenon*, 222.
98 That said, from my vantage point Marion requires the explanatory foundations of a thinker like Lonergan or Doran. His claim that God loves exactly like we do, except with a qualified, albeit infinite difference, strikes me as requiring more robust explanatory distinctions.

6. Incarnate Meaning and Mimetic Desire: Saints and the Desire for God

1 Girard, "The Goodness of Mimetic Desire," 64.
2 Buckley, *Denying and Disclosing God*, chap. 6.
3 I integrate into this chapter several revised sections of my previously published article "Incarnate Meaning and Mimetic Desire: Notes toward the Development of a Theology of the Saints," in *New Voices in Catholic Theology*, ed. Anna Bonta Moreland and Joseph Curran (New York: Crossroad, 2012), 207–20.
4 Buckley, *Denying and Disclosing God*, 130.
5 Buckley, *Denying and Disclosing God*, 130.
6 Lenehan, "Girard and the Tasks of Theology," 114.
7 In what follows, I present the key insights of chapter 9, "The Dialectic of Desire," in Doran's *The Trinity in History*. In his essay "New Paths for a Girard/Lonergan Conversation: An Essay in Light of Robert Doran's *Missions and Processions*," *Method: Journal of Lonergan Studies*, n.s., 4.1 (2013), Grant Kaplan says that Doran's book "continues the most serious engagement with mimetic theory carried out over the last two decades by Lonergan scholars" (24).
8 Doran, *The Trinity in History*, 199. See also *CWL* 12, 139.
9 Doran, *Theology and the Dialectics of History*, 46.
10 See Feingold, *The Natural Desire to See God*, xxiv.
11 Lonergan, *The Triune God: Systematics*, *CWL* 12, 647.
12 Doran, *The Trinity in History*, 197.
13 "The romantic lie valorizes all instances of originality and spontaneity as indicators of personal superiority. The romantic construal of desire is that

of a straight line running between a desiring subject and an intrinsically valuable desired object" (Doran, *The Trinity in History*, 207).
14 See chap. 8, "Autonomous Spiritual Processions," in Doran, *The Trinity in History*.
15 Doran, *The Trinity in History*, 199.
16 Doran, *The Trinity in History*, 204.
17 Doran, *The Trinity in History*, 206. For a sustained discussion of "interdividual psychology," see Girard, *Things Hidden*, 283–431.
18 Hefling, "About What Might a 'Girard-Lonergan Conversation' Be?," 104.
19 Doran, *The Trinity in History*, 217.
20 Doran, *The Trinity in History*, 217.
21 Kaplan, "New Paths for a Girard/Lonergan Conversation," 38.
22 Girard, *When These Things Begin*, trans. Trevor Cribben Merrill (East Lansing: Michigan State University Press, 2014), 12
23 Girard, *When These Things Begin*, 12.
24 Kaplan, "New Paths for a Girard/Lonergan Conversation," 38.
25 Lonergan, *Method in Theology* (New York: Herder and Herder, 1972), 57.
26 John Henry Newman, *An Essay in Aid of a Grammar of Assent* (Notre Dame: University of Notre Dame, 1979), 89.
27 Lonergan, *Method in Theology*, 73.
28 Lonergan, "The Analogy of Meaning," in *Philosophical and Theological Papers 1958–1964*, CWL 6, ed. Robert Croken et al. (Toronto: University of Toronto Press, 1996), 188.
29 Lonergan, *Method in Theology*, 73.
30 Lonergan, "Time and Meaning," in *Philosophical and Theological Papers 1958–1964*, CWL 6, ed. Robert Croken et al. (Toronto: University of Toronto Press, 1996), 94–121. See also Georges Morel, *Le Sens de l'existence selon s. Jean de la Croix* (Paris: Aubier, 1960–61).
31 Lonergan, "Time and Meaning," 102.
32 Buckley, *Denying and Disclosing God*, 108.
33 Buckley, *Denying and Disclosing God*, 119.
34 Buckley, *Denying and Disclosing God*, 117.
35 Buckley, *Denying and Disclosing God*, xv.
36 See Lonergan, *Method in Theology*, 73.
37 See Rosenberg, "The Drama of Scripture: Reading Patristic Biblical Hermeneutics through Bernard Lonergan's Reflections on Art," *Logos: A Journal of Catholic Thought and Culture* 11.2 (Spring 2008): 126–48; and "Lonergan on the Transcendent Orientation of Art," *Renascence: Essays on Values in Literature* (Spring 2009): 141–51. I draw selectively from these essays in a slightly adapted presentation.
38 Lonergan's theory of art is worked out most carefully in "Art," in *Topics in Education: The Cincinnati Lectures of 1959 on the Philosophy of Education*, CWL

10, ed. Robert M. Doran and Frederick E. Crowe (Toronto: University of Toronto Press), 208–32.
39 Lonergan, "Art," 224–5. I expand on this theme more thoroughly in "Lonergan on the Transcendent Orientation of Art."
40 Lonergan, "Art," 216.
41 Lonergan, "Art," 217.
42 Lonergan, *Method in Theology*, 63.
43 Lonergan, "Art," 229.
44 Lonergan, *Method in Theology*, 63.
45 Lonergan, "Art," 222.
46 Lonergan, "Art," 222.
47 Frances Young, *Biblical Exegesis and the Formation of Christian Culture* (Peabody: Hendrickson, 2002), 158.
48 Cunningham, *A Brief History of the Saints*, 139–40. Cunningham is drawing from Frances Young's *The Art of Performance: Towards a Theology of Holy Scripture* (London: Darton, Longman, and Todd, 1990).
49 Cunningham, *A Brief History of the Saints*, 140.
50 Cunningham, *A Brief History of the Saints*, 140.
51 Girard, *Things Hidden Since the Foundation of the World* (London: Continuum, 2003), 431.
52 For a helpful snapshot of his account of the negative mimetic desire and scapegoating, see Girard, *I See Satan Fall Like Lightening*, trans. James G. Williams (Maryknoll: Orbis, 2001), especially chaps. 1–8.
53 René Girard, *Violence and the Sacred*, trans. Patrick Gregory (Baltimore: Johns Hopkins University Press, 1977), 146.
54 Girard, "The Goodness of Mimetic Desire," 63. See also Brian D. Robinette, *Grammars of Resurrection: A Christian Theology of Presence and Absence* (New York: Crossroad, 2009), chap. 7.
55 Girard, "The Goodness of Mimetic Desire," 64.
56 Girard, "The Goodness of Mimetic Desire," 64.
57 Girard, *I See Satan*, 15.
58 Girard, *I See Satan*, 16.
59 For a sustained discussion of "interdividual psychology," see Girard, *Things Hidden*, 283–431.
60 Hefling, "About What Might a 'Girard-Lonergan Conversation' Be?," 104.
61 Hefling, "About What Might a 'Girard-Lonergan Conversation' Be?," 104.
62 Hefling, "About What Might a 'Girard-Lonergan Conversation' Be?," 104.
63 René Girard, *Deceit, Desire, and the Novel: Self and Other in Literary Structure*, trans. Yvonne Freccero (Baltimore: Johns Hopkins University Press, 1965), 9.

64 Girard, *Deceit, Desire, and the Novel*, 9.
65 Girard, *Deceit, Desire, and the Novel*, 9. Though these categories of internal and external mediation are helpful in a suggestive manner, Neil Ormerod has noted their predominantly "descriptive" rather than "explanatory" character: "It is difficult to grasp just what constitutes 'distance' and how it is measured, and how much 'distance' is required to move from one category to the other" ("Doran's *The Trinity in History*: The Girardian Connection," *Method: Journal of Lonergan Studies*, n.s., 4.1 [2013]: 56).
66 Girard, *Deceit, Desire, and the Novel*, 10.
67 Buckley, *Denying and Disclosing God*, 129. For other Buckley-Girard connections, see Grant Kaplan, *René Girard, Unlikely Apologist: Mimetic Theology* (Notre Dame, IN: University of Notre Dame Press, 2016), 178–83.
68 Buckley, *Denying and Disclosing God*, 129.
69 Buckley, *Denying and Disclosing God*, 129.
70 Buckley, *Denying and Disclosing God*, 129.
71 Buckley, *Denying and Disclosing God*, 129.
72 *The Autobiography*, trans. Parmananda R. Divarkar, in *Ignatius of Loyola: Spiritual Exercises and Selected Works*, ed. George E. Ganss (New York: Paulist, 1991), 70.
73 Cunningham, *A Brief History of the Saints*, 66.
74 Grant Kaplan, "Saint versus Hero: Girard's Undoing of Romantic Hagiology," in *The Postmodern Saints of France: Refiguring 'The Holy' in Contemporary French Philosophy*, ed. Colby Dickinson (London: T&T Clark, 2013), 153–67.
75 Kaplan, "Saint versus Hero," 155.
76 Kaplan, "Saint versus Hero," 156.
77 Kaplan, "Saint versus Hero," 159.
78 Kaplan, "Saint versus Hero," 159.
79 Kaplan, "Saint versus Hero," 159. See also Girard, *I See Satan*, chaps. 9–10.
80 Kaplan, "Saint versus Hero," 159. See also Girard, *I See Satan*, 189ff.
81 Girard, *The Scapegoat*, trans. Yvonne Freccero (Baltimore: Johns Hopkins University Press, 1986), 207.
82 Kaplan, "Saint versus Hero," 160.
83 Kaplan, "Saint versus Hero," 160.
84 Kaplan, "Saint versus Hero," 162.
85 Kaplan, "Saint versus Hero," 162.
86 Neil Ormerod, "Desire and the Origins of Culture: Lonergan and Girard in Conversation," *Heythrop Journal* 54.5 (September 2013): 788.
87 Ormerod, "Desire and the Origins of Culture," 789.
88 Ormerod, "Desire and the Origins of Culture," 789–90.

89 Ormerod, "Desire and the Origins of Culture," 790. See also Girard, *I See Satan*, 65–6. On page 66 Girard writes: "What reconciles them ... is nothing else than projecting on the victim all their fears in the beginning and subsequently all their hopes once they become reconciled. These are disorders characteristic of human groups that paradoxically, as they become more and more aggravated, afford humans the means of creating forms of organization. These new forms emerge from a crisis of violence and then put an end to it. Lynchings restore peace at the expense of the divinized victim. This is why they are associated with manifestations of this divine figure and the communities recall them in transfigured accounts that we call 'myths.'"
90 Ormerod, "Desire and the Origins of Culture," 790.
91 Ormerod, "Desire and the Origins of Culture," 790. Ormerod's critique here parallels John Milbank's concern that Girard offers more of a pre-Christian, agonistic metaphysics than a peaceful ontology of Christianity. See Milbank, *Theology and Social Theory*, 2nd ed. (Malden: Blackwell, 2006), 395ff.
92 Ormerod, "Desire and the Origins of Culture," 791.
93 Ormerod, "Desire and the Origins of Culture," 791.
94 Ormerod, "Desire and the Origins of Culture," 791.

7. The Metaphysics of Holiness and the Longing for God in History: Thérèse of Lisieux and Etty Hillesum

1 Ormerod, "Grace-Nature Distinction," 535.
2 Etty Hillesum, *An Interrupted Life: The Diaries, 1941–1943 and Letters from Westerbork*, trans. Arnold J. Pomerans with introduction and notes by Jan G. Gaarlandt (New York: Holt, 1996), 3.
3 Joann Wolski Conn, "A Feminist View of Thérèse," in *Carmelite Studies 5: Experiencing Saint Thérèse Today*, ed. John Sullivan (Washington, DC: ICS, 1990), 139.
4 Conn, "A Feminist View of Thérèse," 129.
5 Wanda Tomassi, "Etty Hillesum: A New Kind of Sanctity," in *Saints and Sanctity Today*, ed. Maria Clara Bingemer, Andres Torres Queiruga, and Jon Sobrino (London: SCM, 2013), 108.
6 Tomassi, "Etty Hillesum," 108.
7 Ormerod, "The Metaphysics of Holiness: Created Participation in Divine Nature," *Irish Theological Quarterly* 79.1 (2014): 68–82.
8 Feingold, *The Natural Desire to See God*, 434.
9 Doran, *The Trinity in History*, 204.

10 Doran, *The Trinity in History*, xi.
11 Doran, *The Trinity in History*, 75.
12 Doran, *The Trinity in History*, 75. In chapter 20 of *Insight*, Lonergan identified a "heuristic structure for identifying the divine solution to the problem of evil before suggesting that this structure points to the explicit revelation of God in Israel and Christianity" (721–2). See also Doran, *The Trinity in History*, 76.
13 Ormerod, "The Metaphysics of Holiness," 68–82.
14 Ormerod, "The Metaphysics of Holiness," 69.
15 Ormerod, "The Metaphysics of Holiness," 75.
16 Ormerod, "The Metaphysics of Holiness," 76.
17 Doran, *The Trinity in History*, 137, 138.
18 Ormerod, "The Metaphysics of Holiness," 76–7.
19 Ormerod, "The Metaphysics of Holiness," 77.
20 Ormerod, "The Metaphysics of Holiness," 77.
21 Ormerod, "The Metaphysics of Holiness," 78.
22 Thomas R. Nevin, *Thérèse of Lisieux: God's Gentle Warrior* (Oxford: Oxford University Press, 2006), 28.
23 Balthasar, *Two Sisters in the Spirit: Thérèse of Lisieux and Elizabeth of the Trinity* (San Franciso: Ignatius, 1992).
24 Balthasar, *Two Sisters in the Spirit*, 11.
25 Balthasar, *Two Sisters in the Spirit*, 9.
26 Balthasar, *Two Sisters in the Spirit*, 10.
27 St Thérèse of Lisieux, *Story of a Soul*, trans. John Clarke (Washington, DC: ICS, 2005), 16.
28 Mary Frohlich, introduction to *Thérèse of Lisieux: Essential Writings* (Maryknoll: Orbis, 2013), 14.
29 Frohlich, introduction to *Thérèse of Lisieux*, 14–15.
30 Balthasar, *Two Sisters in the Spirit*, 237, 238.
31 Balthasar, *Two Sisters in the Spirit*, 238–9, 241.
32 Balthasar, *Two Sisters in the Spirit*, 243.
33 Balthasar, *Two Sisters in the Spirit*, 284.
34 Balthasar, *Two Sisters in the Spirit*, 272, 273.
35 Balthasar, *Two Sisters in the Spirit*, 277.
36 Balthasar, *Two Sisters in the Spirit*, 278, 280.
37 Balthasar, *Two Sisters in the Spirit*, 284, 285.
38 Balthasar, *Two Sisters in the Spirit*, 288.
39 Balthasar, *Two Sisters in the Spirit*, 298.
40 St Thérèse of Lisieux, *Story of a Soul*, 294.
41 St Thérèse of Lisieux, *Story of a Soul*, 299, 302.

42 Ormerod, "The Metaphysics of Holiness," 77.
43 Balthasar, *Two Sisters in the Spirit*, 194–5.
44 Balthasar, *Two Sisters in the Spirit*, 195.
45 Balthasar, *Two Sisters in the Spirit*, 196.
46 Balthasar, *Two Sisters in the Spirit*, 197.
47 Balthasar, *Two Sisters in the Spirit*, 197.
48 Balthasar, *Two Sisters in the Spirit*, 198.
49 Balthasar, *Two Sisters in the Spirit*, 199.
50 Balthasar, *Two Sisters in the Spirit*, 200, 201.
51 *Thérèse of Lisieux: Essential Writings*, 169.
52 Balthasar, *Two Sisters in the Spirit*, 77.
53 Balthasar, *Two Sisters in the Spirit*, 201.
54 The citations here are from St Thérèse of Lisieux, *Story of a Soul*, 151–4.
55 Frohlich, introduction to *Thérèse of Lisieux*, 21.
56 In terms of the feeling/choice distinction, Jeremy Wilkins' reflection based in Lonergan is pertinent: "Love may be a feeling, but its proof is in its love-motivated action, and it is by attending to the data over time that one finds a criterion for discerning between fine sentiments and genuine being in love. No particular physiological event, of whatever elation or anguish, can serve as the criterion and touchstone of authentic love. That criterion is rather ongoing self-displacement into another, and, when it is a question of religious love, it is ongoing self-displacement into God and others for God's sake. In the concrete order of this fallen world, agape adheres to the Law of the Cross – the transformation of evil to good through self-giving love – not only as its precept but also as its statistical rule. The Dalai Lama's steadfast commitment to meeting evil with good is more relevant data on conversion than reports of the physiological states or 'experiences' he may undergo while meditating. Mother Teresa's perseverance in loving service despite the stark aridity, and the hard consolation that marked so much of her later interior life bears more eloquent witness to her sanctity than any spiritual 'favors' she might once have received, and belies her own judgment on the state of her faith" ("Grace and Growth," 732–3).
57 St Thérèse of Lisieux, *Story of a Soul*, 346.
58 Thomas R. Nevin, *The Last Years of St. Thérèse: Doubt and Darkness, 1895–1897* (Oxford: Oxford University Press, 2013), 181.
59 Balthasar, *Two Sisters in the Spirit*, 339.
60 St Thérèse of Lisieux, *Story of a Soul*, 333.
61 St Thérèse of Lisieux, *Story of a Soul*, 334.
62 St Thérèse of Lisieux, *Story of a Soul*, 340.
63 Frohlich, "Desolation and Doctrine in Thérèse of Lisieux," 270. Frohlich is challenging Balthasar's interpretation that she experienced a "half-dark night."

Though space does not permit, there is much more to say about Thérèse as sage and as mystic – the other types of holiness in Ormerod's schema. Her designation as a Doctor of the Church, for example, opens up fruitful paths for exploring her life and writings from the angle of wisdom. She, indeed, displayed her own kind of existential theology and her own kind of unique exegesis of the Word of God.

64 Annemarie S. Kidder, introduction to *Etty Hillesum: Essential Writings* (Maryknoll: Orbis: 2009), 9.
65 Meins G.S. Coetsier, *Etty Hillesum and the Flow of Presence* (Columbia: University of Missouri Press, 2008), 18.
66 Coetsier, *Etty Hillesum and the Flow of Presence*, 19, 20.
67 Kidder, introduction to *Etty Hillesum*, 10.
68 The following description of Etty's relationships is drawn from Eva Hoffman, foreword to Hillesum, *An Interrupted Life*, ix–x.
69 Richard R. Gaillardetz, "Sexual Vulnerability and a Spirituality of Suffering," *Pacifica* 22 (February 2009): 78.
70 Coetsier, *Etty Hillesum and the Flow of Presence*, 32.
71 Gaillardetz, "Sexual Vulnerability and a Spirituality of Suffering," 78.
72 Ormerod, "The Metaphysics of Holiness," 81.
73 http://w2.vatican.va/content/john-paul-ii/en/encyclicals/documents/hf_jp-ii_enc_07121990_redemptoris-missio.html.
74 It is pertinent to note the influence of the following essay of Frederick E. Crowe's on Doran's thinking in this regard: "Son of God, Holy Spirit, and World Religions," *Appropriating the Lonergan Idea*, ed. Michael Vertin (Toronto: University of Toronto Press, 2006): 324–43.
75 Doran, *The Trinity in History*, 78.
76 Doran, *The Trinity in History*, 78.
77 http://w2.vatican.va/content/benedict-xvi/en/audiences/2013/documents/hf_ben-xvi_aud_20130213.html.
78 Pope Benedict is citing Hillesum, *An Interrupted Life*, 97.
79 Tomassi, "Etty Hillesum: A New Kind of Sanctity," 106.
80 Ormerod, "The Metaphysics of Holiness," 76.
81 Hillesum, *An Interrupted Life*, 332.
82 Hillesum, *An Interrupted Life*, 74.
83 Hillesum, *An Interrupted Life*, 61.
84 Hillesum, *Essential Writings*, 119.
85 Balthasar, *Two Sisters in the Spirit*, 219.
86 Hillesum, *An Interrupted Life*, 19.
87 Hillesum, *An Interrupted Life*, 163.

88 Hillesum, *An Interrupted Life*, 9–10.
89 Hillesum, *An Interrupted Life*, 36.
90 Hillesum, *An Interrupted Life*, 46–7.
91 Hillesum, *An Interrupted Life*, 67.
92 Hillesum, *An Interrupted Life*, 68.
93 Hillesum, *An Interrupted Life*, 68. In terms of her further reflection on simplicity, she mused: "A poem by Rilke is as real and as important as a young man falling out of an airplane. That's something I must engrave on my heart. All that happens happens in this world of ours, and you must not leave one thing out for the sake of another. Now go to sleep. Accept your inner conflicts, try to bridge them, to simplify them, for then your life will become simpler as well" (*An Interrupted Life*, 41–2).
94 Kidder, introduction to *Etty Hillesum*, 15.
95 Kidder, introduction to *Etty Hillesum*, 16.
96 Kidder, introduction to *Etty Hillesum*, 15.
97 Kidder, introduction to *Etty Hillesum*, 16.
98 Tzvetan Todorov, *Facing the Extreme: Moral Life in the Concentration Camps*, trans. Arthur Denner and Abigail Pollak (New York: Holt/Metropolitan Books, 1996).
99 Todorov, *Facing the Extreme*, 198.
100 Todorov, *Facing the Extreme*, 209.
101 Tzvetan Todorov, *Facing the Extreme*, 208.
102 Todorov, *Facing the Extreme*, 209.
103 Hillesum, *An Interrupted Life*, 11.
104 Hillesum, *An Interrupted Life*, 84.
105 Hillesum, *An Interrupted Life*, 86.
106 Hillesum, *An Interrupted Life*, 95.
107 Hillesum, *An Interrupted Life*, 95.
108 Hillesum, *An Interrupted Life*, 97.
109 Hoffman, foreword to Hillesum, *An Interrupted Life*, x.
110 Hillesum, *An Interrupted Life*, 5.
111 Gaillardetz, "Sexual Vulnerability and a Spirituality of Suffering," 86.
112 Gaillardetz, "Sexual Vulnerability and a Spirituality of Suffering," 89. Dante masterfully exhibits this transformation of eros into agape in Canto 9 of the *Paradiso*. See his discussion of Cunizza, a woman known as a promiscuous child of Venus. Cunizza later in life transformed this dominant eros into a commitment to compassion and social concern. See also James Collins, *Pilgrim in Love: An Introduction to Dante and His Spirituality* (Chicago: Loyola University Press, 1984), 226ff.
113 Feingold, *The Natural Desire to See God*, 434.

8. Distorted Desire and the Love of Deviated Transcendence

1 Oakes, "The *Surnaturel* Controversy," 652–3.
2 See Alison, *The Joy of Being Wrong*, 47.
3 Braman, *Meaning and Authenticity*, 49–50.
4 Braman, *Meaning and Authenticity*, 50.
5 Doran, *What Is Systematic Theology?*, 126.
6 Boyle, *Who Are We Now? Christian Humanism and the Global Market from Hegel to Heaney* (Notre Dame: University of Notre Dame Press, 1998), 155–59. See Frederick G. Lawrence, "The Economic Good of Order and Culture in Relation to Solidarity, Subsidiarity, and Responsibility," in *The Fragility of Consciousness: Faith, Reason, and the Human Good*, ed. Randall S. Rosenberg and Kevin M. Vander Schel, chap. 9 (Toronto: University of Toronto Press, 2017). See also Dominic F. Doyle, *The Promise of Christian Humanism: Thomas Aquinas on Hope* (New York: Crossroad, 2012).
7 Alasdair MacIntyre, "Three Perspectives on Marxism," *Ethics and Politics: Selected Essays*, vol. 2 (Cambridge: Cambridge University Press, 2006), 149.
8 Pope Francis, *Evangelii Gaudium* (2013), http://w2.vatican.va/content/francesco/en/apost_exhortations/documents/papa-francesco_esortazione-ap_20131124_evangelii-gaudium.html, 2. Henceforth cited as *EG*.
9 John Paul II, *Solicitudo Rei Socialis* (1987), http://w2.vatican.va/content/john-paul-ii/en/encyclicals/documents/hf_jp-ii_enc_30121987_sollicitudo-rei-socialis.html, 28.1. Henceforth cited as *SRS*.
10 Robert M. Doran, *Theology and the Dialectics of History*, 358.
11 John Paul II, *Centesimus Annus* (1991), http://w2.vatican.va/content/john-paul-ii/en/encyclicals/documents/hf_jp-ii_enc_01051991_centesimus-annus.html, 36.3 (henceforth cited as *CA*); Benedict XVI, *Caritas in Veritate* (2009), http://w2.vatican.va/content/benedict-xvi/en/encyclicals/documents/hf_ben-xvi_enc_20090629_caritas-in-veritate.html, 51 (henceforth cited as *CV*).
12 Lonergan, in his *Macroeconomic Dynamics: An Essay in Circulation Analysis* (ed. Frederick G. Lawrence, Patrick H. Byrne, and Charles C. Hefling, Jr, *CWL* 15 [Toronto: University of Toronto Press, 1999]), conceives of democracy and free enterprise as an educational project: "Now to change one's standard of living in any notable fashion is to live in a different fashion. It presupposes a grasp of new ideas. If the ideas are to be above the level of currently successful advertising, serious education must be undertaken. Finally, coming to grasp what serious education really is and, nonetheless, coming to except that challenge constitutes the greatest challenge to the modern economy" (119).

13 Thomas Aquinas, *Summa Theolgiae*, II-II, q. 94, a. 1.
14 *Summa Theolgiae*, II.II. 81.1.
15 *Summa Theolgiae*, II.II.92.1.r.
16 *Summa Theolgiae*, II.II.11.1.
17 *Summa Theolgiae*, II.II, 94.1.
18 Girard, *I See Satan*, 92.
19 Girard, *I See Satan*, 92.
20 Girard, *I See Satan*, 96.
21 See Girard, *I See Satan*, chap. 8.
22 Doran, *Theology and the Dialectics of History*, 116. Doran is appropriating the work of Joseph Schumpeter here.
23 Girard, *I See Satan*, 98–9.
24 In his book *We Become What We Worship: A Biblical Theology of Idolatry* (Downers Grove: InterVarsity, 2008), the biblical scholar G.K. Beale reflects on the constitutive nature of human beings as "imaging creatures." "It is not possible to be neutral on this issue," he writes; "we either reflect the Creator or something in creation" (16). Beale's thesis is that "What people revere, they resemble, either for ruin or restoration" (16).
25 James K.A. Smith, *Desiring the Kingdom: Worship, Worldview, and Cultural Formation* (Grand Rapids: Baker Academic, 2009), 26–7.
26 Smith, *Desiring the Kingdom*, 50. For a helpful complement (and even at times a corrective) to Smith's account from a position influenced heavily by Lonergan, see Steven D. Cone and R.J. Snell, *Authentic Cosmopolitanism: Love, Sin, and Grace in the Christian University* (Eugene: Pickwick, 2013). Cone and Snell write: "We will not devote much attention to worship, cultural practices, conditions of social life, or embodiment. This is not, however, hostility or oversight of those realities, but rather a close read of what it means to be conscious lovers. To be sure, our project can, and should, be supplemented by the sort of reflections Smith and others provide, just as we claim that our project can be thought of as a supplement or sustained deliberation about one aspect of his," namely "intentionality" (6). While appreciative of Smith's project as a whole, they also point out his misrepresentation and oversimplification of certain thinkers. Although they are on common ground on an "anthropology of love," they point out that Smith uses a common narrative that lumps "Plato with Descartes' anthropology of the 'thinking thing," antipathy to the body, and deeply unchristian account of the created realm. As for Aquinas, he comes off terribly, supposedly creating a zone for reason autonomous from, and at potentially at odds with, revelation, and with a semi-Pelagian optimism concerning reason" (16).

27 Smith, *Desiring the Kingdom*, 57.
28 Smith, *Desiring the Kingdom*, 58.
29 Smith, *Desiring the Kingdom*, 35.
30 Smith, *Desiring the Kingdom*, 24.
31 Smith, *Desiring the Kingdom*, 95–6.
32 Smith, *Desiring the Kingdom*, 101.
33 Lonergan, "Sacralization and Secularization," in *Philosophical and Theological Papers 1965–1980*, CWL 6 (Toronto: University of Toronto Press, 2004), 259–81.
34 For his analysis of Chenu and Daniélou, Lonergan is relying on Claude Geffre, "Descralization and the Spiritual Life," *Concilium* 19 (1966): 111–31.
35 Boersma, *Nouvelle Théologie and Sacramental Ontology*, 11–12.
36 Boersma, *Nouvelle Théologie and Sacramental Ontology*, 12.
37 Lonergan, "Sacralization and Secularization," 264.
38 Lonergan, "Sacralization and Secularization," 264.
39 Lonergan, "Sacralization and Secularization," 265.
40 Lonergan, "Sacralization and Secularization," 265.
41 Lonergan, "Sacralization and Secularization," 266.
42 Lonergan, "Sacralization and Secularization," 280.
43 Kelton Cobb, *The Blackwell Guide to Theology and Popular Culture* (Malden: Blackwell, 2005), 7.
44 Juilet Schor, *Born to Buy: The Commercialized Child and the New Consumer Culture* (New York: Scribner, 2004), 11.
45 Schor, *Born to Buy*, 13.
46 Schor, *Born to Buy*, 17.
47 Lonergan, "Sacralization and Secularization," 268.
48 Lonergan, "Sacralization and Secularization,"268–9.
49 Lonergan, "Sacralization and Secularization," 269.
50 Doran, *The Trinity in History*, 253.
51 Doran, *The Trinity in History*, 228.
52 Smith, *Desiring the Kingdom*, 54.
53 Audio interview with Robert Harrison, http://french-italian.stanford.edu/opinions/girard.html.
54 Girard, *I See Satan*, 8.
55 Girard, *I See Satan*, 8.
56 Girard, *I See Satan*, 8–9.
57 Girard, *I See Satan*, 15.
58 Audio interview with Robert Harrison, http://french-italian.stanford.edu/opinions/girard.html.
59 Girard, *Evolution and Conversion: Dialogues on the Origins of Culture* (London: Bloomsbury Academic, 2008), 80.

60 Girard, *Evolution and Conversion*, 80.
61 Girard, "Eating Disorders and Mimetic Desire," *Contagion* 3 (1996): 10. Girard writes: "The politically correct reading of this phenomenon is that the rich young people regard their own superior buying power with a feeling of guilt, and they desire, if not to be poor, at least to look poor. This interpretation is too idealistic. The real purpose is a calculated indifference to clothes, an ostentatious rejection of ostentation. The message is: "I am beyond a certain type of consumption. I cultivate more esoteric pleasures than the crowd." To abstain voluntarily from something, no matter what, is the ultimate demonstration that one is superior to that something and to those who covet it" ("Eating Disorders and Mimetic Desire," 10). He says this about the impact on competition: "The wealthier we are, the more precious the objects must be for which we deign to compete. Very rich people no longer compare themselves through the mediation of clothes, automobiles, or even houses. The more wealthy we are, in other words, the less grossly materialistic we can afford to be in a hierarchy of competitive games that become more and more rarefied as the escalation continues. Ultimately this process may turn into a complete rejection of competition, which is not always but may be the most intense competition of all" ("Eating Disorders and Mimetic Desire," 10–11).
62 Girard, *I See Satan*, 181.
63 Girard, *Evolution and Conversion*, 79.
64 Girard, *Evolution and Conversion*, 79.
65 Girard, *Evolution and Conversion*, 80.
66 Girard, *Evolution and Conversion*, 80.
67 Girard, *Evolution and Conversion*, 80.
68 Girard, *Evolution and Conversion*, 80.
69 Girard, *Evolution and Conversion*, 79.
70 St Augustine, *Confessions*, 64.
71 Lonergan, "Horizons," *CWL* 17, 20.
72 Lonergan, *Method in Theology*, 122.
73 Lonergan, *Method in Theology*, 344.
74 Doran, *Theology and the Dialectics of History*, 117.
75 Doran, *Theology and the Dialectics of History*, 118.
76 Doran, *Theology and the Dialectics of History*, 96–7.
77 Doran, *Theology and the Dialectics of History*, 97.
78 For a fuller account see, St Augustine, *City of God*, trans. Henry Bettenson (London: Penguin, 2003). For a snapshot of the two cities, see *The Essential Augustine*, ed. Vernon J. Bourke (Indianapolis: Hackett, 1964), 227–8.
79 Doran, *The Trinity in History*, 246.
80 Doran, *Theology and the Dialectics of History*, 488.

81 See Doran, *Theology and the Dialectics of History*, 42–63.
82 Walter E. Conn, "Affective Conversion: The Transformation of Desire," in *Religion and Culture: Essays in Honour of Bernard Lonergan, S.J.*, 261–76.
83 Walker Percy, *Love in the Ruins: The Adventures of a Bad Catholic at a Time Near the End of the World* (New York: Picador, 1971), 6. See also Smith, *Desiring the Kingdom*, 124.
84 Lonergan, *Method in Theology*, 111.

Conclusion

1 Guarino, "Nature and Grace: Seeking the Delicate Balance," 151.
2 Mulcahy, "Aquinas's Notion of Pure Nature," 218.
3 David L. Schindler, "Introduction to the 1998 Edition," in Henri de Lubac, *The Mystery of the Supernatural*, trans. Rosemary Sheed (New York: Crossroad, 1998), xxx.
4 Benedict XVI, *A Reason Open to God: On Universities, Education and Culture*, ed. J. Steven Brown (Washington, DC: Catholic University of America Press, 2013).
5 The language of "superstructure" comes from Robert M. Doran, *Theology and the Dialectics of History*, 94–9.
6 Benedict XVI, *A Reason Open to God*, 245.
7 Benedict XVI, *A Reason Open to God*, 245.
8 Benedict XVI, "The Regensburg Lecture," appendix to James V. Schall, *The Regensburg Lecture* (South Bend: St. Augustine's Press, 2007), no. 46, 142.
9 Lonergan, "Natural Knowledge of God," 130.
10 Lonergan, "Natural Knowledge of God," 130.
11 Doran, *What Is Systematic Theology?*, 126.
12 Lawrence S. Cunningham, *A Brief History of Saints* (Malden: Blackwell, 2005), 136.
13 Cunningham, *A Brief History of Saints*, 136.
14 Lawrence S. Cunningham, "Saints," in *The New Dictionary of Theology*, ed. Joseph A. Komonchak et al. (Collegeville: Liturgical Press, 1987), 927.
15 This story is recounted in Paul Elie, *The Life You Save May Be Your Own: An American Pilgrimage* (New York: Farrar, Straus and Giroux, 2003), 28.

Bibliography

Alison, James. *The Joy of Being Wrong: Original Sin through Easter Eyes*. New York: Crossroad, 1998.
– *Raising Abel: The Recovery of the Eschatological Imagination*. New York: Crossroad, 1996.
Augustine. *City of God*. Translated by Henry Bettenson. London: Penguin, 2003.
– *Confessions*. Translated by Henry Chadwick. Oxford: Oxford University Press, 1998.
– *The Confessions*. Edited by David Vincent Meconi. Translated by Maria Boulding. San Francisco: Ignatius, 2012.
– *The Essential Augustine*. Edited by Vernon J. Bourke. Indianapolis: Hackett, 1964.
Balthasar, Hans Urs von. *Glory of the Lord: A Theological Aesthetics*, vol. 5: *The Realm of Metaphysics in the Modern Age*. Translated by Oliver Davies et al. San Francisco: Ignatius, 1991.
– *Theo-Logic I: Truth of the World*. Translated by Adrian J. Walker. San Francisco: Ignatius, 2000.
– *The Theology of Henri de Lubac: An Overview*. San Francisco: Ignatius, 1991.
– *The Theology of Karl Barth*. Translated by Edward T. Oakes. San Francisco: Ignatius, 1992.
– *Two Sisters in the Spirit: St. Thérèse of Lisieux and Elizabeth of the Trinity*. San Francisco: Ignatius, 1992.
Barron, Robert. *Exploring Catholic Theology: Essays on God, Liturgy, and Evangelization*. Grand Rapids: Baker Academic, 2015.
Beabout, Gregory R. "Response to Randall Rosenberg." In *Concepts of Nature: Ancient and Modern*, edited by R. J. Snell and Steven F. McGuire, 225–35. Lanham: Lexington, 2016.

Beale, G.K. *We Become What We Worship: A Biblical Theology of Idolatry*. Downers Grove: InterVarsity, 2008.

Benedict XVI. *Caritas in Veritate*. 2009. http://w2.vatican.va/content/benedict-xvi/en/encyclicals/documents/hf_ben-xvi_enc_20090629_caritas-in-veritate.html.

– *A Reason Open to God: On Universities, Education and Culture*. Edited by J. Steven Brown. Washington, DC: Catholic University of America Press, 2013.

– "The Regensburg Lecture." In James V. Schall, *The Regensburg Lecture*, 130–48. South Bend: St. Augustine's Press, 2007.

– *Spe Salvi*. 2007. http://w2.vatican.va/content/benedict-xvi/en/encyclicals/documents/hf_ben-xvi_enc_20071130_spe-salvi.html.

Berry, Wendell. *The Art of the Commonplace: The Agrarian Essays of Wendell Berry*. Edited by Norman Wirzba. Berkeley: Counterpoint, 2002.

Betz, John. "After Barth: A New Introduction to Erich Przywara's *Analogia Entis*." In *The Analogy of Being: Invention of the Antichrist or the Wisdom of God?*, edited by Thomas Joseph White, 35–87. Grand Rapids: Eermands, 2010.

Blackwood, Jeremy W. "Eighteen Days in 1968: An Essay on the Maturation of Lonergan's Intentionality Analysis." *Method: Journal of Lonergan Studies* 3.2 (Fall 2012): 1–26.

– "Sanctifying Grace, Elevation, and the Fifth Level of Consciousness." *Method: Journal of Lonergan Studies,* n.s., 2.2 (2011): 143–61.

– "Trinitarian Love in the Dialectics of History." *Method: Journal of Lonergan Studies*, n.s., 4.1 (2013): 1–16.

Boersma, Hans. "Analogy of Truth: The Sacramental Epistemology of *Nouvelle Théologie*." In Flynn and Murray, *Ressourcement*, 157–71.

– *Nouvelle Théologie and Sacramental Ontology: A Return to Mystery*. New York: Oxford University Press, 2009.

Bonino, Serge-Thomas. "The Theory of Limbo and the Mystery of the Supernatural in St. Thomas Aquinas." In *Surnaturel: A Controversy at the Heart of Twentieth-Century Thomistic Thought*, edited by Serge-Thomas Bonino and translated by Robert Williams and Matthew Levering, 117–54. Ave Maria: Sapientia, 2009.

Boyle, Nicholas. *Who Are We Now? Christian Humanism and the Global Market from Hegel to Heaney*. Notre Dame: University of Notre Dame Press, 1998.

Braine, David. "The Debate between Henri de Lubac and His Critics." *Nova et Vetera,* English ed., 6 (2008): 543–90.

Braman, Brian J. *Meaning and Authenticity: Bernard Lonergan and Charles Taylor on the Drama of Authentic Human Existence*. Toronto: University of Toronto Press, 2008.

Brotherton, Joshua R. "The Integrity of Nature in the Grace-Freedom Dialectic: Lonergan's Critique of Báñezian Thomism." *Theological Studies* 75.3 (2014): 537–63.

Buckley, Michael J. *At the Origins of Modern Atheism*. New Haven: Yale University Press, 1987.
– *Denying and Disclosing God: The Ambiguous Progress of Modern Atheism*. New Haven: Yale University Press, 2004.
Bushlack, Thomas J. *Politics for a Pilgrim Church: A Thomistic Theory of Civic Virtue*. Grand Rapids: Eerdmans, 2015.
Byrne, Patrick "Consciousness: Levels, Sublations, and the Subject as Subject." *Method: Journal of Lonergan Studies* 13 (1995): 131–50.
Coakley, Sarah. *God, Sexuality, and the Self: An Essay "on the Trinity."* Cambridge: Cambridge University Press, 2013.
Cobb, Kelton. *The Blackwell Guide to Theology and Popular Culture*. Malden: Blackwell, 2005.
Coetsier, Meins G.S. *Etty Hillesum and the Flow of Presence*. Columbia: University of Missouri Press, 2008.
Coffey, David M. "*Quaestio Disputata*: Response to Neil Ormerod, and Beyond." *Theological Studies* 68.4 (2007): 900–15.
Cole, Basil. "Is Limbo Ready to Be Abolished? Limbo Revisited." *Nova et Vetera*, English ed., 6.2 (208): 403–18.
Collins, James. *Pilgrim in Love: An Introduction to Dante and His Spirituality*. Chicago: Loyola University Press, 1984.
Cone, Steven D., and R.J. Snell. *Authentic Cosmopolitanism: Love, Sin, and Grace in the Christian University*. Eugene: Pickwick, 2013.
Conn, Joann Wolski. "A Feminist View of Thérèse." In *Carmelite Studies 5: Experiencing Saint Thérèse Today*, edited by John Sullivan, 119–39. Washington, DC: ICS, 1990.
Conn, Walter E. "Affective Conversion: The Transformation of Desire." In *Religion and Culture: Essays in Honour of Bernard Lonergan, S.J.*, edited by Timothy P. Fallon and Phillip Boo Riley, 261–76. Albany: SUNYPress, 1987.
Cooper, Adam G. *Naturally Human, Supernaturally God: Deification in Pre-Conciliar Catholicism*. Minneapolis: Fortress, 2014.
Crowe, Frederick E. "Son of God, Holy Spirit, and World Religions." In *Appropriating the Lonergan Idea*, edited by Michael Vertin, 324–43. Toronto: University of Toronto Press, 2006.
Crysdale, Cynthia. "Revisioning Natural Law: From the Classicist Paradigm to Emergent Probability." *Theological Studies* 56.3 (September 1995): 464–84.
Crysdale, Cynthia, and Neil Ormerod. *Creator God, Evolving World*. Minneapolis: Fortress, 2013.
Cullen, Christopher M. "The Natural Desire for God and Pure Nature: A Debate Renewed." *American Catholic Philosophical Quarterly* 86.4 (2012): 705–30.

Cunningham, Lawrence S. *A Brief History of Saints*. Malden: Blackwell, 2005.
- "Saints." In *The New Dictionary of Theology*, edited by Joseph A. Komonchak et al, 925–9. Collegeville: Liturgical Press, 1987.

Dadosky, John D. "Desire, Bias, and Love: Revisiting Lonergan's Philosophical Anthropology." *Irish Theological Quarterly* 77.3 (2012): 244–64.
- *The Eclipse and Recovering of Beauty: A Lonergan Approach*. Toronto: University of Toronto Press, 2014.
- "Is There a Fourth Stage of Meaning?" *Heythrop Journal* 51.5 (2010): 768–80.
- "Midwiving the Fourth Stage of Meaning: Lonergan and Doran." In *Meaning and History in Systematic Theology: Essays in Honor of Robert M. Doran, S.J.*, edited by John D. Dadosky, 71–92. Milwaukee: Marquette University Press, 2009.
- "'Naming the Demon': The 'Structure' of Evil in Lonergan and Girard." *Irish Theological Quarterly* 75.4 (2010): 355–72.
- "Woman without Envy: Toward Reconceiving the Immaculate Conception." *Theological Studies* 72.1 (2011): 16–40.

Daniélou, Jean. "The Present Orientations of Religious Thought." *Josephinum Journal of Theology* 18.1 (2011): 51-62.

de Lubac, Henri. *At the Service of the Church: Henri de Lubac Reflects on the Circumstances That Occasioned His Writings*. San Francisco: Ignatius, 1992
- *Augustinianism and Modern Theology*. Translated by Lancelot Sheppard. New York: Crossroad, 2000.
- *A Brief Catechesis on Nature and Grace*. San Francisco: Ignatius, 1984.
- "Catholic Action." In *Theology in History*, 241–3.
- *Christian Resistance to Anti-Semitism: Memories from 1940–1944*. Translated by Elizabeth Englund. San Francisco: Ignatius, 1990.
- "The Church in Crisis." *Theology Digest* 17.4 (1969): 312–25.
- *The Drama of Atheist Humanism*. San Francisco: Ignatius, 1995.
- "Internal Causes of the Weakening and Disappearance of the Sense of the Sacred." In *Theology in History*, 223–40.
- *Letters of Étienne Gilson to Henri de Lubac*. Annotated by Henri de Lubac. San Francisco: Ignatius, 1988.
- "Letter to My Superiors." In *Theology in History*, 428–39.
- *The Mystery of the Supernatural*. Translated by Rosemary Sheed. New York: Crossroad, 1998.
- "The Mystery of the Supernatural." In *Theology in History*, 281–316.
- *Paradoxes of Faith*. San Francisco: Ignatius, 1987.
- *Surnaturel: Études historiques*. Paris: Aubier, 1946.
- *A Theologian Speaks*. Interview by Angelo Scola. Los Angeles: Twin Circle, 1985.

- *Theology in History*. Translated by Anne Englund Nash. San Francisco: Ignatius, 1996.
- "The Total Meaning of Man and the World." *Communio: International Catholic Review* 35 (Winter 2008): 613–41.

Doran, Robert M. "Consciousness and Grace." *Method: Journal of Lonergan Studies* 11 (1993): 51–75.
- *Theology and the Dialectic of History*. Toronto: University of Toronto Press, 1990.
- *The Trinity in History: A Theology of the Divine Missions*, vol. 1: *Missions and Processions*. Toronto: University of Toronto Press, 2012.
- *What Is Systematic Theology?* Toronto: University of Toronto Press, 2005.

Doyle, Dominic F. *The Promise of Christian Humanism: Thomas Aquinas on Hope*. New York: Crossroad, 2012.

Duffy, Stephen J. *The Graced Horizon: Nature and Grace in Modern Catholic Thought*. Collegeville: Liturgical, 1992.

Dunne, Tad. "Being in Love." *Method: Journal of Lonergan Studies* 13 (1995): 161–75.

Elie, Paul. *The Life You Save May Be Your Own: An American Pilgrimage*. New York: Farrar, Straus and Giroux, 2003.

Feingold, Lawrence. *The Natural Desire to See God According to St. Thomas Aquinas and His Interpreters*. Ave Maria: Sapientia, 2010.

Flanagan, Joseph. *Quest for Self-Knowledge: An Essay in Lonergan's Philosophy*. Toronto: University of Toronto Press, 1997.

Flynn, Gabriel. "Introduction: The Twentieth-Century Renaissance in Catholic Theology." In Flynn and Murray, *Ressourcement*, 1–19.

Flynn, Gabriel, and Paul D. Murray, eds. *Ressourcement: A Movement for Renewal*. New York: Oxford University Press, 2012.

Francis, Pope. *Evangelii Gaudium*. http://w2.vatican.va/content/francesco/en/apost_exhortations/documents/papa-francesco_esortazione-ap_20131124_evangelii-gaudium.html.

Frohlich, Mary. "Desolation and Doctrine in Thérèse of Lisieux." *Theological Studies* 61 (2000): 261–79.
- Introduction to *Thérèse of Lisieux: Essential Writings*, 13–31. Maryknoll: Orbis, 2013.

Gaillardetz, Richard R. "Sexual Vulnerability and a Spirituality of Suffering: Explorations in the Writing of Etty Hillesum." *Pacifica* 22 (February 2009): 75–89.

Garrigou-Lagrange, Reginald. "Where is the New Theology Leading Us?" *Josephinum Journal of Theology* 18.1 (2011): 63–78.

Gaudium et Spes. http://www.vatican.va/archive/hist_councils/ii_vatican_council/documents/vat-ii_const_19651207_gaudium-et-spes_en.html.

Geffre, Claude "Descralization and the Spiritual Life." *Concilium* 19 (1966): 111–31.
Girard, René. *Deceit, Desire, and the Novel: Self and Other in Literary Structure*. Translated by Yvonne Freccero. Baltimore: Johns Hopkins University Press, 1965.
– "Eating Disorders and Mimetic Desire." *Contagion: Journal of Violence, Mimesis, and Culture* 3 (1996): 1–20.
– *Evolution and Conversion: Dialogues on the Origins of Culture*. London: Bloomsbury Academic, 2008.
– *The Girard Reader*. Edited by James G. Williams. New York: Crossroads, 1996.
– *I See Satan Fall Like Lightning*. Translated by James G. Williams. Maryknoll: Orbis, 2001.
– *Mimesis and Theory: Essays on Literature and Criticism, 1953–2005*. Edited by Robert Doran. Stanford: Stanford University Press, 2008.
– *The Scapegoat*. Translated by Yvonne Freccero. Baltimore: Johns Hopkins University Press, 1986.
– *Things Hidden Since the Foundation of the World*. Translated by Stephen Bann and Michael Metteer. Stanford: Stanford University Press, 1987.
– *Violence and the Sacred*. Translated by Patrick Gregory. Baltimore: Johns Hopkins University Press, 1977.
– *When These Things Begin*. Translated by Trevor Cribben Merrill. East Lansing: Michigan State University Press, 2014.
Grumett, David. "De Lubac, Grace, and the Pure Nature Debate." *Modern Theology* 31.1 (January 2015): 123–46.
– "Henri de Lubac: Looking for Books to Read the World." In Flynn and Murray, *Ressourcement*, 236–49.
Guarino, Thomas G. "Nature and Grace: Seeking the Delicate Balance." *Josephinum Journal of Theology* 18.1 (2011): 151–62.
Hart, David Bentley. *The Beauty of the Infinite: The Aesthetics of Christian Truth*. Grand Rapids: Eerdmans, 2003.
– *The Experience of God: Being, Consciousness, Bliss*. New Haven: Yale University Press, 2013.
Healy, Nicholas J. "Henri de Lubac on Nature and Grace: A Note on Some Recent Contributions to the Debate." *Communio: International Catholic Review* 35 (Winter 2008): 535–64.
Hedrick-Moser, Erick H. "The Formation of Jean Daniélou's Vision for Catholicism in Secular France, 1925–1950." Doctoral diss., Saint Louis University, 2015.

Hefling, Charles C. "About What Might a 'Girard-Lonergan Conversation' Be?" In *Lonergan Workshop Journal*, vol. 17, edited by Frederick Lawrence, 95–123. Chestnut Hill: Boston College, 2002.
– "Revelation and/as Insight." In *The Importance of Insight: Essays in Honour of Michael Vertin*, edited by John J. Liptay and David S. Liptay, 97–115. Toronto: University of Toronto Press, 2006.
Hengel, John van den. "God with/out Being." *Method: Journal of Lonergan Studies* 12 (1994): 251–79.
Henrici, Peter. "A Sketch of von Balthasar's Life." In *Hans Urs von Balthasar: His Life and Work*, edited by David L. Schindler, 7–43. San Francisco: Ignatius, 1991.
Hillesum, Etty. *Etty Hillesum: Essential Writings*. Maryknoll: Orbis, 2009.
– *An Interrupted Life: The Diaries, 1941–1943 and Letters from Westerbork*. Introduction and notes by Jan G. Gaarlandt. New York: Holt, 1996.
Himes, Brian. "Lonergan's Position on the Natural Desire to See God and Aquinas' Metaphysical Theology of Creation and Participation." *Heythrop Journal* 54 (2013): 767–83.
Hoffman, Eva. Foreword to Etty Hillesum, *An Interrupted Life: The Diaries, 1941–1943 and Letters from Westerbork*, with introduction and notes by Jan G. Gaarlandt, vii–xii. New York: Holt, 1996.
Horner, Robyn. *Jean-Luc Marion: A Theo-logical Introduction*. Burlington: Ashgate, 2005.
Hughes, Glenn C. "Image, Art, and Cosmopolis." In *Language of the Heart: Lonergan, Images, and Feelings*, Lonergan Workshop 11, edited by Frederick Lawrence, 1–19. Boston: Boston College, 1995.
Hütter, Reinhard. *Dust Bound for Heaven: Explorations in the Theology of Thomas Aquinas*. Grand Rapids: Eerdmans, 2012.
Ignatius of Loyola. *The Autobiography*. In *Ignatius of Loyola: Spiritual Exercises and Selected Works*, edited by George E. Ganss and translated by Parmananda R. Divarkar, 65–111. New York: Paulist, 1991.
International Theological Commission. "The Hope of Salvation for Infants Who Die Without Being Baptized." http://www.vatican.va/roman_curia/congregations/cfaith/cti_documents/rc_con_cfaith_doc_20070419_un-baptised-infants_en.html.
Jacobs-Vandegeer, Christian. "Sanctifying Grace in a Methodical Theology." *Theological Studies* 68.1 (2007): 52–76.
John Paul II. *Centesimus Annus*. 1991. http://w2.vatican.va/content/john-paul-ii/en/encyclicals/documents/hf_jp-ii_enc_01051991_centesimus-annus.html.
– *Fides et Ratio*. http://w2.vatican.va/content/john-paul-ii/en/encyclicals/documents/hf_jp-ii_enc_14091998_fides-et-ratio.html.

- *Redemptoris Missio*. http://w2.vatican.va/content/john-paul-ii/en/encyclicals/documents/hf_jp-ii_enc_07121990_redemptoris-missio.html.
- *Solicitudo Rei Socialis*. http://w2.vatican.va/content/john-paul-ii/en/encyclicals/documents/hf_jp-ii_enc_30121987_sollicitudo-rei-socialis.html.

Kaplan, Grant. "New Paths for a Girard/Lonergan Conversation: An Essay in light of Robert Doran's *Missions and Processions*." *Method: Journal of Lonergan Studies*, n.s., 4.1 (2013): 23–38.
- *René Girard, Unlikely Apologist: Mimetic Theory and Fundamental Theology*. Notre Dame: University of Notre Dame Press, 2016.
- "Saint versus Hero: Girard's Undoing of Romantic Hagiology." In *The Postmodern Saints of France: Refiguring "The Holy" in Contemporary French Philosophy*, edited by Colby Dickinson, 153–67. London: T&T Clark, 2013.

Kasper, Walter. *Theology and Church*. Translated by Margaret Kohl. New York: Crossroad, 1989.

Kerr, Fergus. "French Theology: Yves Congar and Henri de Lubac." In *The Modern Theologians: An Introduction to Christian Theology in the Twentieth Century*, 2nd ed., edited by David F. Ford, 105–17. Malden: Blackwell, 1997.
- *Twentieth Century Catholic Theologians: From Neoscholasticism to Nuptial Mysticism*. Malden: Blackwell, 2007.

Kidder, Annemarie S. *Etty Hillesum: Essential Writings*. Maryknoll: Orbis: 2009.

Komonchak, Joseph A. "Humani Generis and Nouvelle Théologie." In Flynn and Murray, *Ressourcement*, 138–56.
- "Theology and Culture at Mid-Century: The Example of Henri de Lubac." *Theological Studies* 51 (1990): 579–602.

Lamb, Matthew L. *Eternity, Time, and the Life of Wisdom*. Ave Maria: Sapientia, 2007.
- *Solidarity with Victims: Toward a Theology of Social Transformation*. New York: Crossroad, 1982.

Lawrence, Frederick G. *The Fragility of Consciousness: Faith, Reason, and the Human Good*. Edited by Randall S. Rosenberg and Kevin M. Vander Schel. Toronto: University of Toronto Press, 2017.

Lenehan, Kevin. "Girard and the Tasks of Theology." In *Violence, Desire, and the Sacred*, vol. 1: *Girard's Mimetic Theory across the Disciplines*, edited by Scott Cowdell, Chris Fleming, and Joel Hodge. New York: Bloomsbury, 2012.

Leo XIII. *Aeterni Patris*. http://w2.vatican.va/content/leo-xiii/en/encyclicals/documents/hf_l-xiii_enc_04081879_aeterni-patris.html.

Levering, Matthew, and Reinhard Hütter, eds. *Ressourcement Thomism: Sacred Doctrine, the Sacraments, and the Moral Life*. Washington, DC: Catholic University of America Press, 2010.
- *Scripture and Metaphysics: Aquinas and the Renewal of Trinitarian Theology*. Malden: Blackwell, 2004.

Levinas, Emmanuel. *Totality and Infinity*. Translated by Alphonso Lingis. Pittsburgh: Duquesne University Press, 1969.
Lonergan, Bernard J.F. *Collection*. In *Collected Works of Bernard Lonergan* (CWL) 4, edited by Frederick E. Crowe and Robert M. Doran. Toronto: University of Toronto Press, 1993.
– *Early Latin Theology*. In *CWL* 19, edited by Robert M. Doran and H. Daniel Monsour and translated by Michael G. Shields. Toronto: University of Toronto Press, 2011.
– *Grace and Freedom: Operative Grace in the Thought of St. Thomas Aquinas*. In *CWL* 1, edited by Frederick E. Crowe and Robert M. Doran. Toronto: University of Toronto Press, 2000.
– *Insight: A Study of Human Understanding*. In *CWL* 3, edited by Frederick E. Crowe and Robert M. Doran. Toronto: University of Toronto Press, 1992.
– "*Insight* Revisited." In *A Second Collection*, *CWL* 13, ed. W.F.J. Ryan and Bernard J. Tyrrell. Toronto: University of Toronto Press, 1996.
– *Macroeconomic Dynamics: An Essay in Circulation Analysis*. In *CWL* 15, edited by Frederick G. Lawrence, Patrick H. Byrne, and Charles C. Hefling, Jr. Toronto: University of Toronto Press, 1999.
– *Method in Theology*. New York: Herder and Herder, 1972.
– *The Ontological and Psychological Constitution of Christ*. In *CWL* 7, translated by Michael G. Shields. Toronto: University of Toronto Press, 2002.
– *Phenomenology and Logic: Lectures on Mathematical Logic and Existentialism*. In *CWL* 6, edited by Philip J. McShane. Toronto: University of Toronto Press, 2001.
– *Philosophical and Theological Papers 1958–1964*. In *CWL* 6, edited by Frederick E. Crowe and Robert M. Doran. Toronto: University of Toronto Press, 1996.
– *Philosophical and Theological Papers 1965–1980*. In *CWL* 17, edited by Robert C. Croken and Robert M. Doran. Toronto: University of Toronto Press, 2004.
– *A Second Collection*. *CWL* 13, edited by W.F.J. Ryan and Bernard J. Tyrrell. Toronto: University of Toronto Press, 1996.
– *A Third Collection: Papers by Bernard Lonergan, S.J.* Edited by Frederick E. Crowe. New York: Paulist, 1985.
– *Topics in Education*. In *CWL* 10, edited by Frederick E. Crowe and Robert M. Doran. Toronto: University of Toronto Press, 1993.
– *The Triune God: Systematics*. In *CWL* 12, edited by Robert M. Doran and H. Daniel Monsour and translated by Michael G. Shields. Toronto: University of Toronto Press, 2007.
– *Verbum: Word and Idea in Aquinas*. In *CWL* 2, edited by Frederick E. Crowe and Robert M. Doran. Toronto: University of Toronto Press, 1997.
Long, D. Stephen. *Speaking of God: Theology, Language, and Truth*. Grand Rapids: Eerdmans, 2009.

Long, Steven A. *Natura Pura: On the Recovery of Nature in the Doctrine of Grace*. New York: Fordham University Press, 2010.
Loughlin, Gerard. "*Nouvelle Théologie*: A Return to Modernism?" In Flynn and Murray, *Ressourcement*, 36–50.
MacIntyre, Alasdair. "Three Perspective on Marxism." In *Ethics and Politics: Selected Essays*, vol. 2, 145–58. Cambridge: Cambridge University Press, 2006.
Malloy, Christopher J. "De Lubac on Natural Desire: Difficulties and Antitheses." *Nova et Vetera*, English ed., 9.3 (2011): 567–624.
Maloney, Raymond. "De Lubac and Lonergan on the Supernatural." *Theological Studies* 59 (2008): 509–27.
Mansini, Guy. "The Abiding Significance of Henri de Lubac's *Surnaturel*." *The Thomist* 73.4 (2009): 593–619.
– "Henri de Lubac, the Natural Desire to See God, and Pure Nature." *Gregorianum* 83.1 (2002): 89–109.
– "Lonergan on the Natural Desire in the Light of Feingold." *Nova et Vetera*, English ed., 5.1 (2007): 185–98.
Marion, Jean-Luc. *Cartesian Questions: Method and Metaphysics*. Chicago: University of Chicago Press, 1999.
– *On Descartes' Metaphysical Prism: The Constitution and Limits of Onto-theo-logy in Cartesian Thought*. Translated by Jeffrey L. Kosky. Chicago: University of Chicago Press, 1999.
– *The Erotic Phenomenon*. Translated by Stephen E. Lewis. Chicago: University of Chicago Press, 2007.
Marsh, James. "Why Lonerganian Philosophers Should Read Lonergan's and Doran's Theology." *Method: Journal of Lonergan Studies*, n.s., 4.1 (2013): 39–45.
McCormack, Bruce L. "Karl Barth's Version of an 'Analogy of Being': A Dialectical No and Yes to Roman Catholicism." In *The Analogy of Being: Invention of the Antichrist or the Wisdom of God?*, edited by Thomas Joseph White, 88–144. Grand Rapids: Eermands, 2010.
Milbank, John. *The Suspended Middle: Henri de Lubac and the Debate Concerning the Supernatural*. Grand Rapids: Eerdmans, 2005.
– *The Suspended Middle: Henri de Lubac and the Renewed Split in Modern Catholic Theology*. 2nd ed. Grand Rapids: Eerdmans, 2014.
– *Theology and Social Theory*. 2nd ed. Malden: Blackwell, 2006.
Miller, Mark T. *The Quest for God and the Good Life*. Washington, DC: Catholic University of America Press, 2013.
Mongrain, Kevin. "Theologians of Spiritual Transformation: A Proposal for Reading René Girard through the Lenses of Hans Urs von Balthasar and John Cassian." *Modern Theology* 28.1 (January 2012): 81–111.

Mudd, Joseph C. *Eucharist as Meaning: Critical Metaphysics and Contemporary Sacramental Theology*. Collegeville: Liturgical Press, 2014.
Mulcahy, Bernard. *Aquinas' Notion of Pure Nature and the Christian Integralism of Henri de Lubac: Not Everything is Grace*. New York: Peter Lang, 2011.
Murphy, Francesca Aran. "Gilson and the *Ressourcement*." In Flynn and Murray, *Ressourcement*, 51–64.
Murphy, Nancy, and William R. Stoeger. *Evolution and Emergence: Systems, Organisms, Persons*. Oxford: Oxford University Press, 2007.
Murphy, Jr, William F. "Thomism and the *Nouvelle Théologie*: A Dialogue Renewed?" *Josephinum Journal of Theology* 18.1 (2011): 4–36.
Narcisse, Gilbert. "The Supernatural in Contemporary Theology." In *Surnaturel: A Controversy at the Heart of Twentieth-Century Thomistic Thought*, edited by Serge-Thomas Bonino and translated by Robert Williams and Matthew Levering, 295–309. Ave Maria: Sapientia, 2009.
Nevin, Thomas R. *The Last Years of St. Thérèse: Doubt and Darkness, 1895–1897*. Oxford: Oxford University Press, 2013.
– *Thérèse of Lisieux: God's Gentle Warrior*. Oxford: Oxford University Press, 2006.
Newman, John Henry. *An Essay in Aid of a Grammar of Assent*. Notre Dame: University of Notre Dame, 1979.
Nygren, Anders. "Eros and Agape." In *Eros, Agape, and Philia: Readings in the Philosophy of Love*, edited by Alan Stroble, 85–95. Paragon House, 1998.
Oakes, Edward T. "Catholic Eschatology and the Development of Doctrine." *Nova et Vetera*, English ed., 6.2 (2008): 419–46.
– "The *Surnaturel* Controversy: A Survey and Response." *Nova et Vetera*, English ed., 9.3 (2011): 625–56.
Ormerod, Neil. "Addendum on the Grace-Nature Distinction." *Theological Studies* 75.4 (2014): 890–8.
– *Creation, Grace, and Redemption*. Maryknoll: Orbis, 2007.
– "Desire and the Origins of Culture: Lonergan and Girard in Conversation." *Heythrop Journal* 54.5 (September 2013): 784–95.
– "Doran's *The Trinity in History*: The Girardian Connection." *Method: Journal of Lonergan Studies*, n.s., 4.1 (2013): 47–59.
– "The Grace-Nature Distinction and the Construction of a Systematic Theology." *Theological Studies* 75.3 (2014): 515–36.
– "The Metaphysics of Holiness: Created Participation in Divine Nature." *Irish Theological Quarterly* 79.1 (2014): 68–82.
– "Questioning Desire: Lonergan, Girard and Buddhism." *Louvain Studies* 36.4 (2014): 356–71.
Peacocke, Arthur. "Biological Evolution – A Positive Appraisal." In *Evolutionary and Molecular Biology: Scientific Perspectives on Divine Action*,

edited by Robert John Russell, William R. Stoeger, and Francisco J. Ayala, 357–76. Vatican City State: Vatican Observatory Publications/Berkeley: Center for Theology and the Natural Sciences, 1998.

Percy, Walker. *Love in the Ruins: The Adventures of a Bad Catholic at a Time Near the End of the World*. New York: Picador, 1971.

– *The Moviegoer*. New York: Fawcett Columbine, 1960.

– "Symbol as Need." In *The Message in the Bottle: How Queer Man Is, How Queer Language Is, and What One Has to Do with the Other*, 288–97. New York: Noonday/Farrar, Straus, and Giroux, 1985.

Pereira, José. "Thomism and the Magisterium: From *Aeterni Paris* to *Veritatis Splendor*." *Logos: A Journal of Catholic Thought and Culture* 5.3 (2002): 147–83.

Pius XII. *Humani Generis*. http://w2.vatican.va/content/pius-xii/en/encyclicals/documents/hf_p-xii_enc_12081950_humani-generis.html.

Pottier, Bernard. "Daniélou and the Twentieth-Century Patristic Renewal." In Flynn and Murray, *Ressourcement*, 250–62.

Przywara, Erich. *Analogia Entis: Metaphysics; Original Structure and Universal Rhythm*. Translated by John R. Betz and David Bentley Hart. Grand Rapids: Eerdmans, 2014.

Rober, Daniel A. *Recognizing the Gift: Toward a Renewed Theology of Nature and Grace*. Minneapolis: Fortress, 2016.

Robinette, Brian. "Deceit, Desire, and the Desert." In *Violence, Transformation, and the Sacred*, edited by Margaret Pfeil and Tobias Winright. Maryknoll: Orbis, 2011.

– *Grammars of Resurrection: A Christian Theology of Presence and Absence*. New York: Crossroad, 2009.

Rosenberg, Randall S. "The Drama of Scripture: Reading Patristic Biblical Hermeneutics through Bernard Lonergan's Reflections on Art." *Logos: A Journal of Catholic Thought and Culture* 11.2 (Spring 2008): 126–48.

– "From Pure Nature to Concrete Subject: The Question of God in the Secular Age." In *Concepts of Nature: Ancient and Modern*, edited by R.J. Snell and Steven F. McGuire, 199–224. Lanham: Lexington, 2016.

– "Guarding a Metaphysics of the Whole Person: Walker Percy and Bernard Lonergan." *Gregorianum* 95.3 (2014): 577–96.

– "Incarnate Meaning and Mimetic Desire: Notes toward the Development of a Theology of the Saints." In *New Voices in Catholic Theology*, edited by Anna Bonta Moreland and Joseph Curran, 207–20. New York: Crossroad, 2012.

– "Lonergan on the Transcendent Orientation of Art." *Renascence: Essays on Values in Literature* 61.3 (Spring 2009): 141–51.

– "Text-Based Friendships and the Quest for Transcendence in a Global-Consumerist Age." In *Grade and Friendship: Theological Essays*, edited by M. Shawn Copeland and Jeremy D. Wilkins, 213–35. Milwaukee: Marquette University Press, 2016.

Ryan, Peter F. "How Can the Beatific Vision Both Fulfill Human Nature and Be Utterly Gratuitous?" *Gregorianum* 83.4 (2002): 717–55.

Schindler, David L. *Heart of the World, Center of the Church: Communio Ecclesiology, Liberalism, and Liberation*. Grand Rapids: Eerdmans, 1996.

Sciglitano, Anthony. "Leaving Neo-Scholasticism Behind: Aspirations and Anxieties." *Josephinum Journal of Theology* 18.1 (2011): 216–39.

Schor, Juliet. *Born to Buy: The Commercialized Child and the New Consumer Culture*. New York: Scribner, 2004.

Smith, James K.A. *Desiring the Kingdom: Worship, Worldview, and Cultural Formation*. Grand Rapids: Baker Academic, 2009.

Sokolowski, Robert. *Introduction to Phenomenology*. Cambridge: Cambridge University Press, 1999.

Stebbins, J. Michael. *The Divine Initiative: Grace, World-Order, and Human Freedom in the Early Writings of Bernard Lonergan*. Toronto: University of Toronto Press, 1995.

Stoeger, William R. "Contemporary Physics and the Ontological Status of the Laws of Nature." In *Quantum Cosmology and the Laws of Nature: Scientific Connections on Divine Action*, edited by Robert John Russell, Nancy Murphy, and C.J. Isham, 209–34. Vatican City State: Vatican Observatory, 1993.

– "Physics and Astronomy in a Catholic Framework." In *Teaching the Tradition: Catholic Themes in Academic Disciplines*, edited by John J. Piderit and Melanie M. Morey. Oxford: Oxford University Press, 2012.

Swafford, Andrew Dean. *Nature and Grace: A New Approach to Thomistic Ressourcement*. Eugene: Pickwick, 2014.

Thérèse of Lisieux. *Story of a Soul*. Translated by John Clarke. Washington, DC: ICS, 2005.

– *Thérèse of Lisieux: Essential Writings*. Selected with an introduction by Mary Frohlich. Maryknoll: Orbis, 2003.

Todorov, Tzvetan. *Facing the Extreme: Moral Life in the Concentration Camps*. Translated by Arthur Denner and Abigail Pollak. New York: Holt/Metropolitan Books, 1996.

Tomassi, Wanda. "Etty Hillesum: A New Kind of Sanctity." In *Saints and Sanctity Today*, edited by Maria Clara Bingemer, Andres Torres Queiruga, and Jon Sobrino. London: SCM Press, 2013.

Torell, Jean-Pierre. *Christ and Spirituality in St. Thomas Aquinas*. Translated by Bernhard Blankenhorn. Washington, DC: Catholic University of America Press, 2011.

– "Nature and Grace in Thomas Aquinas." In *Surnaturel: A Controversy at the Heart of Twentieth-Century Thomistic Thought*, edited by Serge-Thomas Bonino and translated by Robert Williams and Matthew Levering, 155–88. Ave Maria: Sapientia, 2009.

Tracy, David. *The Analogical Imagination: Christian Theology and the Culture of Pluralism*. New York: Crossroad, 1981.
Tyrrell, Bernard. *Bernard Lonergan's Philosophy of God*. Notre Dame: University of Notre Dame Press, 1974.
Vanier, Jean. *From Brokenness to Community*. Mahwah: Paulist, 1992.
Vertin, Michael. "Lonergan on Consciousness: Is There a Fifth Level?" *Method: Journal of Lonergan Studies* 12 (1994): 1–36.
White, Thomas Joseph. "Imperfect Happiness and the Final End of Man: Thomas Aquinas and the Paradigm of Nature-Grace Orthodoxy." *The Thomist* 78.2 (April 2014): 247–89.
– *Incarnate Lord: A Thomistic Study in Christology*. Washington, DC: Catholic University of America Press, 2015.
– *Wisdom in the Face of Modernity: A Study in Thomistic Natural Theology*. Ave Maria: Sapientia, 2009.
Wicks, Jared. "A Note on 'Neo-Scholastic' Manuals of Theological Instruction, 1900–1960." *Josephinum Journal of Theology* 18.1 (2011): 240–6.
Wilkins, Jeremy. "Grace and Growth: Aquinas, Lonergan, and the Problematic of Habitual Grace." *Theological Studies* 72.4 (December 2011): 723–49.
Young, Frances. *The Art of Performance: Towards a Theology of Holy Scripture*. London: Darton, Longman, and Todd, 1990.
– *Biblical Exegesis and the Formation of Christian Culture*. Peabody: Hendrickson, 2002.

Index

active spiration, 122–3, 159–61, 178
Adam, biblical figure, 20, 21, 49, 50, 56–7, 91
aesthetic compromise, 8, 40, 46, 57–9, 94, 112–14
Alison, James, 68–70, 72, 75, 85, 141, 142, 155
analogy: of being, 53, 77; vs. dialectic, 66–8; of the gift, 46; and knowledge of God, 77–9, 96, 98, 108; of nature and the supernatural, 110–11; for the Trinitarian processions, 122, 141
apostolic sanctity, 160–1, 166, 172, 178
Aquinas, Thomas, St, 3, 18–20, 22–4, 27, 32, 34–5, 37–8, 41, 43–5, 49, 54, 56–7, 67, 72, 89–93, 95–6, 100, 103, 113, 117–18, 120, 122, 136, 142–3, 161, 167, 187, 191, 201
Aristotle, 5, 23, 24, 72, 167
Arnauld, Antoine, 21
Augustine, St, 3, 18, 21, 31, 37, 49, 74, 81, 82, 90, 143, 171, 173, 197, 199, 205
Austen, Jane, 134
authenticity, 84, 106, 148, 186

autonomy: Chenu on, 191–2; vs. created receptivity, 60; Doran on spiritual processions of, 141–2; Girard on, 195; relative, 47, 56, 102, 141, 191, 202; and the Romantic lie, 68, 152; of secular learning, 15, 202

Bach, Johann Sebastian, 181
Bacon, Francis, 106
Baianism, 18, 38
Baius, Michael, 20–1
Balthasar, Hans Urs von, 4, 26, 52, 128, 204
Báñez, Domingo, 19, 41, 44, 93, 94
Barth, Karl, 31, 53, 67
Becker, Ernest, 141
being-in-love, 9, 37, 80, 117–22, 127, 129, 136, 175, 178, 182, 197, 235n32, 245n56
Benedict XVI, Pope, 49, 50, 173, 186, 203; *Caritas in Veritate*, 187; *Spe Salvi*, 50
Berry, Wendell, 128, 133, 134
bias, 9, 75, 84–6, 104–5, 126, 159, 202–3
Bible, the, 15, 27, 30, 134, 148, 171
Blondel, Maurice, 23, 31

Bloy, Léon, 151–2
Boersma, Hans, 29, 34, 190
Bonhoeffer, Dietrich, 180
Bouillard, Henri, 31
Boyer, Charles, 33, 39
Boyle, Nicholas, 185
Braine, David, 55, 56
Brotherton, Joshua, 93, 94
Buckley, Michael, 139, 145, 146, 148, 151–2
Bushlack, Thomas, 61, 103

Cajetan, Thomas (Thomas de Vio), 19, 22, 24, 34, 41, 52, 56, 57, 93
Cano, Melchior, 27
Casel, 31
Cervantes, Miguel de, 143
Chenu, Marie-Dominique, 190
Clairvaux, Bernard, 37
Cobb, Kelton, 192
Comte, Auguste, 16
consciousness: Balthasar on, 128; Doran on the two ways of being conscious, 140–1; historical, 27, 41, 184; Lonergan on conscious intentionality, 5, 6, 72–3, 78–80, 82, 84, 123–5, 146–7, 199; religious, 145; soteriological differentiation of, 159
contemplation/contemplative life, 20, 37, 41, 45, 67, 78, 146, 148, 158, 161–7, 174–5, 178, 180, 187
conversion, 6, 8, 80–1; Alison's anthropology of, 68, 70; intellectual, 70–7, 81–2; moral, 82; religious, 151–2, 168, 173
critical realism, 70–7
Crysdale, Cynthia, 101
culture: and bias, 75; classicist vs. empirical understanding of, 82, 84, 106; consumer, 187, 189, 192, 194, 196, 199; Girard on 149, 152; and loss of wisdom, 70; Ormerod on origins of, 154–5; popular, 192, 194; and scale of values, 106–7, 198–9; as theological category, 8, 9, 29, 35, 83–4, 203–4
Cunningham, Lawrence, 148, 205

Dadosky, John, xi, 130,
Daniélou, Jean, 8, 29–34, 38, 39, 83, 190–2, 199, 201
Darwin, Charles, 30
Day, Dorothy, 161, 205
de Beauvoir, Simone, 29, 30
de Lubac, Henri, 3–4, 7–8, 13–38, 39–43, 46–62, 67, 83–4, 86–90, 92, 94, 97–8, 100, 103, 107–8, 112–14, 116–18, 159, 184, 191, 201, 203
de Toledo, Francisco, 41
Delbrêl, Madeleine, 37
Denis the Carthusian, 41
Descartes, René, 71, 129
desire: conditional, 19–20, 44–5, 49, 65, 93–4; distorted, 69–70, 184; elicited, 19–20, 43, 45, 49, 62, 65, 89, 93–5, 97, 111, 114–15, 119, 141, 219n22; as eros of the mind, 5, 70, 75, 77–87, 114, 142, 202; innate, 7, 9, 19–21, 23, 43–8, 62, 67, 93–7, 111–14, 141–2, 150, 158, 183, 213n63, 219n22; intellectual, 8, 65–6, 68, 70, 73, 77, 86–7, 88, 140, 143, 202; and love, 131–6; mimetic, 7, 9, 68, 139–40, 144, 148–55, 159, 180, 182, 190, 194–7, 204–5; natural, relationship with mimetic, 7, 140–4; sexual, 75, 130, 132–6; socially mediated, 9, 65, 139, 151, 157, 194–5; supernatural, 93,

118–20, 123, 130; unconditional, 44–5, 94, 103, 119, 122
Dominic, St, 33, 152
Doran, Robert, xi, 7, 9, 106, 107, 122–4, 130, 135–6, 140–3, 155, 157–60, 173, 183, 188, 190, 193–4, 198
Dostoevsky, Fyodor, 30, 143, 172, 177
Dreyfus affair, 15
Duns Scotus, 41, 91

Eckhart, Meister, 171
emergent probability, 8, 72, 78, 88–9, 97, 99, 100–8, 112, 115, 126–7, 201–2
Evangelii Gaudium, 185
extrinsicism, 16, 36, 38, 52, 60, 62, 108, 114, 117, 118–20, 125–7

Feingold, Lawrence, xii, 8, 14, 19, 39–62, 65, 89, 93–7, 111–13, 115, 117–19, 124, 135, 158, 183
Ferrariensis, 41
Feuerbach, Ludwig, 145
filiation, 160, 162
finality: de Lubac on, 22, 25, 46–56; Feingold on, 47, 54; horizontal, 108–9, 125; vertical, 8, 89, 97, 99, 102, 107–12, 125–7, 141, 202
Flaubert, Gustave, 143
Foucauld, Charles de, 37
four-point hypothesis, 9, 117; and habit of charity, 123, 157, 160–1; and sanctifying grace, 9, 122–3; and the Trinity, 122–4, 157–62
Fourth Lateran Council, 66
fourth stage of meaning, 124, 235–37
Francis of Assisi, St, 152
Francis, Pope, 185
Frank, Thomas, 196
Freud, Sigmund, 145, 170

Galileo, 100
Galliardetz, Richard, 171, 182
Garrigou–Lagrange, Réginald, 8, 19, 29–34, 38, 39, 56, 94, 113, 201
Gilson, Étienne, 24, 33, 57
Girard, René, 4, 7, 9, 68, 80, 139–56, 157, 159, 175, 179–80, 183–4, 188, 190, 193–7, 200, 205
God: the Father, 45, 104, 123, 149, 153, 160–3, 164, 166, 167, 178; Holy Spirit, 50, 121, 123, 153, 158–61, 166, 171–4; Jesus Christ, 25, 32, 35, 37, 48, 50, 67, 77, 104, 105, 119, 127, 149, 150, 152, 153, 157, 163, 165, 167–8, 172, 173, 175; the Son, 123, 153, 160–1, 166, 178
Gregory of Nyssa, 48

habit of charity: Doran on, 122, 124, 130, 135–6; and Etty Hillesum, 172, 178–82; and four-point hypothesis, 123, 157, 160–1; Lonergan on, 120–2; and the metaphysics of holiness, 160–1, and Thérèse of Lisieux, 162, 166, 167–70
Harrison, Robert, 194
Hart, David Bentley, xii, 78, 79
Healy, Nicholas, 46–8, 58
Hefling, Charles, 150
Heidegger, Martin, 13, 97, 141
Hillesum, Etty, 9, 152, 157–9, 161–2, 164, 170–83, 205
Himes, Brian, 96
Hitler, Adolf, 17, 149, 176, 180
Hobbes, Thomas, 106
Hoffman, Eva, 171
Homer, 134
Huby, Joseph, 19
human good, 8, 40, 46, 55, 59–62, 84–6, 89, 103–7, 154, 194, 202
Hütter, Reinhard, 40–1, 46, 47

idolatry: Alison on, 69–70; Aquinas on, 187–8; Augustine on, 3; consumerism as, 185, 187–90, 198, 200; as deviated transcendence, 188; Lonergan on, 193–4; Pope Francis on, 185,
Ignatius of Loyola, St, 143, 152, 161
incarnate meaning, 9, 140, 143–8, 150, 155, 157, 163, 205
interdividuality, 142, 150, 153, 195
interpersonal, 6, 7, 9, 117, 120, 123–5, 128, 130, 136, 140, 145, 150, 155, 165, 209n14, 235, 32, 235n37
intersubjectivity, 6, 7, 30–1, 72, 117, 128, 140, 142, 144, 150–1, 225n25
Irenaeus of Lyon, 31

Jansenism, 18
Jansenius, Cornelius, 20–2, 41
Joan of Arc, St, 164, 167
John of St Thomas, 19, 56
John Paul II, Pope, 50, 172, 185, 186, 190, 197
John XXIII, Pope, 79
Jungian psychology, 158, 171

Kant, Immanuel, 16, 60, 77, 129, 152
Kaplan, Grant, xi, 142–3, 152–3,
Kasper, Walter, 39
Kierkegaard, Søren, 30–1

Lamentabili sane exitu, 27
Law of the Cross, 180, 181, 199, 236n53, 245n56
Lenehan, Kevin, 7, 140
Leo XIII, Pope, 27, 32; *Aeterni Patris*, 27; *Gravissime Nos*, 27
Levinas, Emmanuel, 132, 134
Locke, John, 106

Lonergan, Bernard, 4–9, 13, 26, 27, 37, 40, 48, 52, 56, 61, 62, 65, 66, 68, 70–87, 88–115, 116–17, 120–2, 124–31, 136, 140–8, 150, 154–5, 160–1, 167, 175, 182, 184, 189–94, 197, 199, 200–5
Long, Steven, 41, 46, 47, 51, 54–6, 60–1, 103, 125, 201
Losski, Nicolai, 31
love: and desire, 131–6; metaphysics of, 125–7; phenomenology of, 62, 124–36; *See also* being-in-love

MacIntyre, Alasdair, 41, 185
Malloy, Christopher, 99, 108, 111
Maloney, Raymond, 111–12
Mansini, Guy, 41, 89, 95, 112, 114
Marcel, Gabriel, 29, 31
Marion, Jean-Luc, 4, 70–2, 97, 117, 127–36, 189, 197
Maritain, Jacques, 94, 113, 151
Maritain, Raïssa, 151
Marxism, 30, 31; neo-Marxism, 34
Maurras, Charles, 15–16, 33
Maximus the Confessor, 52
McCabe, Herbert, 41
mediation: external vs. internal, 150–1, 195, 242n65; social, 151
Medina, Bartolomé de, 19, 41, 93
Merleau-Ponty, Maurice, 29
metaphysics: agonistic, 243n91; Aristotle on, 72; Balthasar on, 236n55; of holiness, 9, 158–9, 183; Lonergan on, 71, 92, 100, 228n89; of love, 125–7; Marion on, 71, 129; neo-scholastic, 29–32; and phenomenology, 201; Przywara on, 224n3
Milbank, John, 14, 35, 58–60, 106, 112–15

mimesis: acquisitive, 75, 142, 195; antagonistic, 153, 180, 182; peaceful, 152–4, 156, 179–80; positive, 142, 159
modernism, 27, 29–32, 40; condemnation of, 27
Möhler, Johann Adam, 37
Molinist controversy, 26
Monchanin, Jules, 37
Mounier, Emmanuel, 30
Mulcahy, Bernard, 26, 35
Murphy, William, 40

Narcisse, Gilbert, 4, 71–2, 88
natural theology, 8, 77–9, 80, 83–4, 87, 203
nature: as emergent probability, 100–3; integral, 3, 56, 61–2, 91–2, 103, 107, 115; Lonergan's scholastic context, 89–92; pure vs. concrete historical, 5, 51–7. *See also* pure nature
Nazism, 16–17, 30, 33, 38, 86, 178–90
neo-scholasticism/neo-Thomism, 3, 7, 13, 32, 39–40, 59; de Lubac's critique of, 24–34; Feingold's proposal, 40–6; Kasper on, 39; and the manual tradition, 27, 66; Oakes on, 39 and the Thomistic consensus, 18–20
Newman, John Henry, 37, 144
Newton, Isaac, 54, 100
Nietzsche, Friedrich, 30, 196
Nouvelle Théologie, 15, 31, 33, 40, 55
Nygren, Anders, 75

Oakes, Edward, 39, 49, 50, 184
obediential potency, 8, 57–9, 62, 89, 118, 173, 202, 223n121; Cajetan on, 24; Lonergan on, 107–14, 121

Origen, 37
Ormerod, Neil, xi, 124, 136, 154, 155, 160–1, 166, 169, 178, 183
Otto, Rudolf, 31

Pascal, Blaise, 129, 170
Pascendi dominici gregis, 27
passive spiration, 122–3, 159–62, 166–8, 178, 180
paternity, 160, 161
Paul, St, 37, 153, 173, 175
Peacocke, Arthur, 110
Pelagius, 49 (Pelagianism 21, 49, 91)
Percy, Walker, 73, 200
Pétain, Marshal, 16
phenomenology: and the Daniélou/Garrigou-Lagrange exchange, 31–2; of desire, 184; Levinas on, 132; Lonergan on, 4–6, 9, 70, 117, 201, 209n18; of love, 62, 124–36; Marion on, 127–9; and metaphysics, 202; of the saints, 9, 157, 162–3; Sokolowski on, 19
Philip the Chancellor, 90
Pius X, Pope, 27, 31, 32,
Pius XII, Pope, 32, 34, 38; *Humani Generis*, 34
postmodernism, 65, 84, 153, 158
Proust, Marcel, 143
pure nature: Baius on, 20; Balthasar on, 51–3; Bushlack on, 61; de Lubac on, 3, 4, 7, 13, 14, 17, 19, 22, 25–6, 33–4, 38, 51–2, 59, 62; Jansenius on, 21; Lonergan on 81, 84, 91–2, 113, 201–2; Milbank on 59–60, 106; in relation to work of Buckley, 60; Ryan on 103; Suárez on, 19; Torrell on, 56–7

question of God, 4, 8, 37, 79–84, 87, 116, 173, 184, 203–4

rationalism, 14, 26–9, 36, 69, 70, 83, 222n90
religious experience, 8, 32, 80–1, 83, 120, 129, 139–40, 145, 151, 155, 165, 172, 182, 201, 204
ressourcement, 3, 8, 19, 29, 33–4, 39–42, 60, 76, 190, 201
Rilke, Rainer Maria, 171–2
Ryan, Peter, 103–4

sacralization: to be fostered, 190, 191, 199; to be resisted, 9, 187, 190–4, 197
sanctifying grace: Baius on 21; de Lubac on, 57; Doran on, 122–4, 130, 135–6, 157; Feingold on, 45–7, 54, 117–19; and four-point hypothesis, 9, 122–3; Lonergan on, 120–4, 129–30; and metaphysics of holiness, 160–2, 166, 172, 174, 183, 205
sanctity *simpliciter*, 160–1, 163–6, 174
Sartre, Jean-Paul, 29, 30, 60
scale of values, 89, 106–7, 197–200, 202
scapegoating, 9, 68, 140, 149, 152–3, 154, 156
Scheeben, Matthias Joseph, 94, 113
Scheler, Max, 31
Schindler, David, 60–1, 103, 201, 203
Schor, Juliet, 192
secularism, 19, 39, 59, 187
secularization: Girard on, 196; Pope Benedict XVI on, 173; to be resisted, 190, 191, 194; to be welcomed, 190–1
self-transcendence, 6, 7, 8, 69, 72, 80, 82–3, 86, 89, 104–5, 114–15, 120–1, 124, 129, 130, 140, 142, 150, 154–5, 175, 202–4. *See also* transcendence

Shakespeare, William, 134, 143
Smith, James K.A., 189, 190, 194
Soto, Dominic, 24, 41
Spier, Julius, 171, 179, 182
Spinoza, Baruch, 106
static essentialism, 81, 98–9, 108, 111, 114
Stebbins, Michael, 99
Stein, Edith, 151
Stoic/stoicism, 49, 166, 179
Stump, Eleonore, 41
Suárez, Francisco, 19, 23, 26, 34, 41, 44, 48, 52, 56, 93
subjectivity: authentic, 83; concrete, 5–9, 50, 53–4, 80, 84–5, 88, 114, 119, 139, 155, 163, 182, 184, 201–4; Daniélou on, 29–31; erotic, 9, 130–5; vs. human nature, 4–5; John Paul II on, 186; Long on, 55; and objectivity, 83
sublation, 108, 111, 232n87
supernatural, the: Aquinas on, 91, 94; de Lubac on the natural desire for, 21–6, 48–9, 54, 59, 117; denial of, 16, 36; Feingold on, 42–6, 60, 117, 119; gratuity of, 34, 51; Lonergan on, 95–6, 98–9, 103, 107–8, 110–15, 202; Long on, 60; as new relation to same end, 117–18, 123–4; and the return to mystery, 29; the saints and, 162; separation of the natural and, 14, 17, 18–21, 116, theorem of, 90; Trinitarian structure of, 122–3
Sylvester of Ferrara, 19, 93

Teilhard de Chardin, Pierre, 31, 37
Teresa of Ávila, St, 93, 151, 162
Thérèse of Lisieux, St, 9, 143, 152, 157–8, 159–69, 170, 172, 174–6, 178, 180, 183, 205

Thomas à Kempis, 171
Torell, Jean–Pierre, 56
Toynbee, Arnold, 193
transcendence: divine, 30, 65–6, 135; false and deviated, 3, 184, 187–90, 192, 194, 198, 200, 204; of grace, 67, 111, 126; limitation and, 100. *See also* self–transcendence
Trinity, the, 42, 95, 130, 136, 172; created analogy for, 141; and four-point hypothesis, 122–4, 157–62

Vanier, Jean, 128, 131
Vatican II, 36, 39, 49, 160, 172, 173; *Gaudium et Spes*, 50, 104, 172; *Lumen Gentium*, 160
Vichy regime, 16–18, 30, 33, 38

Wegerif, Han, 171
White, Thomas Joseph, 67, 77
Wicks, Jared, 27
Wittgenstein, Ludwig, 13, 41

Young, Frances, 147

www.ingramcontent.com/pod-product-compliance
Lightning Source LLC
Chambersburg PA
CBHW030308080526
44584CB00012B/493